BEHAVIORAL PSYCHOLOGY
for teachers

BEHAVIORAL PSYCHOLOGY
for teachers

Julie S. Vargas
West Virginia University

HARPER & ROW, Publishers
New York   Hagerstown   San Francisco   London

Sponsoring Editor: George A. Middendorf
Project Editor: Eleanor Castellano
Designer: Frances Torbert Tilley
Production Supervisor: Kewal K. Sharma
Photo Researcher: Myra Schachne
Compositor: V & M Typographical, Inc.
Printer and Binder: The Murray Printing Company
Art Studio: J & R Technical Services Inc.
Cartoons: Edward Malsberg
Cover: Quinlan Studios

Behavioral Psychology for Teachers

Library of Congress Cataloging in Publication Data

Vargas, Julie S
  Behavioral psychology for teachers.

  Includes index.
  1. Educational psychology.   2. Behavior modification.   I. Title.
LB1051.V327   371.1′02   76-51454
ISBN 0-06-046813-0

To Lisa and Justine

Contents

Measuring Behavior 45

Techniques for Change   105

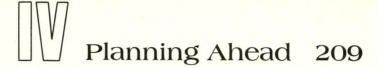

V Teaching Large Numbers of Students   287

Preface

I would like to express my appreciation to the students of Educational Psychology 105, whose successes and failures over the past five years shaped the contents of this text. The debt I owe to B. F. Skinner, the originator of operant psychology, is clear throughout the entire work. I also have incorporated many ideas of Ernest A. Vargas, who made comments on parts of the manuscript and with whom I discussed every major topic. In Part II I have drawn heavily from the workshops and writings of Ogden Lindsley.

I would like to thank Barbara Brock and Winnie Bucklew, who typed various drafts of the manuscript from practically illegible copy, and Dolores Howell, who typed the final version. Finally, I would like to thank my father for his editorial comments, and the following persons who made suggestions which were incorporated into the manuscript: Paul Gratz, West Virginia University; Larry Fraley, West Virginia University; David Myers, Mercer University; James Wasson, West Virginia University; George Middendorf, Harper & Row; and Eleanor Castellano, Harper & Row.

Julie S. Vargas

To the Student

This book is written from the point of view of operant psychology, the science of human behavior. A scientific approach is first of all an attitude —a willingness to see things as they *are* rather than as we wish they would be. It is a willingness, too, to change the way we do things, to try out new ideas and to judge their worth by evidence rather than by opinion. A scientific approach thus encourages the teacher to be a constant learner in order to better help students learn.

Julie S. Vargas

Teaching
and learning

OVERVIEW

If you are planning to teach, or expect sometime to have to
help someone to learn, you need to have a clear idea of what
teaching and learning are. Part I is designed to help you
clarify your thinking.

It discusses teaching and learning and takes up some of
the implications and possibilities of using behavioral psychology in the classroom.

Teaching as changing behavior

OVERVIEW

What is a teacher's job? What do you hope to accomplish with your students? Chapter One looks at teaching from a behavioral viewpoint, showing the challenges, responsibilities, and opportunities that you as a teacher will have.

OBJECTIVES

By the end of the chapter you should be able to:
A. Define teaching according to a behavioral viewpoint and identify definitions with which an operant psychologist would agree.
B. Identify statements about students' learning (or lack of it) which are consistent with an operant approach.

THE SCHOOL COMMITTEE OF THE CITY OF GARDENIA

ASSISTANT DIRECTORS
ELEANOR CASTELLANO
FRANCES TORBERT
HOWARD LEIDERMAN
GEORGE MIDDENDORF
AL ALBOTT

GARDENIA PUBLIC
SCHOOLS

Dear Reader,
I am happy to notify you that you have been assigned as an English teacher in the Gardenia Public schools for the coming school year, to teach in the Hilsbury District.

This agreement is made with the understanding that no change will be made in your assignment, except through a mutual agreement between you and the Board of Education, or unless it becomes necessary to reduce the number of teachers in the school to which you are assigned.

Teachers are reminded that they must have a valid Teaching Certificate on file in the office of the Board of Education before beginning their teaching duties.

If you should have any questions, please do not hesitate to call me.

Sincerely,

William F. Smith

William F. Smith, Director
Secondary Education

WFS/fn

THE CHALLENGE

If you plan to teach, you may someday receive a letter like the one above. What would you do if you received your first letter of appointment today and were expected to begin teaching in one week? Most people would first find out who their students would be (and how many they would have), what they would be expected to teach, and what their schedule would be. Suppose you are told your class is in an inner-city school and you are to teach English to five different classes each day. Some of the problems you will face are similar to those which faced James Herndon. Here is what he wrote about his first day:

The first day there was a girl named Ruth in my eighth grade B class. She was absolutely the craziest-looking girl I've ever seen. Her hair was a mass of grease, matted down flat in some places, sticking straight out in several others. Her face was faintly Arabic, and she was rather handsome. . . . She was very black. Across her forehead a tremendous scar ran in a zigzag pattern from somewhere above the hairline on her left side across to her right eye, cutting into the eyebrow. The scar was dead white. She was about five feet three inches tall, weighed maybe 115 pounds. Not thin, anyway. Her entire figure seemed full of energy and power; she was, every time I saw her, completely alert and ready. She could have been any age from 15 to 25. I once tried to look up her age, there were so many rumors about her from the faculty and from other students, but that fact was absent from her file; on every sheet, the space after Age was simply left blank. No one knew, and apparently no one knew why it was that no one knew. . . .

She sat at the second desk in her row (that first day) and all she did was to sit there and grab all the pencils I handed out for that row and refuse to pass them back. The row burst into an uproar, demanding their pencils. The other rows, not having thought of this themselves, yelled derisively, "that row ain't gittin' any!"

Please pass the pencils back, Ruth, I said, reasonably but loudly, since I wanted to be heard. . . .

Ruth jumped up immediately. Don't go hollowing at me she yelled. You got plenty of pencils! You spozed to give 'em all out! They ain't your pencils! You spozed to give 'em out! I need these pencils!

The class yelled out, Whooooo-ee! They all made the same sound. Everyone stood up. Laughing and yelling Whoo-eee except for the kids in Ruth's row who all screamed, We ain't got no pyenculs!

I advanced on the row. Sit down! I shouted at everybody. I did have plenty of pencils, and I was going to give one to each kid in the row and forget about it. Let her keep the goddam pencils! Who cared? But as I came toward the row, Ruth suddenly flung the handful of pencils out into the room, screeched out No!, and launched herself backwards into space. She actually flew through the air and landed on her back on the floor after crashing some part of her body or head—I couldn't tell—against a desk and a kid or two. Across the room 20 kids dived, shouting for the pencils. No trouble, I thought bitterly, and came over to get her up. That's all I could think of at the time, get this damn girl off the floor. But again, as I moved, she jumped up, full of life, and fled for the door.

You ain't sending me to Miss Bentley, nobody sending me! I go tell her myself what you done, Mr. Herndon!

Bang. She was gone. The class was still squabbling over the pencils but not seriously, and a few were still taunting the row which didn't have any, but only halfheartedly. They were too impressed with Ruth. So was I. I passed out some more pencils, and everyone sat down and awaited excitedly the passing out of paper, enrollment cards and books.[1]

If that were your first day, what would you have done? This book will not tell you exactly what to do or say, but it will give you a method of solving problems that will help you design instruction for any group of students so that they will study and learn more effectively.

[1]James Herndon, *The Way It Spozed To Be*, New York, Bantam, 1969, pp. 3–4. Copyright © 1965, 1968 by James Herndon. Reprinted by permission of Simon & Schuster, Inc.

WHAT ARE YOUR GOALS?

You probably have some idea of what you would like to do as a teacher. You probably would like to motivate your students, to get them excited about the subject or subjects you teach. You might want to help them become more independent, happier, or more creative. Somewhere along the way you probably expect them to learn "content"—facts, principles, and skills which will make them successful in solving problems they will encounter later on.

Whatever you may see as desirable for your students, one thing is certain: you do have goals for them, and you will try to change the way they behave if you believe it will make them more independent, happier, more creative, more productive, and so on. That is your job. Changing behavior is what teaching is all about.

TEACHING—A DEFINITION

Teaching is helping someone to learn. The mother who repeats a word over and over for her baby is teaching. A student who corrects the way a friend sings a song is teaching. We are teaching when we give directions which help someone get to the post office. We teach when we help people learn something they otherwise would not have learned, and also when we help them learn faster or more efficiently

---

Teaching

is changing behavior; it is helping others to learn, or to learn faster, or more efficiently than they could on their own. Teaching may be intentional or unintentional.

---

than they could on their own. Thus we speak of teaching a child to walk, although we know the child will learn anyway, even without our help, or of teaching a person to ride a bike when we suggest methods that the beginner would eventually discover if left alone.

What one person teaches, another person may consider undesirable. One mother may teach her child to hit back when attacked, another may teach her child to "turn the other cheek." One student may teach another a word or expression which teachers would rather they not use. We are teaching when we help others to learn to park illegally without getting caught, or to smoke marijuana, or to avoid paying taxes. The desirability of the behavior learned depends on our point of view. Both "bad" and "good" behavior can be taught, and both are.

Teaching can also be unintentional. Imagine a supermarket checkout line. A seven-year-old boy asks his mother quietly, "May I please have a dime for bubble gum?" She turns and says, "It's too close to dinner time." "Oh," the boy whines, "please. Only *one* dime." Getting no response, he tries again, only louder. "Mom, I just want *one* dime. *Please, please.* You gave me one last time. Don't be mean. *Please,* can't I have just one." He is pulling on her arm now, making it difficult for her to unload the groceries from the cart onto the counter. Finally, in desperation, Mom pulls out a dime. The boy runs off, happy. Mom doesn't like whining or begging, yet, without realizing it, that is what she is teaching. Unintentional teaching also goes on in the classroom. We do not mean to teach students to stray from the topic, to pass notes, to avoid math, or to drop out of school, but what we do may make them more likely to do so. By our definition, then, we are teaching those behaviors.

THE CONTROLLING ENVIRONMENT

What we learn depends on what we encounter. All of our behavior is maintained or altered by our daily experiences, and it shifts according to each environment we enter. Imagine how our friends would react if, in the middle of a lecture, we behaved as we do at a football game. We behave differently when talking to our friends than we do when addressing a stranger. We do things at home we would not do in public and vice versa. We behave, in short, according to the demands of each situation.

If the demands of a situation change, so does our behavior. A lecturer or church preacher may call for audience participation, thus changing the audience response from listening quietly to shouting. A stranger may "put us at ease." Most of us could not imagine undressing at the request of a stranger of the opposite sex. But now imagine that stranger is a famous doctor who is giving us a needed examination for a medical problem. In such a situation most of us would undress, even if we had never seen the person before.

A classroom is an environment with its own demands. The behavior students engage in depends on the "rules of the game" in that class. Whether students study or disrupt others; learn to love or to hate a subject; in short, what students do day after day is determined by what they encounter in the classroom.

What they encounter may or may not be what you, as a teacher, plan. It will affect their behavior in either case. If you do not arrange classroom procedures, the other students (the peer group) will. The standards which emerge then will depend upon the peer group culture, which may or may not be desirable from your point of view.

Some teachers worry about interfering with "natural" development when they deliberately change the way their students behave. A. S. Neill, the author of *Summerhill; A Radical Approach to Child Rearing,* goes so far as to say.

My view is that a child is innately wise and realistic. If left to himself without adult suggestion of any kind, he will develop as far as he is capable of developing.[2]

How far can a child develop without "adult suggestion"? Physically speaking, a human being will die without human help. Adults feed a baby and clothe it. We do everything we can to make it grow up strong and healthy. The foods in the environment a child faces, however, are far from natural. Perhaps in nature children would eat those foods which would most benefit them, but in our society, with its candy and soft drink machines, it is doubtful that they would eat well without "adult suggestion of any kind."

The same is true for behavior. The grabbing, lying, shoving, and so on, which yields immediate "natural" gains, in the long run is harmful for the person who does it. Adult suggestion is needed.

There is no such thing as natural development anymore. What we call "natural" is what we feel will benefit our students. Neill, in fact, recommends taking children away from the family (which one could argue is the most natural environment) and putting them into a special environment. A school, "free" or otherwise, is a special, "artificial" environment, and it is designed to produce behavior which is more desirable than that which the child would learn at home.

Your job as a teacher, then, is to change student behavior. You may try to change it by giving assignments or you may structure the environment to be "open." Whatever the method, your job is to create an environment which produces desirable behavior.

The school environment is artificial in that it is designed to be an improvement over the students' daily world, and it is artificial in another way too. How often have you heard that "school is a preparation for life"? Few people would argue against educating students for happy and productive lives. The problem is that the life for which we must prepare students is largely in the future. We must change their behavior *now* in ways which will benefit them *later*. They must learn to do things for which they have no immediate need. First graders do not need to read to get along in the six-year-olds' world, but they must start now if they are to learn to read for later use. We learn to add and subtract many years before we need to balance our checkbooks or solve practical arithmetic problems in our daily life.

To teach, then, you must arrange immediate reasons for your students for behaviors they will need later. The praise given to a first grader for correctly pronouncing "Run, Dick, Run" is such a reason, as are grades or approval given for writing a term paper well. They are artificial in that they are introduced specifically to promote learning.

[2]A. S. Neill, *Summerhill; A Radical Approach to Child Rearing*, New York, Hart, 1960, p. 4.

The instructional materials you will use in teaching may not be "natural" either. No one environment provides everything you need to teach your students what they need to know. You cannot wait around for erosion, or floods, or pollution in order to teach the principles of ecology. To provide realistic experiences or to demonstrate principles, you bring into the classroom parts of the world that students would not normally encounter in their "natural" day-to-day existence. Such "broadening of horizons" has always been a part of education, artificial though it is. Experience may be the "best teacher" but the teacher should select the best experiences.

WAYS OF CHANGING BEHAVIOR

Changing behavior. It sounds like a goal of George Orwell's *1984*. When we think of changing someone else we think first of using force. But punitive techniques are only one method of control, and in many ways the least effective one. A "healthy" environment also controls the kinds of activities in which people engage. The teacher who provides a "free" atmosphere in which students can express their opinions without being punished is controlling their behavior by making it more likely that they will express opinions. Behavior is also controlled through love. The high school student who goes to great lengths to look attractive for a date or to plan a surprise for someone else is under the control of the person he or she loves. We all spend a lot of time and effort doing things because they please other people. In the classroom teachers may make students study by punishing them if they do not, but they can get far more control with more pleasant methods. Teachers who "inspire" students, for example, get them to study not only while they are watching but even when they leave school. That is real control!

Changing behavior also implies effectiveness. Teachers who fail to change student behavior may hesitate to say that changing behavior was their goal. Instead, by saying that they only wanted to "influence" students, they can point to any small effect as proof of success. Poor teaching can go unexposed.

By denying that their job is to change behavior, teachers avoid taking responsibility for their student's learning. If the student does not learn, teachers can say it is the student's fault. The student doesn't have the ability or the motivation or isn't yet "ready" to learn. But faulty learning is a product of a faulty environment, not faulty genes. We are not born preprogrammed to speak English or Chinese, or to fail math. If we are born with any strong tendency, it is a tendency to learn from our environment. If the student does not learn, the environment is at fault.

What teachers do is an important part of the student's environment, and they are responsible for its effect on student behavior. Teachers who do *not* change a child's selfishness, letting the child "grow out of it" instead, are responsible for the fact that the youngster remains selfish. By refusing to teach writing and reading—say, to a child from an impoverished background—we influence the child's development just as much as a farmer who refuses to interfere with nature by watering a drought-stricken plant. Teachers who do not set out to change behavior are just as responsible for the way students behave as teachers who actively intervene. Both teachers determine the way their students develop.

Students will learn in an unplanned environment, but they may not learn the behaviors they will later need. Teachers can help students more effectively by admitting that they wish to change behavior so that they can concentrate on getting the job done.

THE POSSIBILITIES

Our schools today are not very effective. We do not teach all children even the basic skills of reading, writing, and arithmetic, although these are presumably part of each school's objectives. Textbook series and course outlines acknowledge our lack of effectiveness in their very redundancy. The following excerpts, taken from a popular series on health, provide an example:

Book I for the first grade introduces "the four food groups" as follows:

Foods You Need

"Let me see," said mother,
"What do we need?
There are four kinds of food.
We need some of each kind."

Book II for second graders has a six-page section called "Four Food Groups."

Book III has five pages on the four food groups. By the fourth grade (Book IV) the students read a section called "Using a Food Guide." In Book VII it is called "USDA Recommendation"; and finally, in Book VIII one finds: "The United States Department of Agriculture has defined four basic food groups."

In six different years, students are told they should eat foods from each group each day. The redundancy is undoubtedly deliberate, but it reveals the assumption that the students have not adopted good eating habits as a result of previous years' exposures. The combination of teacher and textbook has, in other words, been ineffective in producing the desired change.

We fail badly in the area of achievement, but we fail even worse in that of attitudes. Students do not have fewer academic skills when they leave school than they had when they entered, but they often leave with more negative attitudes. Most children enter school eager to learn, but it is a rare child who leaves elementary school liking math or grammar. Many students dislike school itself. In the big city schools, the situation is so bad that both students and teachers want to get out. Teachers quit or transfer at a high rate and absenteeism runs high. Newspaper articles like the following appear:

Abandoning the Schools

What can one say of these figures on New York City school absenteeism:

On an average day, fully 25 percent of youngsters enrolled in high school don't go. This figure rises to 30, 40 and even 45 percent in certain schools.

Teacher absenteeism has increased 50 percent in the past three years—to 7.5 percent each day, twice as high as for the city's office workers.

The New York City figures are substantially worse than for other major American cities. In Boston's high schools, for example, average daily attendance is 80 percent. The national average is 90 percent.

Still, the trend is downward. Boston, again, has seen attendance drop steadily one-half percent a year since 1960. The New York decline is only more precipitous and forebodes how city-school life may plummet unless extraordinarily vigorous and fundamental changes are made.

As pointed out in the New York Times this week, youngsters are staying out of school because they know they can't be caught, they're four or five years behind in basic skills, are hooked on drugs, must work, or, if from minority groups, they feel schooling won't really better their lot in life. (40 percent of New York's school-age youngsters are from fatherless welfare families.)[3]

Antagonism toward school and toward intellectual endeavors is pervasive among those who have been educated in our schools; key political figures make derogatory statements about intellectuals, students destroy school property, and the "public" votes down school bond issues. How different our results are from what we put forth as goals—"intellectual curiosity, the development of an appreciation of the scientific approach to problem solving, a concern for the rights of others, an appreciation of the democratic process. . . ."

[3]*The Christian Science Monitor,* February 6, 1970. Reprinted by permission from *The Christian Science Monitor.* Copyright © 1970 The Christian Science Publishing Society. All rights reserved.

For about 200 days of each year after the age of six, students spend roughly half their waking hours in school. What happens to them there cannot fail to have a major influence on their lives. The schools have been blamed for stifling curiosity, killing initiative, and alienating our youth. If the school system can change behavior in such undesirable directions, then they could it not produce desirable behavior?

HOW OPERANT PSYCHOLOGY CAN HELP

Over the past 30 or so years, the science of behavior has shown how the environment controls behavior. There is now considerable knowledge available about what aspects of the environment produce what kinds of changes in behavior.

If, as operant psychologists maintain, student behavior is largely a product of environment, then the failure of the American educational system is a failure of the school environment—in particular what teachers say and do. You, as a teacher, then *can* design a classroom in which your students will be motivated to learn, no matter what their background is. To do so, you must control certain features of classroom procedures and setting. What features are important, and how to change them, is the subject of this book.

SUMMARY

Changing behavior, changing how people approach and interact in their world, is what education is all about. Students are supposed to be different as a result of their school experiences. They are supposed to be able to do things that they could not do before, and they are also supposed to change in more subtle ways. The complex behaviors that we describe by terms such as "positive attitudes," "self-fulfillment," "appreciation," and so on, are part of the changes that education is supposed to bring about.

When you teach, the kind of environment you provide will determine what kinds of changes you produce in your students. Whatever you do, it will make a difference in the way they behave. Some of the changes you produce will be intentional some will not. Some changes will be good, some will be bad. Whether intentional or unintentional, good or bad, the way students behave as a result of your classes is what you have taught them.

Behavioral psychology in general, and operant psychology in particular, shows how behavior changes, and what aspects of the environment are critical for change. Your job as a teacher will be to change behavior. The more skill in analyzing behavior you have, the more you will be able to change those parts of the environment that are responsible for your students' behavior and for your own.

EXERCISES

Concept Check IA—Teaching (Objective A)

Find the four definitions of teaching from the list below with which an operant psychologist would most agree.

1. Teaching is the art of assisting another to learn. It includes providing information (instruction) and situations, conditions, or activities which will facilitate learning.
2. Teaching is regarded as the combination of teachers, students, subject matter content, and materials.
3. Teaching is assisting the development of the powers of the mind by providing amplification systems to which human beings, equipped with appropriate skills, can link themselves.
4. Teaching is the arrangement of contingencies of reinforcement under which a student learns.
5. Teaching is a system of actions intended to induce learning.
6. Teaching is the art of leading students to discover something which they already possess.
7. Teaching is producing a change in the way an individual interacts with the environment.
8. Teaching is organizing and presenting information clearly.
9. Teaching is the meeting of minds.
10. Teaching is whatever one person does that affects either directly or indirectly what another person does.

Answers for Concept Check IA

The four definitions are numbers 1, 4, 7, and 10.

They are the only ones which specify that some change in behavior *must* be produced. Number 4 is by the "father" of operant psychology, B. F. Skinner. Skinner coined the term *operant* in order to distinguish between the kind of behaviorism he was researching and the stimulus-response behaviorism of John B. Watson. This definition is from *The Technology of Teaching*.[4]

Number 2 describes one part of teaching but does not specify the effect on the learner.

Number 3 talks of "the mind," not behavior. Phrases such as "amplification systems to which human beings . . . can link themselves" are not concrete enough for the operant psychologist, who looks for measurable behavior change.

Number 5 would be fine if it did not include the word "intended," which implies that one can teach without producing learning.

Number 6 Although some change in the student is implied, an operant psy-

---

[4]B. F. Skinner, *The Technology of Teaching*, New York, Appleton-Century-Crofts, 1968, p. 64.

chologist would not agree that all behavior is already "possessed." In addition, behavior change is not always "discovery."

Number 8 This is the most common view of teaching, but it focuses entirely on the teacher. A person could "organize and present" in an empty room, but that is not teaching unless someone learns from it.

Number 9 How do minds meet? How do you know when such a meeting has occurred? The operant psychologist avoids using ill-defined terms such as "mind," and looks for change in student behavior.

Concept Check IB—The Operant Approach to Teaching (Objective B)

Which six statements below are most consistent with an operant approach to teaching?

1. The teacher's job is to make sure students can do things they couldn't do before.
2. If students avoid astronomy as a result of having taken Mr. Neptune's astronomy class, then we can say he taught them to avoid astronomy.
3. The failure of a student to learn is a failure in his or her natural development.
4. Students' experiences in school, more than anything else, determine their attitudes toward the subjects they take.
5. "Natural" development can be a harmful concept if it is taken to mean that a student will develop better without human intervention than with it.
6. You can teach a person something without being aware that you are doing so.
7. Only desirable behavior can be taught.
8. The teacher should not try to change the attitudes and values that a student holds, even if the teacher feels they are harmful to the student.
9. "Changing behavior" can mean using positive, rather than punitive techniques.
10. Only some of our behavior is affected by our daily experiences.

Answers for Concept Check IB

The six statements are numbers 1, 2, 4, 5, 6, and 9.

Number 3 attributes lack of learning to "natural development." An operant approach would not omit the environment.

Number 7 If we define teaching as changing behavior, then both desirable and undesirable behavior can be taught. Both are, in fact, being taught all the time. What is desirable or undesirable depends upon our viewpoint, not upon what change can be produced.

Number 8 The operant view is exactly the opposite.

Number 10 *All* of our behavior is being affected all of the time. What we experience either maintains or changes what we do from day to day.

Questions For Further Thought

1. At what point does your idea of teaching agree or disagree with the operant definition?
2. The following statement appeared in a text on teaching. What would an operant psychologist think of it?

"The teacher taught well but the students didn't learn."

Answers and Comments for Questions for Further Thought

1. Naturally there is no "right" answer for your idea of teaching, but the following points frequently arise:
   a. Where the responsibility for learning lies—An operant approach maintains that the school environment controls day-to-day behavior so that much of the responsibility for student learning lies in the environment the teacher creates, not in the student or the home environment.
   b. Whether we have a "right" to change someone's behavior—Given that we can change behavior, should we? Operant psychologists feel that the teacher has a responsibility to change certain behaviors in students.
   c. Whether teaching must involve student behavior—as operant psychologists maintain, or not.
2. It's nonsense. If the students didn't learn, the teacher didn't teach. The teacher may have been active, but whatever he or she did wasn't teaching unless the students learned as a result of it.

Causes of behavior and explanatory fictions

OVERVIEW

We are always "explaining" behavior. Chapter Two looks critically at our "explanations." It defines the criteria for explanation in a science of behavior.

OBJECTIVES

By the end of the chapter you should be able to:

A. Define *functional relationship* and identify or give examples of functional relationships.

B. Take any statement explaining behavior, identify the *dependent* and *independent variables* in it, and

C. Tell whether a statement is an *explanatory fiction* or a *testable explanation*, giving reasons for your choice.

D. Tell whether given explanations of behavior are consistent with an operant point of view or not and tell why or why not.

Teachers have always raised questions about the causes of behavior. Why does Walter refuse to participate? Why does John work so hard sometimes but not at other times? Whenever we ask "Why?" we are looking for causes.

WHAT IS A CAUSE?

A cause of behavior is something upon which behavior depends in a lawful way. Other things being equal, any change in the cause (called the *independent variable*) must produce a change in the behavior we are trying to explain (called the *dependent variable*). The question "Why?" is answered by identifying what is controlling the behavior, what the behavior depends upon. "What causes behavior?" then becomes "Of what is behavior a function?" If John does only those exercises which count toward his grade, John's working is (at least partly) a function of grades. If we change what exercises count toward a grade, we change what exercises John does. We have a *functional relationship* between work and grades.

Functional Relationships. A functional relationship is a relationship in which one variable changes systematically according to the value of another. It has the logical form "If A, then B." For John, whose working is a function of "counting" toward grades, the logical statement is, "If an assignment counts, then John will do it."

A Functional Relationship

is a relationship in which one variable changes systematically according to the value of another.

Any functional relationship holds only within certain limits. If John already has an A in a course, he may fail to do an assignment even if it "counts." More general statements of functional relationships, such as the laws of science, have limits too. It is only when certain conditions are met that a particular functional relationship applies.

Any functional relationship can theoretically be put to an experimental test: manipulate the independent variable and note the effect on behavior. We do this in a casual way when we change the seating of a disruptive student or when we try out a new teaching approach because the old one was not effective enough. Teachers who are dissatisfied with student performance on a particular test might try something different with the next class. Say that they try peer tutoring instead of lecturing. The teachers are varying the independent variable because they believe that student learning is a function of type of instruction. Although the scientist is more systematic, the procedure of trying something and noting results is basically the same.

A Dependent Variable

is a behavior we are trying to explain. It is the variable whose value *depends* upon the value of other variables in a functional relationship.

The variables in a science are observable: they are concepts closely tied to the measurable world. Because of the specificity of variables,

> **An Independent Variable**
>
> is any variable which is different from the dependent variable in that it can change *independently* of it. It is something, in other words, that can change when the dependent variable does not, or can remain the same when the dependent variable changes, or can change in a different direction, or at a different rate. (For any dependent variable, there are thousands of independent variables. In looking for causes of behavior, we look for the particular independent variables of which behavior is a function.)

functional relationships provide powerful tools for prediction and control. Knowing the value of the independent variable, we can predict the value of the dependent variable. If we can control the independent variable, we can control the dependent variable. A functional relationship which holds within certain limits is as close to "cause" as science ever gets.

EXPLANATORY FICTIONS—
EXPLANATIONS THAT DO NOT EXPLAIN

Many of the statements made to explain behavior do not identify causes in the sense described above. Here is an example. During an in-service workshop, an elementary schoolteacher brought up the following problem. She had a student, she said, who did well on weekly spelling quizzes but misspelled badly on his daily compositions—the very same words he had spelled correctly on his spelling tests! Why, she asked, did he misspell when he "knew better"? Table I gives some of the reasons given by the rest of the teachers. Perhaps the statements sound reasonable enough. But if we look at them closely we discover that not one is an explanation in any scientific sense. All they do is state the problem over again.

Explanatory Fictions. No one would be satisfied with the statement "Carol hits because Carol hits" as an explanation because the reason given ("Carol hits") is the same as the behavior we are trying to explain ("Carol hits"). We might vary the words a bit and say "Carol strikes others because she hits others" but that does not improve the explanation. If we rephrase the statement by putting a label on Carol, we have something that *sounds* reasonable: "Carol hits because she is aggressive." But if the evidence we are using to conclude that Carol is aggressive is simply that she hits, we are still only describing the same problem twice. We have what is called an *explanatory fiction*.

In a true explanation the reason, or cause (independent variable), must be *different* from the behavior we wish to explain (dependent vari-

TABLE I Examples of Practicing Teachers' Responses to the Question: "Why Does Paul Spell Correctly on Friday's Test But Then Misspell the Same Words in His Compositions?"

1. Because Paul is careless about spelling on compositions.
2. Because Paul isn't motivated to spell except on tests.
3. Because Paul doesn't proofread.
4. Because Paul is in a hurry.
5. Because Paul isn't interested in spelling correctly in his daily work.
6. Because Paul doesn't apply what he has learned.
7. Because he has a defeatest attitude.
8. Because he doesn't associate—make a connection between a word on Friday and later.
9. Because he's too intent on getting his ideas down in creative writing.
10. Because he doesn't relate Friday's words to follow-up activities.
11. Because he lacks the background in spelling rules.
12. Because he doesn't correlate the idea that spelling is the same as writing.
13. Because he doesn't try.
14. Because he has a perceptual problem.
15. Because he doesn't hear sounds—he has a hearing problem.

able). The test for whether or not it is different is whether or not the same evidence is used for both independent and dependent variables. If we were to measure cause and effect, would we look at the same things? If we must answer "yes," then our statement is not an explanation but an explanatory fiction.

An Explanatory Fiction

is a statement which has the form of an explanation but in which the cause which is given is really only another way of describing the behavior which is supposedly being explained.

Let's look back at why Paul misspells on his compositions. The dependent variable is "misspelling on compositions." It would normally be measured by the number of mistakes made on compositions (perhaps in comparison with the number of correctly spelled words). Let's try our test on the independent variables proposed. Number 1 is "Paul is careless about spelling on compositions." What evidence would we use to judge carelessness? How do we know Paul "isn't motivated to spell except on tests" (Number 2) or he "isn't interested in spelling correctly in his daily work" (Number 5)? The evidence for each of these statements would most likely be "misspelling on compositions," the very behavior we are trying to explain! The statements are all explanatory fictions.

The same case could be made for the other statements in the list, although it is less clear in some. Perhaps we would look at something besides spelling errors to see if Paul proofreads, or perhaps there is evidence other than misspelling for a "perceptual problem" or a "hearing problem" (though why, then, Paul spells correctly on tests is a mystery). But you must remember that these statements were made about a student the teachers did not know. The only information they had was what Paul's teacher had said about his spelling. If we ask, "How do you know Paul doesn't proofread?" and hear, "Well look at his awful spelling," the teacher is using misspelling to explain misspelling and we have an explanatory fiction.

The use of explanatory fiction to explain behavior is like the Indian Theologian's explanation of what holds up the world:

An Indian Theologian was giving a class. He stroked his long beard and said to his students in a serious voice, "The world rests on the back of an elephant." A student shot up his hand. "Sir," he asked, "what does the elephant stand on?" The Theologian peered over his spectacles. "Why, another elephant." Another hand shot up. "Sir, what does *that*. . . ?" But the Theologian interrupted, "Save your breath," he said. "Its elephants all the way down."

In a similar way, explanatory fictions can be generated ad infinitum: "The student doesn't work because *he doesn't feel like working.*" "He doesn't feel like working because *he isn't interested in the subject.*" "He isn't interested in the subject because *he isn't motivated.*" "He isn't motivated because *he has a low 'need to achieve.'*" And so on, "all the way down."

Explanatory fictions are no help to the teacher. Being told that a student doesn't work enthusiastically *because* he or she is not motivated does not tell the teacher what to change. We are no closer to a solution if we are told to motivate Johnny than we were when we knew we had to get him to work harder. In practice, explanatory fictions are worse than no help. Too often they put the blame on the student, thus discouraging the teacher from looking at the environment for the real causes of the problem.

One more example: A college course in educational psychology was converted from a lecture format to self-instructional units through which students could progress at their own pace. About 500 students normally took the course, which was required for certification. The semester started, and for the first few weeks things went smoothly. True, the learning center in which the units were to be taken was nearly empty, but the few students who came seemed to be progressing nicely. Midsemester came and went, and everybody was happy. Then, as the end of the semester drew near, disaster struck. Five hundred students descended on the learning center, waiting in lines 20 and 30 deep for the few copies of materials, for the tests, and for their test scores. Somehow, 300 students made it through by the time grades had to be sent to the registrar. The registrar called up immediately, "There must be some mistake," he said. "Two hundred students are recorded as not having completed your course." The instructors had to admit, "There's no mistake."

Why didn't the students complete the course? It would have been tempting to blame the students by saying they were not motivated to get going soon enough, or they procrastinated too long, or they lacked the self-discipline necessary for individualized instruction. Then, like Pontius Pilate, the instructors could wash their hands of any responsibility. All of these supposed reasons, however, are explanatory fictions. They merely restate the problem. They do not identify the variables which determine how students behave.

To change the situation, the instructors needed to find out what aspects of the course determined the students' progress through it. Three factors identified were: (1) there weren't enough deadlines; (2) there was no advantage (such as grade points) for beginning earlier; and (3) students weren't informed of their progress and its implications. These reasons are not merely another way of describing the problem, they are independent variables. They can be changed—and were. By setting weekly deadlines which had to be met for a good grade and by making progress (or its lack) conspicuous, the instructors reduced the number of incompletes to fewer than a dozen, and many students finished early in the semesters which followed.

TRUTH AND CAUSES

A statement may satisfy the requirement that the cause is different from the behavior explained and still not be a true statement. Advertising provides many examples. If an advertisement states that Mr. Romance proposes to Ms. Smiley because she uses Breatho toothpaste, we are likely to object. "Number of proposals" and "brushing teeth" are clearly measured differently, so the statement is not an explanatory fiction. It is simply not true.

To determine whether or not a statement of a functional relationship is true, we must test it. It is tempting to attribute the cause of a behavior to something which happens to occur at the same time, particularly when it agrees with our beliefs. Suppose, for example, we have a nursery school child who wets her pants Monday, Wednesday, and Friday. If, in talking to her mother, we discover that the child was spanked on those mornings, we are likely to conclude that spanking caused the child to wet her pants. If, however, Mama says that on those days she poured water over a voodoo model of her daughter, we are likely to dismiss the relationship as coincidental. Our judgment is made not upon the evidence, which is equally strong for both "causes," but upon our beliefs. To determine whether or not a functional relationship exists, we could do an experimental test. For the "voodoo doll cause" we would see if Mama could produce wetting by soaking the doll. It is this ability to *test* a statement and not its truthfulness that distinguishes explanation from explanatory fiction.

HOW OPERANT PSYCHOLOGY DIFFERS FROM OTHER APPROACHES TO EXPLAINING BEHAVIOR

In insisting on looking at behavior as a scientific subject matter, operant psychology differs from other approaches to studying behavior. The difference is not primarily in the dependent variables studied. The same kinds of behaviors have interested people throughout history. The difference is in how one goes about explaining behavior. Operant psychology looks at measurable behavior and tries to identify the variables of which that behavior is a function. The following "causes" are therefore rejected.

Hypothetical Constructs—Cognitive Structures and Stages. In contrast to cognitive psychology, operant psychology rules out hypothetical constructs (located *inside* the student) as explanations. Such constructs as *cognitive structures* are demonstrated only by the very kinds of behaviors they are invented to explain. They are classic cases of explanatory fictions.

Some developmental psychologists classify behavior into stages through which a child passes while developing. To say Simone is in the "crawling stage" indicates not only her method of locomotion but a number of other behaviors common in children who crawl. To then say that she sits up but can't walk *because* she is at the crawling stage, however, is an explanatory fiction. Similarly, it is redundant to say that a child can solve certain problems (such as telling that a quantity of liquid does not change when poured from a tall skinny glass into a short fat one) *because* he has reached the "stage of conservation." One identifies the cognitive stage by these very behaviors.

Time. There is a relationship between chronological age and behavior, but the passage of time does not cause behavior. A child does not walk or talk because the youngster is three but because of the physical growth and the learning which have taken place up to that time. Even height and weight are not a function of time. Without food and water no growth would occur. It is what happens during the passage of time that produces change, not the ticking of seconds on a clock.

Future Goals and Expectations. In daily speech we often attribute behavior to some future occurrence, as in the statement, "He goes to school because he will get a degree." Scientifically it is impossible for some event *now* to have a cause which is in the future. If the cause does not occur when the time comes, how do we explain the behavior that did occur? Suppose we say that Sheri goes to driving class in order to pass the driver's test. The behavior (going to class) is attributed to a cause which is to occur afterward (passing the driving test). If Sheri fails the test, Sheri's going to class could not have been caused by passing the test she didn't pass.

Since a future occurrence can't cause behavior, we might be tempted to say that the cause is our expectations. Sheri goes to class not because she *will* pass the test but because she *expects* to pass the test. In naming an expectation, however, we have generated another question: How did the expectancy originate? Perhaps Sheri in the past has passed tests by going to classes. We then have a three-step analysis: Passing Tests in Past → Expectancy of Passing → Going to Class.

Since expectancies are determined completely by past experience, it adds nothing to the analysis to include them. By Ocham's razor (the simplest explanation is best) we can eliminate the middle step. The behavior of going to class can then be seen as a function of experiences with tests in the past. It is not caused by a future event or an expectancy. There is a second reason for eliminating the middle step. We can directly manipulate how often Sheri passes tests, but there is no way to directly manipulate expectancy. An operant approach, therefore, rejects expectancies as independent variables.

"Born That Way." There is no doubt that heredity plays an important role in our behavior. The short boy will not be likely to play professional basketball. His behavior is partly a function of an inborn physiological trait. Differences in activity level, sensitivity to physical stimuli, even what is called "intelligence," are doubtless present at birth. But genetic endowment is overworked as a cause for behavior.

A student who constantly moves about, changing activities, is likely to be called "hyperactive." The implication is that this behavior is inborn, a fixed characteristic, caused by inherited genes. If we follow a hyperactive youth outside school, however, we may discover him working undistractedly for two hours on an old car, or sitting motionless watching TV. His genetic endowment has not changed. The behaviors of concentrating or moving about are not, then, a function of a given genetic plan. Something in the environment is maintaining those behaviors. Similarly, all of us behave differently in different environments.

While our genetic makeup partly determines certain tendencies we have, it cannot account for what we do and when we do it.

WHICH ENVIRONMENT AS A CAUSE?

We live in many different environments, each of which "shapes up" certain behaviors. A teacher behaves differently in class than at a party; a student, differently at home than at school. When explaining behavior in one environment, it is tempting to cite another environment which is currently part of a person's life. The other environment teachers most often use is home environment. In spite of the fact that students work hard in one class and not in another, talk out in one class and not in another, do more work pages one week than they do another week, teachers often explain school behavior by citing the students' home environment. Ask why Joe talks out in history class and we hear, "He has a poor home background." But Joe's behavior varies. The day before a test he may work very hard. Joe's parents and home environment have not changed. It is something in the day-to-day school environment which controls Joe's day-to-day behavior.

Home environment *is* important. A student who has already learned at home much of what is taught at school has an easier time than one with a home environment which does not teach academic skills. All students come into class with established patterns of behavior which have been determined by all of their past experiences, including those at home. Students who already have learned to work hard on assignments, read and write well, and so on, are likely to find learning easier than those who do not have those skills when they enter a class. But what any student continues to do or begins to do differently in the classroom depends upon his or her daily experiences in it. We cannot blame note-passing day after day in our biology class on Ms. Smither's Uncle George's drinking habits at home. We need to look at our own classroom environment to find out what is maintaining behavior.

SUMMARY

Operant psychology is a science of behavior which looks for functional relationships between behavior and factors in the environment in which that behavior occurs. It is an experimental approach to behavior and insists that explanations be testable. It does not, therefore, accept explanatory fictions, which are statements in which the behavior to be explained and its causes refer to the same set of facts. Behavior, according to an operant view, is a product of one's genetic inheritance and experiences since birth. We are always controlled, and how we behave is always changing through our day-to-day interactions with the environment. To find out why we behave in a particular way, then, we look, first of all, at factors in the environment in which that behavior occurs.

EXERCISES

Concept Check IIA—Functional Relationships (Objective A)

Which three statements below describe functional relationships between the underlined variables?

1. The <u>distance</u> traveled equals the <u>rate times the time</u> traveled.
2. Joan <u>passes notes</u> only when <u>near Judy.</u>
3. Tom <u>is a boaster</u> and <u>he brags</u> often.
4. How much <u>work I get done</u> in the morning depends on <u>what time I go to bed the previous night.</u>
5. I really feel that students <u>who come to class late</u> should <u>stay later than the others.</u>

Answers for Concept Check IIA

Functional relationships are stated in numbers 1, 2, and 4.

In Statement 1 distance is a function of rate and time.
In Statement 2 note-passing is a function of nearness to Judy.
In Statement 4 work done is a function of bedtime.

In the others, no lawful relationship is stated between two things. There is no implied "because":

Statement 3 does not relate two variables; two statements are merely joined by "and."
Statement 5 does not specify any lawful relationship between coming late and staying late. The speaker would like to establish such a relationship perhaps, but the statement as it stands does not imply that there is any cause-and-effect relationship.

Concept Check IIB—Dependent and Independent Variables (Objective B)

For each statement, jot down whether the underlined variable is a dependent variable (D) or independent variable (I).

1. Jan <u>completes assignments on time</u> because the teacher gives extra points for promptness.
2. John's <u>blond silky hair</u> is responsible for the teachers liking him.
3. The reason the child developed dependency behaviors was that these behaviors regularly brought <u>attention and concern from the teachers.</u>

4. He <u>types rapidly</u> due to having taken a good typing course.
5. Young drivers, because of <u>immaturity and overconfidence</u>, drive too fast.

Answers for Concept Check IIB

1. D (completing assignments *depends* on points).
2. I (hair color and texture are given as a *cause* for the dependent variable, "teachers liking him").
3. I (attention and concern are given as *causes* for the dependent variable, dependency).
4. D (rapid typing *depends* on having had a good course).
5. I (immaturity and overconfidence are given as *causes* for the dependent variable, "drive too fast").

Concept Check IIC—Explanatory Fictions (Objective C)

Pick the six explanatory fictions from the following list of statements:

1. Erik doesn't seem to do math well—perhaps because of his poor math aptitude.
2. Tom shoots baskets well because he is tall.
3. John, a first grader, clings to his teacher, Ms. Spivens, because he has developed a genuine fear of being separated from her.
4. Mr. Salten refuses to participate in classroom discussions because he lacks the confidence to talk up.
5. One very important part of creativity, the asking of provocative questions, is killed in our schools by the teachers who punish those who ask embarrassing questions—like Tom Edison asking why water runs uphill in some rivers instead of downhill as in most rivers.
6. Sam's lack of progress is due to his lack of readiness.
7. Joe can't understand mathematics because it confuses him.
8. Janet likes science because she is good at it.
9. Richard works hard at physics because he is motivated in it.
10. Myrtle shoves and cuts into lines because she gets farther ahead in them.

Answers for Concept Check IIC

Explanatory fictions are numbers 1, 3, 4, 6, 7, and 9.

In Number 1 one would measure how well Erik does math by how many problems he gets correct and incorrect (and perhaps by how fast he can do them), and that is also the measure of math aptitude. Tests of "math aptitude" have problems to be done. If they differ from classroom problems at all, it is only in having more variety than a single classroom test.

In Number 3 one infers the fear from the clinging behavior: one tells whether a child has "fear of being separated" by whether or not the child clings. The same behavior is described by both variables.

In Number 4 the only evidence for "lack of confidence to talk up" is "not participating in classroom discussions." For both, one would have to count frequency of volunteering, or answering questions, or some similar behavior. This is a classic explanatory fiction—the dependent behavior (not participating) is put inside the student as a trait, "lacking confidence," and then given as a cause.

In Number 6 "lack of progress" would be the evidence used for "lack of readiness."

In Number 7 both "lack of understanding" and having math "confuse him" describe the same behaviors by Joe.

In Number 9 motivation would be assessed by how hard Richard works.

The rest are testable explanations.

In Number 2 "shooting baskets" would be measured by "number of baskets made and missed." Height (the independent variable) would be measured by inches or centimeters. Although one cannot manipulate height, one could see whether, in general, tall players make more baskets than short ones do. (Note that one might find that the statement is not true.)

In Number 5 the dependent variable would be measured by the frequency of "provocative questions"; the independent variable, by the frequency of the teachers' punishment. One could vary the degree of punishment to see how it affected the students' asking of provocative questions.

In Number 8 the dependent variable, "liking science," could be measured by many things, such as positive statements or extra projects done. Being "good at it" would be measured by "achievement." It would be possible to see whether success determines attitudes—by, for example, seeing whether Janet's positive statements or work done changes when she is put into an environment in which she is more "successful."

In Number 10 one could count shoves and/or cuts into line directly. How far ahead Myrtle gets in line could be measured by a simple count from her original position. These two are different.

Concept Check IID—Operant Explanations of Behavior (Objective D)

Which two of the following statements are consistent with an operant approach to explaining behavior?

1. The kinds of experiences a student encounters and has encountered in a subject area determine how hard he or she will work in it.
2. Bess is interested in sex more than most girls her age because of an overactive sex drive.
3. How hard a student will work in school is preprogrammed at birth (by genetic endowment).
4. Man's mind determines his behavior.
5. Our physiological and genetic makeups do have an effect on our behavior.

Answers for Concept Check IID

The statements are numbers 1 and 5.

Number 2 is an explanatory fiction.

Number 3 overemphasizes the role of genetic inheritance. Such specific behaviors as working hard in school are controlled largely by an individual's history. Genetic endowment may determine how experience affects learning, but genes alone do not cause particular behaviors.

Number 4 Operant psychology considers everything that a person does as behavior, including "inner events" such as thinking. While thinking and other behaviors usually associated with "mind" are legitimate *dependent* variables in a science of behavior, the concept of "mind" is avoided, especially as an independent variable. In Number 4 it is used as an independent variable. In more specific statements such a use becomes an explanatory fiction, as in the statement, "He went because he made up his mind to go."

CHAPTER THREE

How we learn

OVERVIEW

This chapter discusses operant learning: why we do the things we do from day to day.

OBJECTIVES

By the end of the chapter you should be able to:

A. Describe how operant learning occurs and identify the necessary conditions for operant learning.
B. Identify an operant in a classroom episode and the preceding and following stimuli, and in one sentence describe the contingencies involved.
C. Define and identify examples of the following:
   1. An operant
   2. Operant conditioning
   3. A stimulus
   4. A response
   5. Contingencies of reinforcement

A FABLE

Once upon a time there was a modern prince who set out to make his fortune. So that people wouldn't recognize him, he grew his hair long and wore old jeans instead of rich robes.

It was September, and the day was believably warm and beautiful. Our hero, whom we shall call Ewan Mea, set out toward the general direction of things happening. As he turned a corner he saw six youths holding the nozzle of a long, fat hose, trying to wash down a pool and fountain head. Others were looking on. The water rushed out with considerable force. Suddenly the hose began to take life, like a dragon who wanted to look around. The nozzle swayed back and forth, breaking loose from two of the youths. Loops of water encircled the onlookers.

"Hey, hold on."

"Come back here."

"Help!" the youths cried. Several concerned people ran to help hold the monster's head, but it playfully turned on them, too, scattering them with its watery bursts.

Two students shielded behind a raincoat moved in on the beast. They held their ground when it swept by them, but they couldn't catch the monster's head.

One or two onlookers ran for the squirming nozzle as others were shaken loose. Water flowed everywhere.

Ewan Mea didn't hesitate. Breaking into a run he shouted, "You're working at the wrong end! Get the faucet. Turn off the water."

He reached the valve first, and with three mighty twists shut off the monster's lifeblood. The hose instantly fell to the ground. Quiet and relief settled down with the last mists of spray.

Most people deal with behavior like the people in the fable who rushed to the nozzle of the hose. They react to the most conspicuous part of a problem but ignore its cause. This chapter presents an analysis of causes from an operant standpoint. It should help you cut through words and actions to the critical factors which control your students' behavior and your own.

A THREE-TERM ANALYSIS OF BEHAVIOR

Imagine that you are in a classroom on your first day of class. Forty-three students have come into the room, and they are already behaving in very different ways. One tall girl is talking animatedly to two others. A short girl is rummaging in an enormous purse; a boy grabs the scarf hanging out of one side of the purse and the girl chases him around the room. Several boys are standing and looking out the window, a few are talking and laughing. Finally, several students have taken their seats and are looking expectantly up to you for words of wisdom.

What is it that determines what each student does? Inheritance, no doubt, plays a part. No student born blind, for example, will be looking out the window. But within the rather broad limits of what is called "normal," it is difficult to trace behavior to inheritance. No one would seriously consider a specific genetic code to be responsible for scarf-grabbing or laughing at this particular moment. To find out what controls our day-to-day behavior, we first decide on a behavior of interest. We isolate a particular *response*. For our example above, we might take "grabbing an article from a female." Next we look at the environment—at the *situation* in which the response occurred and at the *consequence* that followed the response.

The fact that it was 71° F. in the classroom, or that the radiators were banging, or that you could faintly smell spaghetti from the lunchroom are probably not of interest. The part of the environment we consider is any part likely to be functionally related to the response. We look for stimuli preceding or following the response of interest.

A stimulus is any physical object or occurrence in the environment. A chair is a stimulus. A sound is a stimulus. A student running past is a stimulus. Some stimuli are measured physically, in centimeters, decibels, and so on; some, less precisely in words (12 students ran from Defiant Hall to the Administrative Ediface). Stimuli exist whether or not anyone responds to them. They are part of our environment.

A Stimulus

is an environmental event or object which can be physically measured in some way. A chair is a *stimulus,* a magnetic field is a *stimulus,* the chemical substance called perfume is a *stimulus. Stimuli* exist whether or not anyone responds to them.

To analyze behavior, we look at both preceding and following stimuli. We have, then, a *three-term analysis.* For the response "grab" in our example, the three terms are shown in Number 1 in Table I. We name the response *first.* There is no way to identify "preceding stimulus" unless you can answer "preceding what?"

Some other examples of a three-term analysis follow in Table I. Sometimes we respond to a particular stimulus, as when we answer a question. For much of our behavior, however, there is no identifiable

TABLE I   Three-Term Analyses of Some Classroom Behaviors

Preceding stimulus (Situation)	Response(s)	Following stimulus (Consequence)
1. Presence of a "grabable" scarf	Grabs scarf	Girl chases him
2. Teacher: "How does Chaucer portray the Wife of Bath? Sam?"	"I'd sure like to take her on."	Class laughs
3. "Open" classroom science table with tray, sand, water, and clumps of grass (for studying erosion)	Charles looks at the display, picks up a glass of water and pours it down the tray filled with sand.	Sand washes down tray

stimulus which occurs just before we respond. The student in Number 3, Table I, for example, may, at a particular time, pick up a glass which has been sitting on the table all morning. There is no specific preceding stimulus we can identify as we could if someone had told him to pick up the glass. There are identifiable results, however, when his pouring washes away the sand, and this change in stimuli is crucial in learning.

OPERANT CONDITIONING

Behavior which is controlled by changes in the environment is called *operant behavior*. Most of what we do each day is operant. Walking, talking, thinking are all operant. Most of what we teach in school is operant. The process involved in learning or in teaching any of these behaviors is called *operant conditioning*.

Operant Conditioning

is a process in which behavior is "strengthened," in the sense of becoming more likely to occur, through reinforcement.

Operant conditioning is a selection process which works for behavior much as Darwin's "survival of the fittest" works for species. The behaviors which survive out of the thousands of things we do and have done in the past are those which have been in some way effective. Each response, from scratching an itch to composing a poem, is either strengthened, maintained, or weakened by the changes it produces in stimuli. If a response is strengthened, it is likely to occur again. If it continues to be strengthened, it becomes a stable part of behavior.

To find out why a person behaves in a certain way, then, we must

TABLE II   Why Does a Child Cry Over a Skinned Knee?

Preceding stimulus	Response	Following stimulus
Skinned knee (sympathetic teacher present)	Cry	Sympathy

Everyday analysis:

"He cries because it hurts."

Operant analysis:

"He cries because in the teacher's presence, crying over a skinned knee has brought sympathy."

"IF MY TEACHER WAS HERE I'D REALLY CRY UP A STORM!"

Figure 3.1

look at what usually *follows* that kind of behavior. We are not used to this approach. For example, consider an eight-year-old boy who skins his knee on the playground and cries. Asked why the child is crying, most people will say "because he skinned his knee and it hurts." Both the skinned knee and the pain are stimuli which precede the behavior we wish to explain. An *operant analysis*, in contrast, looks not only at the preceding stimuli but at the stimuli which have usually followed the behavior in the past (see Table II).

Now suppose the same boy is playing baseball after school with the big boys. No teacher is around. What kind of consequence would a cry produce in that case? The chances are that instead of sympathy, the boy would be ignored or perhaps ridiculed. It doesn't take long for the child who cries when his teacher is around to learn to "take" a skinned knee without crying when the consequences are not likely to be favorable (see Figure 3.1).

In the first case (Table II) the child does not cry *because* he skinned his knee. He skinned his knee in both cases, and in the second case he learns *not* to cry (see Table III).

TABLE III   Unfavorable Consequences

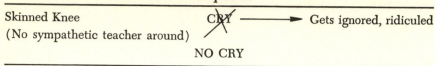

| Skinned Knee | CRY | ⟶ Gets ignored, ridiculed |
| (No sympathetic teacher around) | NO CRY | |

The stimulus which precedes a response is important, however, because of its relationship to the kinds of consequences an action will have. If Jim's teacher decides one day that he is old enough to "act like a man" and no longer shows sympathy when he cries, the teacher will cease to become a stimulus for "crying when hurt." If big boys "baby" a younger boy, giving sympathy when he cries, they will become a stimulus for crying when he's hurt (or when he wants his way).

In the same fashion, a sign "machine broken" on a vending machine is a stimulus usually associated with a lack of payoff for inserting a coin. A school recess bell is a stimulus for running outside. The announcement of a test is a stimulus for studying. The sign, bell, and announcement have control over behavior only insofar as they are associated with consequences. If a person experiences different consequences, the same stimuli will cue different behaviors, as when the broken machine gives two candy bars for the price of one, Mr. Brown requires his students to remain after the bell until *he* dismisses them, or a teacher's tests are so unpredictable that studying is useless.

CONTINGENCIES OF REINFORCEMENT

The relationships between the preceding stimulus, response, and following stimulus are called the *contingencies of reinforcement*. Some of the contingencies above were:

1. In the presence of the sign "machine broken" INSERTING A COIN produces <u>no candy.</u>
2. STUDYING just before a test <u>enables the student to answer questions on the test.</u>

Contingencies of Reinforcement

are the relationships between a kind of response, the stimuli which precede it, and the stimuli which follow it. All three terms must be specified in a statement of contingencies of reinforcement.

Both statements specify relationships between a RESPONSE (shown in capitals), the stimulus which preceded it (shown in regular type), and the stimulus which followed (underlined). The change from preceding to following stimulus is often called the *consequence*, although it need not be caused by the response.

AN OPERANT

It is useful to distinguish between a specific response (for example, one particular time when John hit Sarah) and a category of responses (John's behavior of hitting girls). The latter category of behavior is called *an operant*. An operant is a group of responses which produce the same or similar consequences. Behavior may *look* different and still be part of the same operant. The operant "hitting girls," for example, includes not only slaps but the quick punch, the elbow jab, the two-handed descending book strike, the belt snap, and many others. The responses vary in form but they produce a similar response from the receiving girl and are called "hitting girls."

An Operant

is a group of responses which produce, and are controlled by, similar consequences. Examples are "eating," "talking," and "doing arithmetic." "An operant" is roughly equivalent to the term "a behavior," except that is does not include behavior controlled by a preceding stimulus, such as the behavior in a reflex. "Blinking in response to a loud sound," for example, is not an operant.

Verbs are usually operants. Walking, talking, writing, reading, and thinking are operants. They refer to a group of behaviors which have similar consequences. Moving one's legs is not walking unless the behaver moves (the consequence), "talking" must produce audible sounds, "writing" must produce visible marks. The consequences of reading and thinking are less obvious, but we do not consider it reading when eyes merely pass over words—some change called "understanding" must occur. A similar argument can be made for "thinking."

The consequence of a response follows the response. It cannot affect the particular response which has already occurred. Sarah's jumping to John's poke does not change anything about the act John has already completed. What is strengthened is the *operant* of poking girls. The likelihood of John's poking girls in similar situations in the future increases.

Operant learning is a process much like Darwinian selection is for species. In a given environment those acts which are in some way effective survive and those which are ineffective die out. Over a period of time, patterns of behavior, like species, evolve from the kinds of individual operants that survive.

NECESSARY INGREDIENTS FOR OPERANT LEARNING

Responding. Since operant learning is a process in which certain responses are strengthened, it cannot occur unless the learner is responding in some way. At the very least the learner must be "paying attention." If, in biology class, a male student is daydreaming about motorcycles, he cannot be learning biology, no matter what the teacher is doing. (He may be learning about motorcycles or some other behavior, such as "how to look as though you're paying attention when you're not," but he is not learning biology.)

A quick look at a classroom can reveal a lot about the learning which is taking place. What are the students doing? Are they doing the kinds of things the teacher wants them to learn, or are they sitting while the *teacher* talks, demonstrates, or works out problems? While we can learn directions or rules from a lecture, we ourselves must at some point apply them if we are to learn to solve problems or create. We would not pretend to be effective in teaching swimming, speaking French, or writing poetry by talking about how to do it, but we persist where failure is less obvious. In English, social studies, or science, for example, the teacher may do most of the discussing, writing, evaluating, even creating, while the students spend most of their time sitting and watching.

Immediate Consequences. Student responding is not enough. We do not "learn by doing" alone. We learn when we receive consequences for our behavior. Students must not only act, they must see the effectiveness of their behavior. Some changes in stimuli come naturally from responding. When Ricardo is focusing a microscope, for example, he gets natural consequences for "correct" behavior. He does not need a teacher to tell him he is focusing correctly. For many paper and pencil exercises, students also "know" they are acting correctly because a problem may "come out right" or a problem may be easy for them. If you did Item I below, for example, you wouldn't need anyone to provide feedback.

Item I—An item for which the "right answer" is known.

$$2 + 2 = \underline{\hspace{1cm}}$$

For many responses, however, the *teacher* must provide consequences. Students may not be able to judge their own products or they may judge them incorrectly, like the student who completes an entire page of 40 problems like the ones in Table IV.

You, as a student, may have encountered lessons in which you had little or no idea of what was expected. In such cases, feedback is critical. For example, try Item II below.

TABLE IV   A Common Mistake Made by Students Learning to Add

$$\begin{array}{r} 17 \\ +\ \ 8 \\ \hline 115 \end{array} \qquad \begin{array}{r} 29 \\ +\ \ 8 \\ \hline 217 \end{array}$$

Item II—A task in which the "right answer" is *not* known (assuming the student does not know Hebrew).

Match each Hebrew word with its meaning in English:

דְּיוֹ ____   a. pen
עֵט ____   b. hand
יָד ____   c. ink
סֵפֶר ____   d. book

You could try the item over and over and learn nothing (except perhaps to avoid Hebrew) if you had no way of telling which responses were correct.

Next Step Determined by Student Behavior. Since learning is a process of strengthening existing responses, the teacher must build new behavior by providing consequences for the best of what the student already does. In tutoring, most teachers first find out what the student can do before starting to teach. In teaching nutrition, for example, a tutor would not present "exchange lists" because it was Tuesday and that was Tuesday's lesson. The tutor would find out what the student could already do, and then give slightly more advanced problems that the students would be likely to solve correctly.

In the typical classroom, in contrast, topics covered are often presented without any regard for what students can do already. Chapter 14 is assigned in October because that is October's lesson. Those for whom the lesson is too easy are bored, while those for whom it is too advanced do not learn in class at all. They are forced to learn later in remedial sessions either with the teacher, with friends or parents, or alone with earlier chapters of the book. Many never learn at all.

IMPLICATIONS FOR CLASSROOM MANAGEMENT

In looking at the role of stimulus change in producing and maintaining behavior, we can see the reasons for many problems in classroom control. Look at the kinds of consequences students get for talking with friends or other unassigned activities as opposed to consequences for studying. When there is an immediate reason for working *now*, as in a timed test which counts toward a grade, students for whom a grade is a meaningful consequence work hard. When it really doesn't make much difference whether or not a student works now, or ten minutes from now, or *mañana,* he or she is likely to do other things. And what about misbehavior? What are the consequences for misbehaving? If one student in a room starts to hum or to look out the window, who gets the teacher's attention? Whenever teachers criticize any student, they are providing a consequence for the misbehavior they are criticizing. If teacher attention is reinforcing enough (and it usually is), they are strengthening the unwanted behavior, thus producing a disciplinary problem.

SUMMARY

Operant conditioning is constantly going on. Everything we do either changes, or fails to change the stimuli in our environment. Every experience affects the way we will behave in the future. In the schoolroom, each student's behavior is constantly being shaped by the consequences it produces. The contingencies either maintain behavior from day to day or change it. The teacher may feel the student ought to study—just as one might feel that a hefty shove ought to move a rock. But both student and rock will obey the laws of nature. They act as functions of environmental variables. If students do not behave the way the teacher feels they should, it is because the contingencies are wrong. The rock behaves "the way it should" given its particular circumstances. Similarly, each student behaves the way he or she should, given the contingencies under which he or she exists. Just as one can move a rock more effectively by using physical laws, one can teach more effectively by using psychological laws. As the old saying goes, "Nature, to be commanded, must be obeyed."

EXERCISES

Concept Check IIIA—Operant Learning (Objective A)

Which six statements best describe how operant learning occurs?

1. New responses unfold naturally as we grow older.
2. Repeated exposure to a stimulus forms new stimulus-response bonds.
3. We repeat the kinds of responses that pay off in some way.
4. Any of our actions that are strengthened by the environment survive as part of our behavior while other actions die out.
5. We store information in our heads for later use.
6. The changes in stimuli which immediately follow a response determine the probability of similar responses in the future.
7. In a given situation, acts which are effective tend to be repeated while ineffective ones tend not to be repeated.
8. New responses emerge as our behavior shifts due to the consequences of individual responses.

9. We learn by acting and getting feedback for what we do.
10. We learn by doing something again and again until it "sticks."

Answers for Concept Check IIIA

The best statements are numbers 3, 4, 6, 7, 8, and 9. Each of them specifies that we must *behave* in order to learn and that the consequences of what we do determine what we learn.

Number 1 is not acceptable because it omits the roles of experience and environment altogether.

Number 2 fails to specifically mention that we must respond in order to learn and it does not mention consequences at all.

Number 5 does not mention any consequences. The metaphor of "storing information" is not a good description of what happens when we learn because it implies that we consciously put something inside ourselves. What exactly is "stored"? Electrical impulses? Biochemical substances *do* change when we learn but nothing is "stored." Statement 5 does not convey our continual evolution as we experience the world. Even if "storing information" were a good description, the statement fails to account for what is "stored" and what is not.

Number 10 mentions our "doing" but counts on repetition to produce learning. Without consequences, repetition leads to extinction, not to "sticking." The behavior dies out.

Concept Check IIIB—An Operant (Objective B)

Which of the items below are examples of an operant?
1. An experimental apparatus
2. Eating
3. The one time you mounted a horse
4. The composing of term papers
5. The rumbling of thunder
6. Raining
7. A school psychologist
8. The shock you sometimes get from the school's old soft drink machine
9. All of the actions that open a book
10. What you are doing now (selecting examples of an operant)

Answers for Concept Check IIIB

Examples of an operant are numbers 2, 4, 9, and 10. They each describe a class of behaviors having similar effects.

Number 1 is not behavior at all.

Number 3 describes a single response. The collection of responses called "mounting horses" *is* an operant but a single response is not.

Number 5 and Number 6 are stimuli. Events are not operants. An operant must be the behavior of an animal.

Number 7 The kinds of things a school psychologist *does* are operants, but he himself is not.

Number 8 is a stimulus. It describes what happens *to* you but not a class of your actions.

Concept Check IIIC—Operant Conditioning (Objective C)

In which examples is operant conditioning occurring?
1. You reward another person for some action.
2. You throw a ball and it misses the basket.
3. You throw a ball and it makes the basket.
4. You throw a ball and it makes the basket and your friends cheer you.
5. You talk with your friend.

Answers for Concept Check IIIC

Operant conditioning is occurring in *all* of the examples. In each, you are behaving, and the results of your behavior will condition you, in that your future behavior will be affected by them.

Number 1 specifies a reward, which no doubt affects future behavior.

Number 2 and Number 3 specify natural consequences which will have different effects on future throws, but each of which "shapes" behavior. We tend to repeat the motions which lead to making baskets and to change something in what we do when we miss.

Number 4 adds a social reinforcer, "cheering," to the making of the basket itself. It may make the presence of peers a stimulus for trying especially hard.

Number 5 mentions a friend. Whatever the reactions (or the lack of reactions) you receive for talking, they will condition your verbal behavior.

Concept Check IIID—Stimulus (Objective C)

Which of the following are stimuli?

1. The jabbing of a pencil in your ribs to which you jump.
2. Background music which you hear but to which you do not otherwise respond.
3. A tree falling in the middle of a forest with no one around.
4. A book.
5. The radio waves (no radio present) which are part of your environment right now.

Answers for Concept Check IIID

All five are stimuli because they all are events or objects (matter or energy) in the physical universe which can be measured.

Concept Check IIIE—Response (Objective C)

Which of the following are responses?

1. Answering a particular question.
2. A textbook.
3. Singing a song one day when there is no identifiable stimulus for singing.
4. A printed sheet containing exercises for students to do.
5. Coughing when you swallowed the wrong way.

Answers for Concept Check IIIE

Numbers 1, 3, and 5 are responses. The others are stimuli.

Concept Check IIIF—Contingencies of Reinforcement (Objective C)

Which of the following *specify* all three terms of the contingencies of reinforcement?

1. Sam is a good student who works a great deal.
2. By having a good excuse when your assignment is late, you can get an extension of time.
3. Raising your hand is reinforced by getting called on.
4. When the teacher says, "Stand up," Sarah stands up.
5. "We learn by doing."
What is missing from the other item(s)?

Answers for Concept Check IIIF

Number 2 is the only statement in which all three terms and their relationships are specified.

Number 1 describes a response, "works a great deal," but leaves out both the stimulus (situation) under which Sam does so and the consequence following his response.

Number 3 fails to specify the situation in which the response, "hand raising," is reinforced by "getting called on."

Number 4 does not mention any consequences (stimulus change) following the response "standing up."

Number 5 Although "doing" is necessary for learning, without the preceding and following stimuli, the contingencies for learning have not been specified. A more complete statement might be "We learn by $\overset{1}{doing}$ more often those things which $\overset{2}{have\ been\ reinforced}$ in $\overset{3}{similar\ situations}$ in the past." (1 is the response; 2, the following stimuli or consequences; and 3, the preceding stimuli.)

ANALYSIS PROBLEMS (OBJECTIVE B)

For each student below, pick *one* desirable or undesirable behavior which would concern you as a teacher and:

1. Name a specific response;

2. Write down the preceding stimulus (situation); and

3. The consequence(s) for that response; and

4. In one sentence describe the contingencies of reinforcement for the response.

Example: Jerry
Jerry cries when he is knocked down. The teacher goes over and sympathizes and scolds the bigger boys who pushed Jerry.

Sample Answer:
1. Crying
2. Push by boys (hard enough to knock Jerry down)
3. Sympathy
4. When Jerry is pushed down a cry brings sympathy.

Sam

At the beginning of grammar class, the teacher tells the students to take out paper and a pencil and open their grammar books to the next lesson. The students don't like grammar and they are not enthusiastic. Sam, especially is a procrastinator. Usually he can't find the page, or a piece of paper, or his pencil is broken. He sits flipping through the book, or searching through his desk, or biting off the wood around the lead in his pencil until finally his teacher goes over to see what's wrong. The teacher usually has to find the right page for Sam and has to go get him a piece of paper and a new sharp pencil.

John

John is way beyond the rest of his French class and likes to impress his French teacher. No matter what question the teacher asks in French, John always gives a long, complicated response. He always speaks correctly, rapidly, and with good pronounciation. The French teacher usually replies with some little remark in French that no one else but John understands. It's a kind of game between them.

Answers for Analysis Problems

Sam

There are many responses you could have chosen. The contingencies for four of them are shown below.

Preceding stimulus	Response	Following stimuli
	1. *Flipping through book.*	1. Teacher finds page for Sam. Also Sam gets out of doing grammar for a little while. (A more subtle consequence is seeing a lot of pages in the book and perhaps catching the same page the other students are on. More likely, though,
Teacher's announcement to take out paper and pencil and turn to grammar lesson. (Also presence of book and broken pencil.)		

Preceding stimulus	Response	Following stimuli
		the flipping attracts the teacher's attention and the teacher's attention is the main reinforcer for the behavior.)
	2. *Searching through desk.*	2. Teacher comes over— perhaps bringing new paper to Sam.
Teacher's announcement to take out paper and pencil and turn to grammar lesson. (Also presence of book and broken pencil.)	3. *Biting off wood around pencil point.*	3. Teacher brings him new sharp pencil. (The effects the bite produces on the pencil itself are no doubt reinforcing also. They maintain the particular kind of bites that break off wood but not lead.)
	4. *Doing grammar.*	4. No particular consequence specified. Perhaps that's the problem.

STATEMENT OF CONTINGENCIES FOR SAM

1. Flipping through the book brings teacher attention when a grammar lesson has been assigned.
2. When the teacher assigns a grammar lesson to do, Sam gets the teacher to come over (sometimes bringing him a piece of paper) by searching through his desk.
3. If, instead of doing a grammar lesson as assigned, Sam bites off the wood around his pencil point, the teacher comes over to see what the problem is and sometimes brings him a new pencil.
4. Doing grammar when assigned has no particular positive consequences.

John

The student behavior described is answering French questions. You could have picked several aspects of it or put them all together.

Preceding stimulus	Response	Following stimuli
Teacher's question in French to French class.	1. *Gives long, complicated answer.* 2. *Answers with good pronunciation.* 3. *Answers rapidly.*	1. "Personal" remark from teacher—(one that only John understands). Also, perhaps John is reinforced by being able to say something his classmates do not understand.

STATEMENT OF CONTINGENCIES FOR JOHN

Any statement which specifies that John gets a personal remark from the teacher when he answers questions in French class with rapid, well-pronounced and complicated responses.

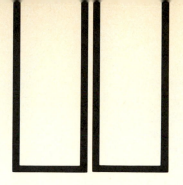

Measuring behavior

OVERVIEW

Dear Ms. Bea Mod,

I am a third grade teacher. One of the children in my class, Paulette, is a terrible problem. She is hyperactive and never stays in her seat very long. She is in the third grade but is reading on the first grade level. Naturally, since she can't read, she is also having trouble with math, spelling, social studies, and health. She is a bully also, always shoving other kids as she passes by them and pulling their hair. It seems I can never get her attention for even a few minutes. What should I do?

Sincerely,

Mr. Hopeful

Mr. Hopeful

Dear Mr. Hopeful,

Parts II and III give suggestions for problems such as yours.

Ms. Bea Mod

Ms. Bea Mod

STEPS IN CHANGING BEHAVIOR

Every teaching situation you encounter will pose one or more problems for you. Maybe a few students disrupt the class. Maybe you want to make sure that your students apply what they learn or that they develop more independence. Whatever change you wish to produce is your "problem."

If you take a minute to jot down four or five steps you follow in solving problems in general, you will probably have a list much like the following (though you may use different words):

1. Clearly define the problem (what do you want to do?).
2. Find out where you are now in terms of progress or resources.
3. Try something—and note results.
4. Revise as necessary.

The procedure for solving behavioral problems is basically the same. Using the language of what is called *precision teaching*, we can represent it in the four steps shown in Table I, which parallel the four steps above.

We first define the problem by *pinpointing* exactly the behaviors we wish to change, then we find out "where we are now" by *recording* and *charting* (or *graphing*) that behavior, we *change* something in what we are doing to see how that works, and we *try, try, again* if we are not successful the first time.

Although precision teaching is only one format for changing behavior, all behavior modification techniques first define the problem in terms of behavior; second, measure and record "entering behavior" (what each student does already); third, try some procedure and continue to record behavior, and fourth, revise as necessary. Part II discusses the first two steps; Part III, the second two.

TABLE I   **Four Steps in Precision Teaching**[1]

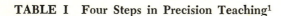

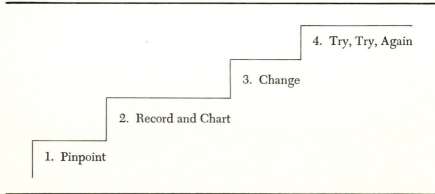

4. Try, Try, Again

3. Change

2. Record and Chart

1. Pinpoint

[1]Ogden Lindsley, Second Annual Trainer's Course in Precise Behavioral Management, Kansas City, Kansas, July, 1969.

This problem-solving approach to changing behavior is not only a method, it is also an outlook, a willingness to judge by what *works*, not by what we like to do or what we already believe. This point is illustrated in the following story:

A famous psychologist had written a book on learning, based on studies using rats. One day one of his students ran into the distinguished man's office, waving a long strip of paper.

"Look," he cried, "look at these results." The paper had the record of a rat's behavior during an experiment. "Look," he repeated, pointing to the record, "this shows that your second chapter is all wrong."

The psychologist looked carefully at the data. "Well," he said after a long pause, "the rat knows best."[2]

A teacher must be as much a scientist as the psychologist was. It is tempting to hold on to a method or point of view because we like it or because it makes us feel that a class is going well. To benefit our students, however, we must see how our actions affect *their* behavior, and for this we need the objectivity that good records give.

[2]The psychologist in the story was B. F. Skinner, the originator of operant psychology. The student was Ogden Lindsley, who later developed precision teaching.

Defining the problem

OVERVIEW

When you are teaching, how do you decide on what behaviors to change? What should you work on first? Chapter Four gives some suggestions.

OBJECTIVES

By the end of the chapter you should be able to:

A. Tell which of several statements of problems are best defined behaviorally, using the following criteria:
    1. Choose one problem at a time.
    2. Pick an active behavior you can count.
    3. Count in small enough units to get a count which will vary daily.
    4. Choose the problem behavior itself or its immediate product rather than your reactions to it or delayed results.
B. Specify a behavior to change from a description of a general problem.

STATING THE PROBLEM IN TERMS OF BEHAVIOR

Before you meet your students, you will undoubtedly have an idea of some of the skills you want them to learn and some general abilities you would like them to develop. As you interact with them, you will discover other behaviors which you will feel need to be changed. In order to be effective at changing behavior, you will have to be clear about what you are doing and about the results of your actions. Teachers who are truly concerned about each individual must keep

TABLE I Some Changes Practicing Teachers Said They Would Like in Their Students[1]

Elementary teachers	Secondary teachers
1. Be more curious and question more	1. Show more interest—volunteer to do work on own
2. Read more	2. Do more independent reading
3. Use better manners	3. Have less concern about grades
4. Talk less	4. Verbalize more in and before class
5. Show more consideration for others	5. Talk less, listen more while others are talking
6. Worry about grades less	6. Show more respect and acts of kindness toward fellow students
7. Show more respect for adults	7. Complain less about what you want them to do
	8. Be more independent and work more on their own

track of each student's progress (or its lack) in each of the behaviors they feel are important. It is a large job.

Most teachers keep track of individual progress in the so-called "content areas." Many public schools require some kind of weekly assessment in each subject, and in many courses across the country, the weekly quiz is standard practice. But what about all the other behaviors we talk about—such as attitudes, self-actualization, motivation, and creativity—all the areas which are not usually considered as course content? Can we say where each student stands in motivation, or how much Susan has improved in motivation this week as compared to last? The answer is certainly "No!" Perhaps it is because these less-tangible behaviors are rarely assessed in any systematic way that they get lost in our schools. In any case, it is the behaviors involved in the nonacademic areas that most concern teachers in the schools.

If one asks practicing teachers what changes they would like to see in their students, they name things such as those in Table I.

A teacher concerned with, say, "curiosity" or "showing interest" should be able to point to any student in the class and tell whether or not that individual has improved in curiosity over the past week. Moreover, if teachers are *really* interested in helping each student "show more interest," they should know *how much* improvement each student has made. Teachers need some measure of "showing interest"—something they can count. They can start by pinpointing some behavior involved in "showing interest" and working to increase that. The high

---

[1]Responses of teachers from in-service workshops conducted by the author in Grafton (elementary school) and Morgantown (high school), West Virginia, 1971.

school teacher (see Number 1 in Table I) pinpointed a measure of "showing interest" when he added "volunteer to do work on own."

A good statement of behavior must be precise, so that it is clear when it does or does not occur. One test for precision is to imagine two people watching the same student and ask whether or not they would agree on when the behavior occurs. Two people might disagree on such vague statements as "showing interest" or "showing respect," but they probably would agree on a more specific behavior such as "how many times Sally volunteered to do work." If a behavior is stated precisely, it is easier for even one person to be sure of the count. A second check on precision is to ask the question, "Can you state improvement in terms of numbers?" It is hard to say how much more Mr. Shaie "was enthusiastic" this week than last, but by pinpointing behavior we can say, for example, "Mr. Shaie spoke up five times more in discussion this week than he did last week." Some examples of behaviors which could be pinpointed for the general concerns in Table I are shown in Table II.

WHAT TO WORK ON FIRST: CHOOSE ONE PROBLEM AT A TIME

You may find, when you first teach, that almost everything goes smoothly. You have only one or two problems, so it is easy to pick

TABLE II Sample Pinpointed Behaviors for Some of the General Goals Listed in Table I

General goal		Possible specific behaviors
For { Be more curious or Show more interest }	You Might Count	{ Questions asked or Projects done outside class
For { Read more or Do more independent reading }	You Might Count	{ Pages read or Statements made about books that were not assigned
For { Show more consideration for others or More respect and acts of kindness toward fellow students or Talk less, listen more while others are talking	You Might Count	{ Offers of help to others or Offers to share or Times let someone else talk without interrupting

something to work on. You may, however, have many problems like those of Mr. Hopeful, who was concerned about Paulette's hyperactivity, reading, math, spelling, social studies, and health; her tendency to bully and her lack of attention.

If you try to work on reading, answering social studies questions, spelling words, hair-pulling, and shoving others all at once, you will probably be unsuccessful. By picking *one* problem—say, vocabulary words correctly read—you can concentrate your efforts, and your students can concentrate theirs. Once you successfully conquer one problem, you can work on the next.

The same principle applies to a large problem, such as use of drugs or illiteracy in an older child. You can't really expect a solution in one try; you must break down your goal into achievable steps and start with a slight improvement as your first goal.

PICK AN ACTIVE BEHAVIOR YOU CAN COUNT

To change behavior you must look at behavior instead of characteristics or states. Paulette may be called "hyperactive" or a "bully" or "inattentive," but it is her *behavior* that gets her into trouble and her behavior that we can change. Stating a problem as a characteristic or state makes it sound unsolvable. To say that someone *is* a bully or *is* hyperactive or *is* unmotivated is to imply that such behavior is a fixed personality characteristic. How does one go about changing what someone *is*? Even if you could change "being a bully" or "being unmotivated," how could you tell how much change occurred? You need something you can count. Eventually you come back to behavior. When you state your problem as behavior, it doesn't sound so inevitable. To say a student "pushes others and takes their things too often" puts the problem of "being a bully" back into perspective. It is really only behavior that needs to be changed. Similarly, you can count how many "problems Sam does without leaving his seat" to tell whether Sam's "hyperactivity" is subsiding or not. There are many specific behaviors which make up motivation. You might choose "volunteering to do extra work," "contributing to discussions," "bringing in material from outside class," or perhaps just "completing assignments without prodding." Whatever you choose, your problem is already closer to being solved when you stop using vague labels and look instead at specific things students do.

One test of whether a pinpointed problem is specific enough is to try to visualize a student engaging in the behavior and to imagine counting each occurrence. If I tell you that Sam is "being hostile," can you visualize what, specifically, he is doing? From that statement you cannot tell, because it is not specific enough. Sam might be making sarcastic remarks, he might be swearing, he might be banging things around. It is difficult to visualize "being hostile," and even more difficult to count it. Do you count "dropping schoolbooks on a desk from a foot high" or not? In contrast, a good statement such as "Sam makes obscene gestures" enables one to visualize pretty well exactly what it is that Sam is doing. One can imagine oneself counting, "That's one, two . . ." because it is clear exactly *what* one is talking about.

Counting of itself doesn't make a behavior active. You can count minutes "staying in one's seat" or "paying attention" but you still do not have a goal that is active. You don't know what Rachael is actually doing while she is in her seat looking at you. Perhaps she is planning a party. Even if she is listening, the point of having her pay attention is to help her add better, discuss the peace movement better, spell better, or whatever. You'd do better to count columns of figures added, contributions to discussions, or properly spelled words.

Active Behavior

is behavior which changes. Running, talking, and writing are active because we can see them progress and change. Even thinking is active because the thinker can "observe" his thoughts changing. However, paying attention and sitting are *not* active because they do not imply change.

It is almost always better to count active behavior rather than minutes spent behaving or minutes of attendance. One Community Action Agency paid dropouts for coming to an Adult Education Program. They came all right, and for the minutes required, but they didn't do very much learning. To get quality of performance (or any performance at all) you need to count what it is that students *do*.

Sometimes it is difficult to pinpoint the specific behaviors you want. While it is easy to count "minutes spent practicing the trumpet" or "minutes spent working on a term paper," it is difficult to say just what the student should be doing. Perhaps the trumpet player is only going over easy pieces when the difficult passages need work. It would be better to count "repetitions of passages needing work." If Miguel wants to increase his speed, he could use a metronome with a particular passage or exercise and record the speed at which he could play it without a mistake. For some projects, several behaviors might be involved. If you were working on a paper, you might want to chart both "pages read" and "lines written." That way you could see not just the time spent but what you had accomplished. Two days of "60 minutes" each might be very different in terms of productivity. By counting "pages read" or "lines written," for example, you could see the difference between, say, 57 pages read in Tuesday's study hour and 15 in

Wednesday's, or between the 93 lines written in a half hour on Thursday and the 10 written in the same time on Friday.

There are only a few times when it is appropriate to count seconds, minutes, or hours. One is when you are counting the time taken to start or to complete a given task. You might be interested in how long it takes a particular child to start work. If so, a count of "time taken to begin" or "time taken to complete the day's assignment" would be appropriate. Time is useful also to measure lateness. If you want to work on getting a student to arrive on time, you could count minutes late (or early) that the person arrives. In both of these cases, we are not interested so much in what behaviors occur during the time we are counting as we are interested in how long it takes before a behavior occurs. In contrast, it is never good to count minutes spent doing something when the behavior of interest is what is accomplished, not how long it takes.

If we work to cut down minutes late or minutes taken to get started, we *increase* activity. In contrast, by counting minutes spent "working" without specifying what is to be accomplished, we encourage taking more minutes but not necessarily accomplishing more. Too often the result is inefficiency and passiveness.

A subtle kind of passiveness is also present when you pick a behavior you *don't* want rather than one you *do* want. If you work to get students to stop getting out of their seats, to stop poking others, to stop talking during class, you are working at *reducing* activity.

It is possible to produce a class of well-mannered, attentive-looking students who don't learn much except the discipline of sitting still. Rather than concentrating on what students are doing wrong, if we look at what students *should* be doing, we are more likely to teach, to get students to solve problems, create plays, and so on. The student who is working hard can't be disrupting the class, so, as an added bonus for producing *desirable* behavior, we reduce disciplinary problems as well. A study by Ayllon and Roberts illustrates this:

Five boys in a fifth grade class of 38 students spent as much time standing, walking around, running, talking out, hitting others, or grabbing their things as they did studying. By getting them to do more workbook exercises, the teachers were able to almost eliminate undesirable behavior. As the authors conclude: "This study demonstrated that a reciprocal relationship may exist between academic performance and disruptive behavior: not the traditionally held 'make them sit still so they will learn,' but rather a 'teach them better and they may sit still' relationship."[2] By building what we want, then, we often also get rid of what we don't want.

[2]Teodoro Ayllon and Michael D. Roberts, "Eliminating Discipline Problems by Strengthening Academic Performance," *Journal of Applied Behavior Analysis* 7, no. 1 (Spring 1976), p. 75.

Events that occur inside the skin, such as "positive thoughts about myself," are called private behaviors. Private events can be active behaviors. They are good statements of behavior if they are specific enough to be counted accurately. Naturally only the behaver can count behavior going on inside his own skin. Your students, then, would have to count their own "creative ideas" or "thoughts about science" or any other private behaviors.

WHAT UNITS TO USE
(Count in Small Enough Units to Get a Count which Will Vary Daily)

It is usually best to count in units small enough so that you can see a change from day to day. "Pages read" is better than "books read" unless you are a voracious reader. "Lines written" is better than "pages written"; "problems done" is better than "assignments completed."

We all need to see progress. It can be very discouraging to work toward a goal that takes months to reach. Suppose you want to be able to read *Crime and Punishment* in Russian. You enroll in Russian I and go to class. It takes you a week to learn the alphabet and the sounds of the letters. If you are counting the pages of *Crime and Punishment* read, all those zeros could get you down. A chart of "Russian words pronounced correctly" would be much more encouraging. Or take the company in California that has such success in curing bed wetters. It doesn't have the family count nights dry. That's too big a step. It has the parents and the child measure the wet spot and count *inches*. When the child goes from 36 to 24 inches, that's progress!

CHOOSE THE PROBLEM BEHAVIOR ITSELF
OR ITS IMMEDIATE PRODUCT

Whenever possible count the behavior itself as it occurs. When that is not possible, count its most immediate product. It is the behavior we can change and it is the behavior that causes difficulties, yet we often measure the delayed results of behavior. For example, people who want to lose weight usually watch the scale instead of watching what they eat. They could count Calories consumed or, to look at the positive side, bites of low-calorie food they substituted for high. Often the results of a day of restricted eating do not show up in the next morning's weigh-in. To starve a whole day and see no progress is discouraging enough to drive a dieter to a banana split. But by counting calories consumed or low-calorie foods substituted for fattening food, the dieting day becomes a successful day, giving encouragement for days to come. Once eating is under control, weight loss will follow.

In the schoolroom you would do better to count the problems done rather than the number of times you must remind a student to get back to work. "Reminding" is as much a measure of your behavior as of your student's, and it will change as your moods and preoccupations change. To encourage self-discipline in a student who fails to complete assignments on time you would do better to count something daily (such as exercises completed) rather than days late handing them in.

CONSULT YOUR STUDENTS

Although you as a teacher have the final responsibility for what your students learn, you will get more cooperation from students if you let them come up with pinpoints *they* would like to work on. As an added bonus, by teaching students how to pick their own goals, you are teaching them to solve their own problems. You are helping them become independent.

SUMMARY

The first step in problem-solving is to define the problem clearly. We need to specify behavior rather than to talk about characteristics or states. To produce active learning, we specify what we want students to *do* in preference to what they should not do or to minutes spent in an activity, both of which often lead to passivity. By looking at active, countable behavior, we also state our problem in a way which enables us to get a good measure of it. By concentrating on one behavior at a time and by measuring the behavior in fine enough units to get a daily variation, we make signs of success likely. How one states a problem largely determines the ease with which it is solved.

EXERCISES

Concept Check IVA—Stating Problems Behaviorally (Objective A)

Which two of the following ten goals are best defined behaviorally?

> **Criteria for defining the problem behaviorally**
> 1. Choose one problem at a time.
> 2. Pick an active behavior you can count.
> 3. Count in small enough units to get a count which will, or can, vary daily.
> 4. Choose the problem behavior itself or its immediate product rather than your reactions to it.

I would like students to:

1. Utilize time more efficiently.
2. Volunteer to answer questions more often.

3. Be less lazy.
4. Solve more problems correctly.
5. Show more commitment to the subject area I teach.
6. Wander around the room less.
7. Hand in term papers on time.
8. Pay closer attention.
9. Demonstrate understanding of the readings.
10. Write answers to questions, and check them, and then use extra time productively.

Answers for Concept Check IVA

The best statements are numbers 2 and 4.

Number 1 Much too vague. How can you count a "utilize time" or tell when one begins or ends?

Number 3 "Be less lazy" is a statement of a characteristic or state and not behavior. Like Number 1, it cannot be counted. In addition it is usually better to state a problem as something to increase, not to decrease. What should the student be doing instead of "being lazy"?

Number 5 is not a behavior. Because the statement starts with the word "show," it *sounds* active, but it is not specific enough. If you try to visualize what someone is actually *doing* when "showing commitment," you may have a hard time. Even if you can see a particular behavior, would others see the same one when they visualize "showing commitment"? A good statement of a behavior is not open to so many different interpretations.

Number 6 isn't too bad a statement. One could define one "wander" as any time a student gets out of his or her seat and does not immediately return. However, the statement is negative, aimed at reducing something, not building it up, so that it could promote passivity. It would be better to count what the student *should* be doing.

Number 7 is specific enough—but it does not meet Criterion 3 because it would happen too infrequently.

Number 8 "Paying attention" is not countable nor is it active.

Number 9 "Demonstrate" is another of those words that sounds behavioral but may not indicate specific behavior. It is not at all clear exactly what a student does to "demonstrate understanding."

Number 10 Too many things tackled at once.

PROBLEM-SOLVING EXERCISES (OBJECTIVE B)

Each of the following describes a behavioral problem in the schools. For each problem, pinpoint the behavior you would work on if it were your problem, indicating what you would count.

Scoring: Score your statement by the directions on the following pages. You will also find sample good statements for comparison, but remember that your approach may be different and still be just as good or even better!

Problem I—Elementary School: Cindy

Cindy is a normal eight-year-old girl in a third grade class with 27 students in it. She is usually cooperative and engages readily in class activities. There is one exception: she takes forever to line up. She lingers at her desk, opens a book, draws on paper or whatever is handy, or even sits down on the floor and takes off her shoe to fix her sock. At first the teacher thought Cindy didn't hear well (or notice that everyone else was already in line), but when the teacher asked Cindy what was she was supposed to do, Cindy replied, "Line up."

Problem 2—Secondary School: Peter

Peter is one of the more capable students in the class, but he has a bad attitude. In any class discussion, instead of giving information that he knows, he answers one question with another question. If the teacher asks what form of government the local city council represents, Peter says something like "You mean they *have* a form of government?" Naturally the rest of the students laugh. Peter's continual smart-aleck behavior makes it almost impossible for the teacher to conduct a serious discussion.

Scoring Directions for Problem-Solving Exercises

Problem 1: Cindy:

This is a case where "seconds taken" *would* be an appropriate measure.

Scoring: If you

1. picked only *one* behavior to change first   _____score 1 point
2. stated the behavior so it could be counted (you can tell when it begins and ends)   _____score 1 point
3. stated the behavior precisely enough so that you feel two observers watching the student would get the same count   _____score 1 point
4. stated the problem as seconds or minutes taken (with the intent of *decreasing* time taken) or picked something you would want to increase   _____score 1 point
5. stated the behavior of the *student,* not the teacher's or peers' reaction to it   _____score 1 point

Problem Total = 5 points

Sample Good Statements	*Sample Poor Statements*
a. Seconds taken to get into line after first direction to "line up" is given	a. Lining up faster (you would need to say how fast "is faster")
b. Number of times Cindy lines up within 30 seconds of being	b. Taking too long to line up
	c. Lingering at desk.

told to do so (there are usually many opportunities during the day)

d. Sitting down on floor (this is specific and countable—but it is negative in that you *don't* want it. It is better to pinpoint what you *do* want)

Problem 2: Peter

Scoring: If you

1. picked only *one* behavior to change first   _____score 1 point
2. stated the behavior so it could be counted (you can tell when it begins and ends)   _____score 1 point
3. stated the behavior precisely enough so that you feel two observers watching the student would get the same count   _____score 1 point
4. stated the problem as a behavior you would want to *increase, not* one you would want to *decrease*   _____score 1 point
5. stated the behavior of the *student,* not the teacher's or peers' reaction to it   _____score 1 point

Problem Total = 5 points

Sample Good Statements

a. Answering questions "seriously"— that is, with factual information
b. Answering teacher's questions with questions (this is specific enough but it would be better to state the problem positively as in "a" above)

Sample Poor Statements

a. Having a bad attitude
b. Smart-aleck behavior
c. Giving information

Recording behavior

OVERVIEW

Chapter Five discusses the importance of recording rather than casually observing behavior. Suggestions are given for recording behavior, particularly in the classroom.

OBJECTIVES

By the end of the chapter you should be able to:

A. Tell why it is important to record behavior frequently and give an example to illustrate your reason.
B. Identify records which show rate of responding and tell what information is provided by *rate* that is lost in *number* or *percent correct*.
C. Calculate rates for given data.
D. Outline how you would observe and record for a given problem —using the principles below:
   1. Pick the most critical behavior.
   2. Record for a long enough period to get a count which will vary daily but which will not be so long that you will get tired of counting.
   3. Make it physically easy to record behavior *as it occurs*.
   4. Record daily.

WHY RECORD?

Imagine that you have graduated from college and have found that jobs are scarce. You find a job teaching in a federal prison for young offenders. You are to teach remedial math. The 15 or 20 students in each of your classes are aged 16 to 21, but they do not know even their basic math facts. Most dropped out of school well before reaching high school. They are not a highly motivated group. When told they are to take remedial math, they say:

"Wha' I godda learn all that stuff fo'?"

"@#$%!&°"

"Man, I had that already ten years ago."

. . . and so on.

You have your problem. You are to teach the "basic math facts." Having read the preceding chapter, you will probably (and wisely) pinpoint "math problems done correctly" as the behavior to work on. Then what?

To know where to start you must determine what each student can and cannot do already: you must find out his or her "entering behavior." To see progress you must record that performance for later reference. You must, in other words, measure behavior and record each student's performance.

While most teachers record grades on work sheets and tests, few bother to record other concerns such as "contributions to discussions." When you are serious about changing behavior, however, you *must* keep records in order to see what change is occurring. Mere opinions of what is getting better or worse are often incorrect, as two researchers describe in the following episodes:

A boy in the laboratory preschool frequently pinched adults.
Attempts by the teachers to ignore the behavior proved ineffective,
since the pinches were hard enough to produce at least an involuntary
startle. Teachers next decided to try to develop a substitute behavior.
They selected patting as a logical substitute. Whenever the child reached
toward a teacher, she attempted to forestall a pinch by saying, "Pat, Davey,"
sometimes adding, "Not pinch," and then strongly approving his patting,
when it occurred. Patting behavior increased rapidly to a high level. The
teachers agreed that they had indeed succeeded in reducing the pinching
behavior through substituting patting. Then they were shown the recorded
data. It showed clearly that although patting behavior was indeed high,
pinching behavior continued at the previous level. Apparently, the teachers
were so focused on the rise in patting behavior that, without the objective
data, they would have erroneously concluded that development of a
substitute behavior was in this case a successful technique.

A second example illustrates a different, but equally undesirable kind of erroneous assumption. A preschool child who had to wear glasses (Wolf, Risley, & Mees, 1964) developed a pattern of throwing them two or three times per day. Since this proved expensive, it was decided that the attendants should put him in his room for ten minutes following each glasses-throw. When the attendants were asked a few days later how the procedure was working, they said that the glasses-throwing had not diminished at all. A check of the records, however, showed that there was actually a marked decrease. The throwing dropped to zero within five days. Presumably, the additional effort involved in carrying out the procedure had given the attendants an exaggerated impression of the rate of the behavior. Recorded data, therefore, seem essential to accurate objective assessments of what has occurred.[1]

Teacher judgments on handwriting, reading, algebra, and so on, are seldom much better. How can one teacher remember exactly what letters each child can write in cursive, or what novels each student has read, or an individual's specific problems with algebra when there are many students in one class? Yet these precise bits of information are what you need to know.

RECORDING RATE

Teachers are interested not only in what each student does but in how often it is done. There is a great difference between the student who reads 50 pages a month and the one who reads 50 pages a day. A student who talks out of turn is a disciplinary problem only if he or she interrupts often. Even "hitting others" is only a problem if it occurs at a high rate. An occasional punch—say, once a semester—is not of great concern unless it lays someone out flat. Even then it is likely to be dismissed as an accident unless it is part of a pattern of aggressive or hostile behavior. We judge aggressive or hostile behavior, in turn, by how frequently a student grabs, shoves, and so on.

When we say that students know a subject, we mean that they are likely to respond correctly. Take, for instance, "knowing" math facts. We are interested not only in whether students can say "49" when shown "7 x 7" but in the likelihood that they will do so. Teaching, then, is not only producing new behavior, it is also changing the likelihood that a student *will* respond a certain way. Since we cannot see a likelihood, we look instead at how frequently a student does something. We see how fast he can add. The student who does problems correctly at a higher rate is said to know addition facts better than one who does them at a lower rate.

Rate

of behavior is the number of times a given operant occurs within a specified time period. Rate is often reported in "responses per minute," "responses per hour," or "responses per day."

---

[1]Florence R. Harris, Montrose M. Wolf, and Donald M. Baer, "Effects of Adult Social Reinforcement on Child Behavior," in *Child Development: Readings in Experimental Analysis*, eds. Sidney W. Bijou and Donald M. Baer, New York, Meredith, 1967, p. 157.

TABLE I   Typical Teacher's Grade Book

	Monday	Tuesday	Wednesday	Thursday	Friday
Bill	✓	✓	+	✓	
Frank	—	✓	—	—	Abs.
Justine	+	+	+	+	+
Jack	✓		✓	✓	
Lisa M.		✓	✓	✓	+
Lisa V.	+	+	+	+	+
Jonathan	+	✓	✓	✓	+

Abs. = Absent

✓ = Handed in

+ = Better than average

— = Worse than average

In spite of the importance of rate, the conventional grade book ignores rate altogether. The grade book in Table I, for example, is typical of the kinds of records teachers keep.

Justine is obviously a "good" student, but what is she learning? The grade book shown in Table I gives little information. Even if the teacher had recorded the number of problems correct, we could not see whether or not Justine is improving. Look at Table II, for example. Justine always gets all problems correct. Even though she does not improve in number of problems correct each day, however, she is probably doing them faster. By recording time taken, as well as problems correct, we can get a measure which will show that change. Table III records rate and shows that Justine is doing problems twice as fast on Friday as on Monday.

TABLE II   Grade Book Showing Number of Problems Correct of Twenty Given

	Monday	Tuesday	Wednesday	Thursday	Friday
Bill	18	16	19	15	
Frank	5	14	7	8	Abs.
Justine	20	20	20	20	20
Jack	14		15	18	17

TABLE III   Grade Book Showing Rate of Problems
Correct Per Minute

	Monday	Tuesday	Wednesday	Thursday	Friday
Bill	9	8	10	7	
Frank	2	6	3	4	Abs.
Justine	10	10	12	14	20
Jack	7		7	8	12

She is improving tremendously, but only measures of rate show that change.

HOW TO CALCULATE RATE

To measure rate we need two things: (1) the number of times the pinpointed behavior occurs; and (2) the number of minutes, hours, etc., during which we were counting. By dividing occurrences by units of time we get rate: ten books read a month, six hits per hour, ten problems a minute, and so on (see Table IV).

HOW TO OBSERVE AND RECORD RATE

If you take ten teachers into a classroom and then ask them to describe what went on, you will get ten different answers. Some incidents such as "a boy tipped over his desk" will be reported by everyone, but other less obvious behavior such as whispering, or solving problems, or rhymes written will be reported by some and not by others.

As a teacher you certainly cannot count the rate of all behavior all the time. How, then, do you see what is really going on?

First, you must zero in on the most critical behaviors. Most teachers will tell you they are interested in academic performance, but without systematically checking on each student's performance, they tend to *see* disciplinary problems. Sandy's 16 lines of poem written can go unnoticed a long time in the back row, but Mark's thrown eraser may literally "hit you between the eyes." By pinpointing the specific behaviors you *want,* you will counteract the tendency to have your attention diverted from measuring the critical skills you are teaching.

TABLE IV   How to Calculate Rate

$$\text{Rate} = \frac{\text{Number of occurrences}}{\text{Number of minutes (hours, etc.)}}$$

or

$$\text{Number of minutes} \sqrt{\text{Number of occurrences}}$$

Second, you must get a count. It seems like a simple task. But when you are in the middle of an exciting class—say, a good simulated debate in Congress—it is a nuisance to count. Since the important thing is to see daily progress, it is more important to get *some* count every day than to get a complete or extremely accurate count for only part of the week. To make it likely that you will get daily counts, you must minimize the effort involved. You can make it easier by having students count their own behavior or by counting for only a small part of each period. Either way, you can get a daily count with little effort.

Student Recording. Students *can* record as accurately as teachers. Whether they will or not depends on the consequences for getting a correct number. When students have a part in setting their own goals, they are more likely to count accurately than when goals are set solely by the teacher. This is particularly true when the behavior counted is socially undesirable. Jill may count her interruptions willingly if *she* picked interruptions to work on, but if you tell her, "Why don't you count the number of times you interrupt so we can decrease it?" you will probably get incorrect counting or outright refusal.

On the other hand, if you have students count something positive, like their creative thoughts or their contributions to discussions, they usually settle down to counting accurately enough to see change from day to day. If they inflate Thursday's figure too much, they ruin the chance of improving on Friday. Over the long run, then, you can see trends and periodic fluctuations in behavior.

Counting Only Part of the Time. There may be things you would like to count yourself but which involve a lot of effort. Your students' bad grammar may bother you, but you don't want to ask them to count it. You may want to get an indication of motivation by the number of science-related statements your students make to you *outside* of class. Only by counting them yourself can you get a realistic figure.

You probably won't feel like counting all the time, so don't. Count only part of the time but do it *each day*. Count the usage of "isn't or aren't" versus "ain't" during after-lunch recess, or during the first ten minutes of class, or for half an hour when you have a discussion.

How Long to Count Each Day. Since the reason for counting is to show change from day to day and week to week, you should count long enough each day to get figures that change. If for 17 days in a row you get no "ain'ts," you are counting for too short a time each day or you have a solved problem. If, on the other hand, your counts vary (say 27, 3, 6, 13), you have plenty of variation to show change and needn't be afraid that you are counting for too short a time period each day.

The cue that you have picked too long a period each day is your fail-

Figure 5.1

ure to count. If you forget one or two days a week, or forget to count part of the time you were supposed to count, you probably selected too long a time period. Try counting for a shorter period each day.

Recording a Count. You've pinpointed a problem. You've decided when and how long to count the behavior in which you are interested. You are standing in the classroom and the pinpointed response occurs. Now what? If recording is not to interfere with your other teaching procedures, it, too, must be made easy. If you must hunt for a pencil and look through your books for a scrap of paper, you will be likely to say to yourself, "Oh, I'll remember that and write it down later." Suddenly you find you are measuring your memory, not your students' behavior.

Teachers have used all kinds of devices to overcome the problem of recording behavior *as it occurs.* One popular device is a golf counter worn on the wrist (see Figure 5.1).[2] A piece of paper scotch-taped to the inside cover of a grade book works well too. Whatever your method—if it works, fine; but if your counts are getting lost or forgotten, try something else.

RECORDING QUALITY OF STUDENT PERFORMANCE

Although we have stressed rate because of its sensitivity and importance for skill development, one needn't time everything. The art teacher

[2]Based on an idea by Susan Tucker, course manager for Educational Psychology 105, West Virginia University, Morgantown, West Virginia, 1972–1974.

may be concerned not only with the student's ability to control the brush (which involves rate) but with what is created with that skill. How many pictures are completed in an hour may not be important. The same could be said of the engineer designing a bridge, or of the writer, or of the composer. Mastering the skills with which we create may involve increasing speed and precision, but quality in the product is not determined by behaving rapidly.[3] Timing such things as writing or inventing leads to glibness, not quality, and they are better taught and assessed without the pressure of timing.

It is harder to judge quality than quantity but it is just as important to record quality. To judge quality, it is helpful to develop criteria which a good product should meet. An example is Number 4 at the end of Table V on page 69, and Chapter 12 gives some suggestions on how to go about setting criteria. Even with criteria, much subjectivity remains—and perhaps some should remain. But with a checklist (even when some subjectivity is involved), we become more consistent in our evaluations. Changes in what we record from day to day are thus more likely to reflect change in student behavior and less likely to reflect our moods or prejudices. The art teacher who goes from easel to easel analyzing what each student has done and giving suggestions, for example, can better help each student by checking for specific strengths and weaknesses. With set criteria the teacher is less likely to overlook a problem in the use of color because of a student's excellence in perspective or to fail to see improvement in one aspect because another one still needs work. With a checklist, progress becomes more visible to both teacher and student (see Figure 5.2). The student is less likely to repeat only what he or she already does well and to avoid areas that need work. Furthermore, the teacher with a checklist is more likely to be specific in suggestions and comments, so that the student is given help not only with *what* needs improvement but in *how* to improve.

It is just as important to evaluate frequently when judging quality as it is when judging quantity. There is no way to see daily progress without daily evaluation, whether it be in the rate of problems solved or in the number of criteria met.

OTHER METHODS OF CLASSROOM OBSERVATION

There are many methods of measuring performance. When counting over a time period is appropriate, it will give the greatest accuracy for

[3]It is interesting to note that many tests of creativity, such as the "uses test," do involve rate. In the uses test, you write down as many different uses of a commonplace object, such as brick, as you can think of within a fixed time. Your creativity score is based upon the number of unusual uses (such as grind up the brick and use the powder for rouge) that you have written in the time period. "Unusual" is defined as uncommon, that is, a use not given often by others.

Figure 5.2 In this Verbal Skills Center, each student's folder serves as a checklist. It lets both teacher and student see daily progress and serves as a record of what skills the student has mastered. (Whittie Elementary School, Pontiac, Michigan. Courtesy of New Century Education Corporation.)

the least effort. That is why it is stressed here. Other ways are listed in Table V (along with the method we have discussed).[4]

TABLE V   Recording Methods

Name and description	Example
1. *Recording Rate of Response* Counting the number of times a response occurs during a specified period of time. Usually converted to responses per minute. a. can be done as the behavior occurs or b. later, from student products	1. "Susan: 30 acceptable cursive letters in 10 minutes" (or 3 acceptable letters per minute.) a. counted *as she wrote* or b. counted later from her paper
2. *Recording Time to Completion* Counting how long it takes a student to complete a specified act or unit of work. (Data can be converted to a rate if desired.)	2. "Susan: 10 minutes to complete handwriting assignment." (If the assignment has 30 letters in it, the rate is 30/10, or 3 acceptable letters per minute.)
3. *Time-Sampling and Time-Ruled Checklists* Every so many seconds, or at set intervals, a person looks to see what a student is doing and classifies it in preset categories. a. Time-sampling is usually used only by a person other than the teacher, such as a student observer. Unlike #1 and #2, it is not feasible for a teacher to do while teaching.	$$\boxed{O}\,\boxed{O}\,\boxed{I}\,\boxed{I}\,\boxed{O}\,\boxed{O}\,\boxed{I}\,\boxed{I}\,\boxed{W}\,\boxed{W}\,\boxed{W}\,\boxed{I}\,\boxed{O}\,\boxed{O}\,\boxed{O}$$ W = working on handwriting I = not working, but in seat O = not working and out of seat
4. *Checklists for Quality of Performance* Daily work, assignments, or other products are evaluated by checking or rating them against criteria that have been set up beforehand.	*Susan's handwriting* *December 4* _____1. Letters vary no more than ⅛ inch from a guideline drawn at the tops and bottoms of small letters. _____2. Closed letters (a, o, p,

[4]Based on Judith E. Favell, "The Power of Positive Reinforcement and Other Topics: How to Design and Implement Behavior Modification Programs," *Western Carolina Center Papers and Reports in Mental Retardation* 3, no. 5 (April 1973), pp. 5–20.

TABLE V (Continued)

Name and description	Example
a. Numbers may be assigned for quality on each criterion with or without samples.	etc.) are round and similar in shape and size.
	_____3. Student's handwriting has *individuality* (that is, he or she forms some letters consistently in a way which is different from standard form yet which is legible.)
5. *Testing* Set a time aside and have the student do an assigned task; grade it according to rate or quality of work. Tests may or may not be timed. a. The main problem with testing is that it usually occurs too infrequently to give a measure of daily progress, or it is graded on a curve so that one cannot tell what the student actually did.	"Susan: Grade of B for handwriting" (based on comparison with the rest of the students' handwriting.)

PRECISION TEACHING IN PRACTICE—AN EXAMPLE

The following is an account of a class at Kennedy Youth Center near Morgantown, West Virginia. It is one teacher's solution to the problem posed at the beginning of this chapter.

Mr. Sampson's Remedial Math Class

"Here, I'll show you how I run this class," says Mr. Sampson, a young man is his late twenties. "I'm not really a math teacher but they needed someone to take this class. This is the first time I've worked in an institution like this."

Turning toward his class, he announces, "Two minutes. Better get your stuff ready."

A big six-foot student heads for a large file, "Outa my way, man," he says as he squeezes past another student.

"That's Carver,' says Mr. Sampson. "He couldn't add two and two when he came here three weeks ago. You should see him now."

Five students beat Carver to the box, a cardboard carton with 30 well-worn manila folders in it. Each student flips to a different folder and takes out a work sheet.

"Hey, Tes' Six missin'. Mr. Sampson, there's no mo' Tes' Six."
It's Carver again.

"Hold on, Carver," Mr. Sampson answers. "Test Six is there—the
tab is just torn off."

Carver finds the folder, gets his sheet, and goes to a desk, as do the
other students. He puts his paper face down on the desk, waiting.

Mr. Sampson looks at the school clock. He waits while the second hand
slowly moves around to 10, to 11—

"OK, begin."

There is a flutter of papers turning over, then silence, except for the
sounds of pencils. The students work at top speed. Carver starts Row Two.

"They have to do almost one problem a second correctly in order
to pass," Mr. Sampson whispers. "We require 42 a minute to pass. Few
visitors can pass the division facts test." He watches the students and the
clock. "Ok, stop," he announces.

A couple of loud "Oh's!" are heard. The students come up to Mr.
Sampson, crowding around his desk, papers in hand. Mr. Sampson pulls out
a folder of answer sheets and runs quickly over the students' papers.
Three pass. One is jubilant and punches his neighbor in joy, one sighs
with relief, one says gruffly, "About time." The rest count up their right
answers. Each goes to a chart on the wall.

"What are those?" you ask.

"Those are progress charts."

He takes you to Carver's chart (Figure 5.3). "Every day the students
chart their rate of problems correct. The horizontal black line is at 42
per minute. They have to get over that line to earn 'privilege' points and
to pass on to the next test. The tests get harder—look here. When they pass
one and start a new one, they drop below the black line. Then they gradually
improve. Come over here. I'll show you the sequence."

A chart marked "'Curriculum" (Table VI) is posted on the wall.
"At first some cheated a bit when they plotted their own performance,"
Mr. Sampson continues. "They would put their dot too high. But they
couldn't put it over the black line because I check on that. So they'd put it
just underneath. But if a dot was put too high on Monday, they'd have
trouble beating it on Tuesday. So now they sometimes make mistakes,
but I don't have too much trouble with cheating.

"OK, let's get busy now," he says. The boys quiet down, but not

**TABLE VI   Math Facts Curriculum for the Part
Carver Covered on His Chart**

1. Addition facts to total sum of 20.
2. Subtraction facts to 20 (also in the form, $10 + \underline{} = 17$).
3. Addition and subtraction mixed.
4. Multiplication tables—ones and twos.
5. Multiplication tables—threes.
6. Combinations (multiplication ones, twos, and threes).

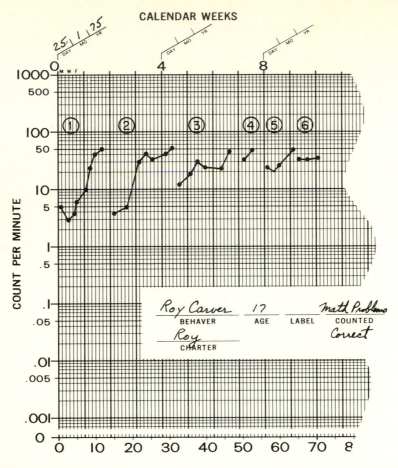

Figure 5.3   Carver's Chart.

much. You look over the class. The students don't look much different from those in a regular school. Some are working in workbooks, two are doing flash cards, and some are "goofing off." What a difference from the beginning of class when every student was working as hard as he could! But on the wall are charts attesting to the daily improvement in learning basic math facts.[5]

SUMMARY

As a teacher you must be both artist and scientist; you must be able to create teaching strategies, but you must also objectively assess how well your methods produce learning. The more sensitive you are to your

[5]This fictional account is based on an actual math class taught by Jerry Miller at the Kennedy Youth Center (a correctional institution for young federal offenders). The chart is a real one, but the student's name has been changed.

students' behavior and to changes in their behavior, the better teacher you will be.

The reason we measure anything is to make ourselves aware of subtle differences we couldn't see before. In measuring student behavior, we discover individual strengths and weaknesses that we may have only been dimly aware of or may not have seen at all. By recording frequently, we can see each student's progress (or its lack) when it is helpful—*while* the student is learning. We become sensitive to individual needs in a way which is impossible without measurement.

Our records are a check on *our* behavior as much as they are a check on our students'. They help to keep us honest and fair. We can't so easily pass out grades like political favors when hard evidence of actual performance stares us in the face. Nor can we fool ourselves about how much students are learning. We may feel wonderful after leading an exciting discussion—but how much did it really benefit each student? Without records, it is easy to forget about the quiet or shy individual. The "squeaky wheel" gets the grease. With records, on the other hand, no one is likely to be ignored. The records draw our attention to each student's learning.

Not all kinds of records are equally sensitive to change in student behavior. The most sensitive is rate. By recording the rate of active behavior we want, such as problems correct per minute, we keep closely in touch with student progress. Whatever we record, we can see learning best if we record *something* each class period. Since recording can be tedious, we must be careful not to attempt so much of it that we give up in frustration. To make it likely that we will get a daily measure, we can make it easy to evaluate. We can use a checklist if we are interested in quality of performance. For rate, we can have students count, we can count for only part of a period, we can wear a counter, or we can use an ever-present grade book to mark down each instance of behavior as it occurs. When we notice gaps in our records, it is time to try something different—to find the system that works for us.

There is no way that we can keep in our heads all the strengths and weaknesses of 15 or 30 or 200 students. We need records. The more sensitive and frequent records we make, the more we are likely to treat each student as an individual.

Records keep us focused on *student* problems and progress. To put it the other way around, our concern for each student's learning is shown in the care with which we keep records.

EXERCISES

Concept Check VA—Which of the Following Records in Figure 5.4 Are Records of Rate? (Objective B)

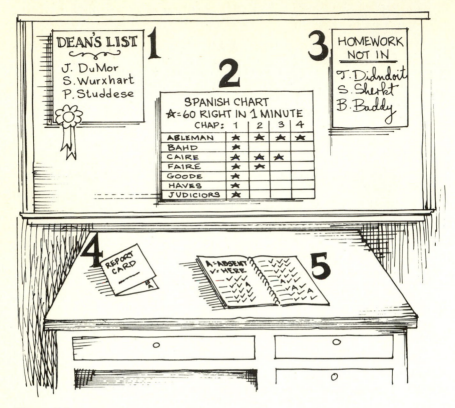

Figure 5.4

Answers for Concept Check VA

There is only one record of rate in the picture—Number 2. Sixty right in one minute is a rate because it specifies a behavior (doing problems) and the time period over which one is counting (which may or may not be one minute). A star means the student can solve problems at a rate of 60 per minute.

Number 1 The criteria for getting on the dean's list are not always the same, but they usually involve grades (see Number 4).

Number 3 This is just a list of those who didn't hand in homework. No time is specified and no count of behavior is taken. One could get a rate on homework done by counting the number of exercises done per day, or, if students have a study hall in which they can do homework, you could count exercises completed per minute while in the study hall.

Number 4 A grade does not specify the number of behaviors per unit of time that a student can perform. In fact, few report cards mention countable behaviors at all. They may say "grasps historical concepts well," but they do not say what the student can do. It is difficult to get a meaningful rate for some subjects, such as history, but if the teacher looks at what students do on tests, at least some behaviors can be found that can be counted. On a simple level, one might get a rate on matching "famous figures" with their contributions to society or matching names of movements with the people associated with them. On a more complex level, the teacher could ask for an essay response and (to take one example) look at the number of statements relating current events to events in a particular time period studied.

Number 5 One might argue that attendance measures the rate per day of coming to class. Counting classes attended might have meaning for a student who cuts some classes but not others. Such a record could vary daily from zero to the number of classes the student has scheduled. Any *individual* class attendance record, such as the one in the picture, however, does not specify the time period and does not permit rates other than 1 (for "here") and 0 (for "absent"), even if it is assumed that the time period covered is one day.

ANALYSIS PROBLEMS (OBJECTIVE B)

Imagine that you teach a high school typing class with 18 students in it. You feel that the students are too careless. You decide to post all errorless papers to see whether or not that makes a difference in the students' performance.

A. If it did make a difference, which method below would best show it?
B. What is wrong with the other methods? In particular, what information on improvement would you lose with each of the other three methods?

1. Counting percent of words typed correctly each day on a daily typing performance test and recording percent correct.
2. Timing the students' typing on a daily typing performance test and recording the number of correct and incorrect words they type for each minute on the average.
3. Measuring the amount of time out of the period that each student actually works on typing and recording minutes spent working.
4. Having students time themselves for a daily typing quiz and recording the number of minutes it takes them to type the whole thing with no errors.

Answers for Analysis Problems

The best method is Number 2. By recording rate of correct and incorrect words typed you can see improvement both in rate and in accuracy.

COMMENTS: This problem is like a study that was actually done in which 100 percent correct arithmetic papers were posted. Methods A (percent correct) and B (rate correct) were compared to see which better showed significant differences in performance. Statistically, change which would occur by chance only 1 time in 20 (.05 level of significance) was shown five times better using rate than percent correct. Large changes, which would occur only 1 time in 10,000 (.0001 level of significance), showed up 40 times more when using rate than when using percent correct. Clearly, then, rate was the more sensitive measure.[6]

Number 1 In using percent correct, you lose completely any information on how fast the student is typing.

Number 3 First of all, this is really impractical if you have more than two students. Can you see yourself with a dozen or so stopwatches, clicking them on and off as each student works or stops working? Secondly, you do not get a rate of behavior. "Minutes spent working" does not tell you how fast or how well a student types, and it cannot, therefore, show improvement in typing performance.

Number 4 The problem with Number 4 is that you only can see improvement in the rate of typing papers with *no* errors. You lose any information on any student who makes even one mistake. You cannot see, for example, improvement in accuracy from typing half of the words incorrectly to typing only one or two words incorrectly in a whole page. Nor can you see improvement in rate in any student who makes any mistakes at all. Considering the typing quality of students in typing classes, you might end up with very little data, period.

PROBLEM-SOLVING EXERCISES (OBJECTIVE D)

For each problem below, describe (in no more than three sentences):

1. When and how long the behavior would be counted.
2. How often it would be recorded.
3. How, physically, each count should be registered.

Problem 1—Elementary School: Sandra

Sandra was falling behind in spelling. The teacher felt that it was due to the fact that she did not complete the 10–15 items in each day's spelling assignment during the 20 minutes allotted to spelling. By Friday's test, then, Sandra had less practice writing the words than other students.

The teacher chose "spelling items completed correctly" as the behavior to work on.

Problem 2—High School Counseling: Jerry

Jerry was having problems talking to females. He had come voluntarily to a small weekly counseling group of two boys and three girls led by the high school counselor. Even in the group, however, he had a hard time looking at a female when he spoke to her and he would only say about five words at a

---

[6]These statistics were presented by Ogden Lindsley at the Second Annual Trainer's Course in Precise Behavioral Management, Kansas City, Kansas, July, 1969.

time to a female. He chose (with the counselor's guidance) "words spoken to female peers while looking at them" as his pinpoint.

Comments and Sample Solutions for Problem-Solving Exercises

Problem 1: Sandra

The most straightforward procedure would be to count items done correctly at the end of each spelling period and to write down that number where it wouldn't get lost. Either the teacher or Sandra could do it. Whatever method you used, however, you should have specified daily counting.

Problem 2: Jerry

You could either work on the problem during counseling sessions or have Jerry work on it outside the sessions (or both).

IN COUNSELING SESSIONS

There are many methods. You need to count Jerry's behavior *each* session for a period of time that is long enough to get numbers which will vary but that is not so long that it will monopolize the sessions for the counselor or for the others. If Jerry counts, he could count for all of the session or for only part. If the counselor or other students count, however, they should not count longer than about ten or fifteen minutes. Jerry's problems are not likely to be interesting enough to others to get accurate counting for longer than that. Whatever method, each word should be counted as it occurs. The numbers involved are not yet large, so marks on a slip of paper or any other immediate recording will do. It might be good to use something less conspicuous than a counter, which clicks.

OUTSIDE OF COUNSELING SESSIONS

If Jerry wishes (and only if then) he might count "words spoken looking at females" during the day. It is more important that he get a count each day than that he count all day long. You might suggest counting for a short period, such as over the dinner hour. For daily counting, some recording device kept on one's person is a must. Otherwise counts will get lost. Gadgets, such as wrist counters, are best, since they do not necessitate getting out a pencil or pen, or fumbling around with scraps of paper, calendars or notebooks.

SELF-PROJECT—CHANGING YOUR OWN BEHAVIOR (PART I)

To get the feel of recording behavior daily, you can do a project in which you change your own behavior.

Suggestions for doing a "self-project"

1. Start now. Even if you don't plan to try to change right away, pinpoint a behavior you would like to change and start counting. Then, when you do get around to trying to change, you'll have a good idea of your usual rate and its daily variations.
2. Plan exactly what you are going to do, answering the questions in the list below.

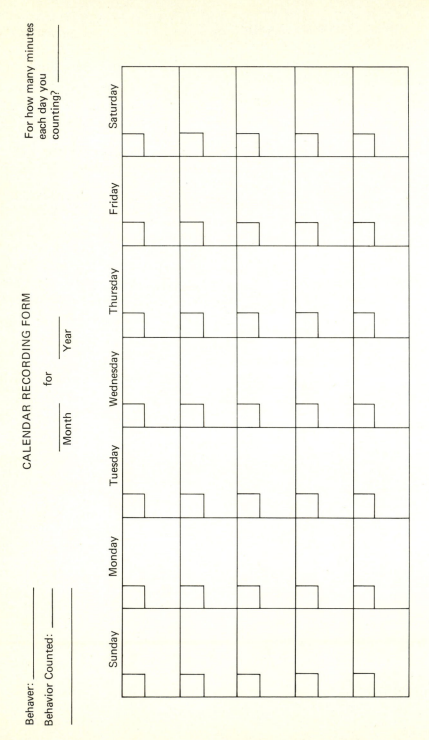

Figure 5.5

Plan for starting a "self-project"
Questions to Answer

1. What precisely is the behavior?

2. If Number 1 is something you would like to do less often, can you also think of something you would like to do *instead?*

3. For how many minutes each day will you count?

4. How will you record each instance of behavior when it occurs?

5. Where will you record each day's total?

Comments

1. Pinpoint the behavior as specifically as you can. Your pinpointed behavior should be active and countable:
   —can you tell easily when one instance occurs?
   —would two people interpret your pinpoint the same way?

2. If you build up a good alternative pattern of behavior, you are more likely to have long-lasting results than if you try to cut down on a behavior you wish you would do less.

3. Don't be too ambitious. If, for example, you are counting "happy thoughts about the future" or "encouraging comments to my roommate," you may wish to count for only a small part of the day. Whatever you choose should not take so much time or effort that it is a burden.

4. Make it easy to record on the spot. A wrist counter or pocket note pad and pencil which are carried *on the body* encourage an accurate record.

5. So that you do not lose data, you should have a definite spot for recording each day's total. If, like most people, you have trouble remembering dates, you may wish to record each day's data on a calendar. Figure 5.5 on page 78 can be duplicated and used for any month. The upper left-hand corners are intended for dates; the rest of the space, for recording.

Graphing

OVERVIEW

This chapter describes several different types of graphs and gives the reasons for using them.

OBJECTIVES

By the end of the chapter you should be able to:

A. Identify examples of the following graphs:
   1. Percent—line and bar
   2. Frequency—line and bar
   3. Rate—equal interval and equal ratio
   4. Cumulative record
B. Tell what kinds of information can or cannot be read from each of the following graphs:
   1. Percent
   2. Frequency
   3. Rate
   4. Cumulative record
C. Name an appropriate graph for a given purpose and graph sample data on it.

WHY GRAPH?

A graph is a way to show data. When we graph data on behavior, we are usually interested in how behavior changes over a period of time. A good graph should show the kinds of changes we are interested in. It should represent the data accurately so that the conclusions we would draw from looking at the graph would be the same as those we

TABLE I   Three Week's Data on Pam's Reading of
Flash Cards on Short Vowel Sounds

| Date | Words used | Number | | Time taken | Rate | |
		Correct	In-correct		Correct	In-correct
January 5	sit, sat, pin, pan, tip, tap, bat, bit, hat, hit, big, bag, has, his, wag, wig, mat, mit, nip, nap	4	16	10 min.	.4	1.6
7	Same 20 words	14	6	15 min.	.9	.4
9	Same 20 words	12	8	12 min.	1.0	.7
12	Same 20 words	20	0	12 min.	1.7	—
14	Same 20 words	20	0	10 min.	2.0	—
16	Same 20 words	20	0	6 min.	3.3	—
19	Added 10 new words set, pen, bat, mat, pet, beg, leg, pot, pit, pat	22	8	10 min.	2.2	.8
21	Same 30 words	30	0	10 min.	3.0	—
23	Same 30 words	30	0	5 min.	6.0	—

would draw from a detailed analysis of the data themselves or from the actual observation of the behavior as it occurred.

The reason we graph is to see clearly what is going on. Take about ten seconds to look over the data in Table I.

Now cover up the data and see if you can describe Pam's progress each week. Most people find it difficult to do. Looking back again at the data, you will probably see something like that shown in Table II.

PERCENT, FREQUENCY, AND RATE GRAPHS: WHAT THEY DO AND DO NOT SHOW

It it hard to see what is going on in a table of numbers, so we graph data to show changes that are occurring. Not all graphs show all changes, however. Figure 6.1 shows Pam's data using six kinds of graphs commonly used in the behavioral sciences. All of the graphs show improvement from the first week to the last, but they differ in the other information they show. The data show marked improvement in rate during the second week and an increase in correct words from Friday

TABLE II   Week by Week Description of Pam's Progress

		Additional comment
WEEK 1	Definite improvement in accuracy.	The first day (Monday the 5th) Pam could have been reading the consonants but guessing at the vowel sounds since her score is about what one would get by chance by guessing at vowels. The next two days she is doing better than chance—with more words correct than incorrect.
WEEK 2	Improved during the week in speed (rate).	Pam seems to have "caught on" on Monday (all correct).
WEEK 3	Improved in accuracy and in rate.	She probably got all the original 20 correct on Monday plus two of the new words. Then she learned the new words too.

the 16th to Monday the 19th. These two points are marked A and B respectively on the graphs.

Percent Correct Graphs. The percent correct graphs don't show either improvement in rate or increase in number of words when new words are added to the list. They are the least informative of the graphs shown.

> **A Percent Graph**
>
> is a graph of the percent of correct responses, of opportunities taken, of times that a response occurred out of the times checked, and so on. Percent graphs do not show how many responses were made or how rapidly responses were made.

Frequency Graphs. The frequency graphs, on the other hand, have number of words (correct and incorrect) on the vertical axis so that

> **A Frequency Graph**
>
> is a graph showing the number (that is, the frequency) of times something occurred during each session that a count was taken. For example, a frequency graph might have on its vertical axis the number of responses, number of opportunities taken, number of correct and incorrect problems solved, and so on.

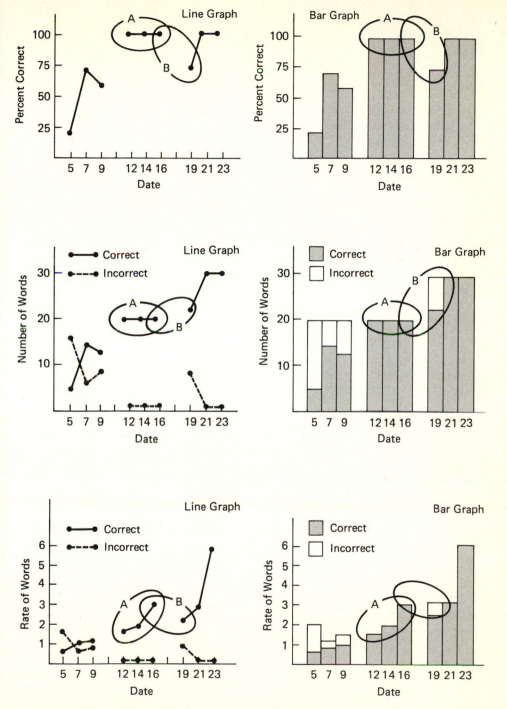

Figure 6.1 Six Line and Bar Graphs of the Data in Table 1.

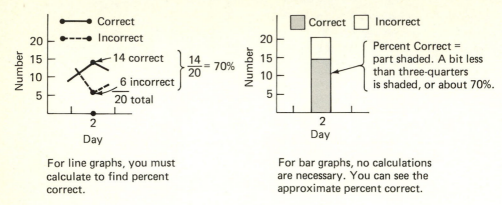

For line graphs, you must calculate to find percent correct.

For bar graphs, no calculations are necessary. You can see the approximate percent correct.

Figure 6.2 Comparison of Frequency Line and Frequency Bar Graphs in Answering "What Is the Percent Correct?"

they *do* show the increase from Friday the 16th to Monday the 19th. You can read information on the number of times something occurred directly from any frequency graph. The frequency graph, however, does *not* show changes in rate (for example during Week 2—shown as A in the graphs).

All of the information you can get from percent graphs can also be seen in frequency graphs. You can calculate percent correct from the numbers in the frequency line graph, and percent correct is very clear in the frequency bar graph, since it is the portion of the bar that is not shaded (see Figure 6.2).

Frequency graphs are also less misleading than percent graphs be-

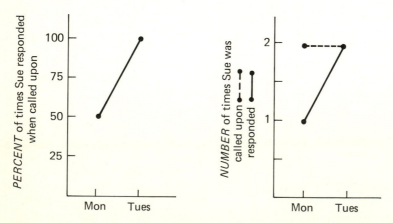

Figure 6.3 How Percent Correct Can Make a Small Change Look like a Large One by not Showing the Numbers Involved.

cause they make it difficult to misrepresent change. The two graphs in Figure 6.3 show how one could exaggerate improvement by basing percent correct on a very small total number so that a minor change would look like a large one. A gain of only one response out of a total of two is 50 percent improvement!

On a frequency graph the numbers involved are shown on the vertical axis, so one is more likely to notice that the gain involved only one response. Since a frequency graph shows everything that a percent graph shows and gives the numbers involved in addition, frequency graphs are generally preferable to percent graphs.

Rate Graphs. Neither percent nor frequency graphs show improvement in *rate*, such as the gain made during Week 2. For that, we need to graph rate (graphs 3 in Figure 6.1). Unfortunately, the rate graphs do

---

A Rate Graph

is a graph of rate, that is, of the number of responses made *per unit of time,* such as problems correct per minute, number of contributions per hour, or number of words read per minute.

---

not show the addition of new words so that, at B, it looks as though the student dropped in performance. A way to get both total number and rate on the same graph is to add the missing information, as in graphs A and B in Figure 6.4. Depending on what you wish to show, you could choose Graph A, which emphasizes the total number of words used, or Graph B, which emphasizes changes in rate.

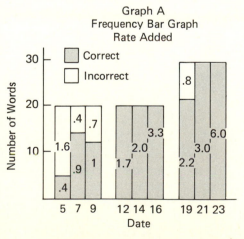
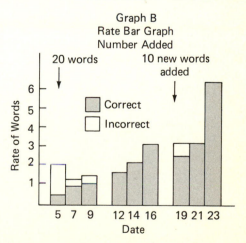

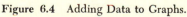

Figure 6.4 Adding Data to Graphs.

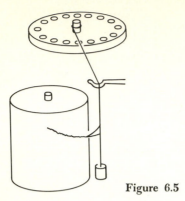

Figure 6.5

THE CUMULATIVE RECORD

The six graphs given so far show each day's behavior as one or two lines or one bar. There are times when more detail is desired. We could break down each day into smaller time periods or we could use an ongoing record to show each response as it occurs.

One such record is the *cumulative record*. It was discovered by accident by B. F. Skinner. Skinner had invented an apparatus in which a rat running down a runway would make a mark, or "pip," on a strip of paper which was moving. The distance between pips showed how much time the rat had taken between one response and the next. Skinner describes the next step in the development of the cumulative record:

A third unformalized principle of scientific practice: Some people are lucky. The disc of wood from which I had fashioned the food magazine was taken from a storeroom of discarded apparatus. It happened to have a central spindle, which fortunately I had not bothered to cut off. One day it occurred to me that if I wound a string around the spindle and allowed it to unwind as the magazine was emptied [Figure 6.5], I would get a different kind of record. Instead of a mere report of the up-and-down movement of the runway, as a series of pips as in a polygraph, I would get a curve. And I knew that science made great use of curves, although, so far as I could discover, very little of pips on a polygram. The difference between the old type of record at A [Figure 6.6] and the new at B may not seem great, but as it turned out the curve revealed things in the rate of responding, and in changes in that rate, which would certainly otherwise have been missed[1].

The modern cumulative record consists of a line drawn slowly and evenly across a strip of paper (see Figure 6.7). At each response the line moves up. The more rapidly the individual responds, the more

[1]B. F. Skinner, "A Case History in Scientific Method," in *Cumulative Record,* 3rd ed., New York, Appleton-Century-Crofts, 1972, pp. 108–109.

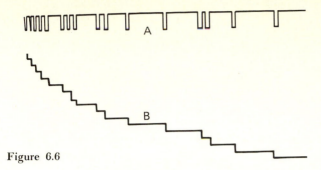

Figure 6.6

rapidly the line moves up, so that the *slope* of the line indicates rate of responding. Figure 6.8 shows a cumulative record of a boy's "cooperative responses" and his "commands" to his mother—first (baseline), where they interacted, as they usually did; and then (treatment) where the mother was instructed to reinforce only cooperative behavior. During

Figure 6.7   A Modern Cumulative Recorder. (Courtesy of Ralph Gerbrands Company, Inc.)

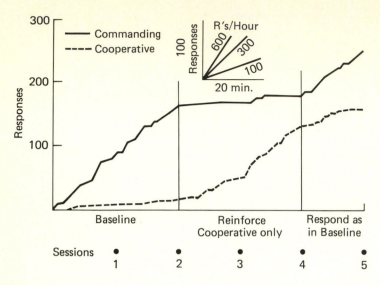

Figure 6.8 Rate Measures of Danny's Commanding and Cooperative Behavior over Baseline and Therapy Sessions.[2]

baseline, the boy commands at a high rate of nearly 300 times per hour (see the little box for rates for different slopes). He cooperates, on the other hand, at a very low rate. When contingencies change during treatment (sessions 2–4), commands drop off almost immediately and cooperative responses rise.

A Cumulative Record

is a graph of the running total of responses made. New responses are added on to the old total so that, in a cumulative record, the data line can only go up. How fast it goes up depends on the rate of responding—the more rapid the responding, the steeper the climb. A horizontal line indicates no responding.

Note that because a cumulative record "cumulates" responses, the line cannot go down. *No* responding is shown by a horizontal line. You cannot *subtract* responses in a cumulative record. For this reason it is usually used to record responses made, rather than skill level. Once made, a response is a part of history: unlike a skill, which can be forgotten, it cannot be subtracted.

[2]Robert G. Wahler, Gary H. Winkel, Robert F. Peterson, and Delmont C. Morrison, "Mothers as Behavior Therapists for Their Own Children," in *Child Development: Readings in Experimental Analysis,* eds. Sidney W. Bijou and Donald M. Baer, New York, Meredith, 1967, p. 247.

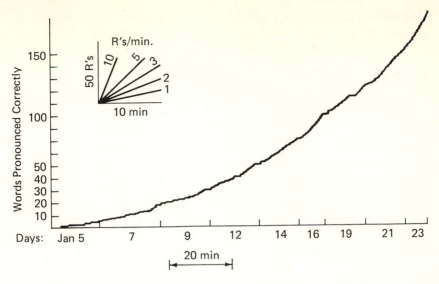

Figure 6.9 One Possible Cumulative Record for the Data in Table 1.

A cumulative record of the data used for the graphs from Figure 6.1 might look like Figure 6.9. The vertical lines separate each day.

Normally teachers don't use such a detailed record as Figure 6.9. One might, however, want to show cumulative responding day by day. For example, rather than showing sit-ups done each day as in Graph A, Figure 6.10, a coach might prefer to emphasize the total as in Graph B.

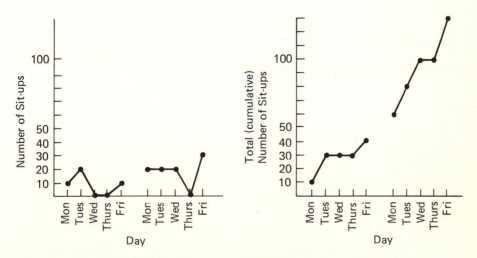

Figure 6.10 The Same Data Graphed as Response per day and as Cumulative Responses per day.

A Cumulative Graph Is Used When Total Number of Responses Is Important. On this graph, students plotted their points earned, showing their progress toward their grades for a nine-week period.

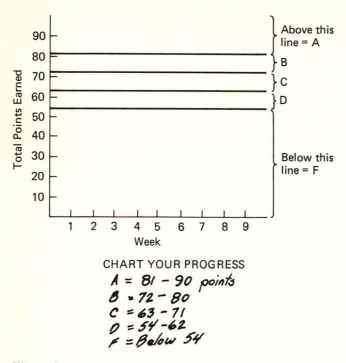

Figure 6.11

Similarly a teacher might have each student keep a cumulative record of assignments completed, quizzes passed, grade points earned, and so on (Figure 6.11).

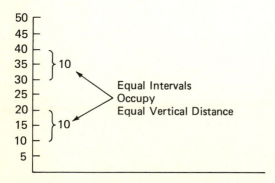

Figure 6.12   An Equal-Interval Graph.

EQUAL-RATIO GRAPHS

All of the graphs we have discussed so far are called *equal-interval graphs* because equal intervals (such as between 10 and 20 and between 30 and 40) occupy the same vertical distance on the graph (Figure 6.12). When we ask, "How much has Janet improved?" we may be interested in the *interval,* or difference, between her prior performance level and her present level. We answer in that case by adding or subtracting. We might, for example, subtract her beginning typing level of 20 words per minute from her present level of 60 words per minute and say, "She has improved 40 words per minute." When the differences we are interested in can be found by subtracting, an equal interval graph is appropriate.

An Equal-Interval Graph

is a graph which has the intervals between numbers equally spaced up and down the vertical axis. When you add or subtract a certain amount, you move up or down the same distance, no matter where you start on the graph.

We may, however, be less interested in the *number* gained than in the *ratio* of change. We may want to know if the student has doubled his or her performance or if the student has done something only half as often as when we started. When we ask how many *times* better the student performs, we are asking for ratios, not intervals. Instead of adding or subtracting to get the answer, we must multiply or divide. To take the example of Janet's typing, we may not care how *many* words correct per minute she has gained but rather how many times faster she can now type. To find out, we take her present rate of 60 words per minute correctly typed and *divide* by her initial rate of 20 words per minute, and answer. "She types three times faster now."

To show ratios—rather than intervals—an *equal-ratio graph* is used. Whereas in an equal interval graph, the horizontal lines are equally spaced (to give equal intervals), in an equal-ratio graph, lines are spaced logarithmically so that equal ratios (number of *times* more or less) span equal distances on the graph. The distances between 1 and 2, 2 and 4, 100 and 200 are the same on an equal-ratio graph because the ratio (times 2) is the same. An equal-interval and equal-ratio graph are compared in Figure 6.13.

An example may help to clarify the uses of equal interval and equal ratio graphs. Suppose you are to teach physical fitness to high school

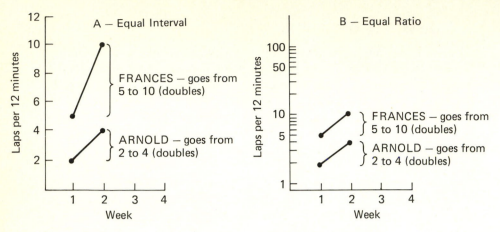

Figure 6.13   Comparison of Equal-Interval and Equal-Ratio Graphs.

An Equal-Ratio Graph

is a graph which has numbers spaced on the vertical axis so that *ratios* will be equal up and down the graph. If you multiply or divide by a certain amount (that is, change by a certain ratio) you move up or down the same distance, no matter where on the graph you start.

---

students who are not going out for football or any of the other specific programs offered at the school. Jogging is part of your program. The first day you see how many laps around the high school track the students can run in 12 minutes. The results are not impressive. Most can make five laps, but there is tremendous variation from student to student. You decide that a reasonable goal is for your students to double the number of laps they can run in 12 minutes. You are talking ratios. What happens if you plot progress on an equal interval graph? Chubby Arnold, who at first gave out after only two laps decides to really work. He cuts out milkshakes, comes to all practices, and doubles his performance (see figure 6.13). Frances, who started at five laps, works hard, and also doubles her performance. On an equal-*interval* graph (Graph A, Figure 6.13), Frances's record is much more impressive than Arnold's, because the *number* gained was greater. The ratio gained, however, was the same, and it may very well have taken the same effort from the two students to improve the same ratio. An equal-interval graph can be very discouraging to the student who, like Arnold, starts out at a low level. It seems fairer to use a ratio graph. On a ratio graph (Graph B, Figure 6.13) Arnold's record looks the same as Frances's.

THE DAILY BEHAVIOR CHART

A standard ratio graph for teachers is the daily behavior chart. It was developed in 1965 by Dr. Ogden Lindsley while he was working with practicing teachers.

Lindsley found that the teachers didn't have any reliable measure of their students' behavior and that their casual feelings about what worked and what did not work were often inaccurate. Knowing that rate (or frequency) is the most sensitive measure of behavior, he started teachers timing and counting. The teachers came back with rates of this behavior and that behavior—but what a time they had trying to graph their rates! Each teacher labeled the axes of the graph differently and they all complained about the time it took to figure them out. Lindsley's response was to print up a standard graph. The daily behavior chart is a ratio graph that can handle any behavior occurring at a rate of between one a day and 1000 a minute—and 1000 a minute is really moving![3]

The daily behavior chart has movements per minute along the vertical axis and days along the horizontal axis. The heavy vertical lines are Sundays. One chart covers 20 weeks, which is half of the usual school year. By keeping one line for each calendar day (whether or not any data are collected) overall patterns can be seen. For example, if Fridays are always bad days, a dip will show at the same place each week. Similarly, vacations and days absent show clearly. Rates are plotted in "count per minute." If you have a count of five problems completed correctly in an hour, you must convert it to problems correct per minute before graphing it on the daily behavior chart. The same is true for a count per day. Since there are almost 1000 minutes in a 16-hour day, we can divide by 1000 to convert a daily count into behaviors per minute. A simpler method is to relabel the vertical axis with the daily equivalents of behaviors per minute as is done in Figure 6.14. Then we needn't bother with fractions, we can just plot directly.

Once mastered, the daily behavior charts are easy to use and informative. A glance tells us how much a student is improving in both rate and in accuracy (see Figure 6.15).

Where progress is reinforcing, posting charts is highly motivating for students. Unlike most posted charts, the daily behavior chart is as rewarding to the slower student as to the faster one. Slower students'

---

[3]Daily behavior charts are six-cycle semilog graphs. "Semi" because only the vertical lines are spaced on a log scale (horizontal, or "day" lines, are equally spaced), and six-cycle because there are six log cycles from top to bottom. Semilog paper with various numbers of cycles can be bought at most office supply houses because it is widely used in engineering. The daily behavior charts can be ordered from:

Precision Media
Box 3222
Kansas City, Kansas 66103

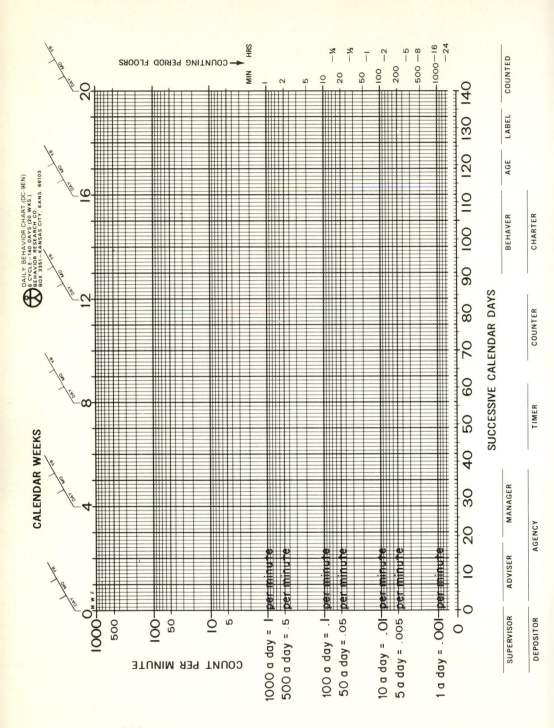

Figure 6.14

A Daily Behavior Chart Relabeled for Counting All Day. (Courtesy of Ogden Lindsley.)

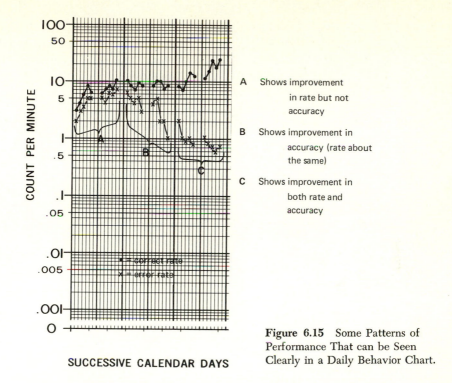

A Shows improvement
    in rate but not
    accuracy

B Shows improvement in
    accuracy (rate about
    the same)

C Shows improvement in
    both rate and
    accuracy

COUNT PER MINUTE

SUCCESSIVE CALENDAR DAYS

Figure 6.15 Some Patterns of Performance That can be Seen Clearly in a Daily Behavior Chart.

records show just as much improvement as faster students' records because they show the *ratio* of change from one's starting rate.

SUMMARY

Good teachers are sensitive to their students' behavior. In teaching anything, we constantly ask ourselves questions about student progress. "Are the students ready to go on? Does anyone need review? Does anyone need more of a challenge? What will most benefit each student now?" These questions are answered by looking at student behavior.

The more we know about student behavior, the more we can make decisions based upon *their* needs rather than upon our own inclinations or guesses. We need records so that we have as much information as possible. We *graph* data to see more clearly the trends and changes that the data show.

The particular record forms we design determine what we look for in our students and thus what we see in their behavior. Similarly, the kind of graph we use determines what we see about the data. If we graph *percent correct*, we can see progress in accuracy but we cannot see changes in rate of performance. Unless we write in the numbers involved, a percent graph also obscures the number of *times* a response occurred. It is the least informative kind of graph.

The *frequency graph* emphasizes the numbers of responses involved. It shows accuracy as well as numbers, so that it is preferable to the percent graph in being closer to the actual data. The frequency graph does not, however, show changes in rate unless the time period each day is the same or unless daily rates are written on the graph.

The *rate graph* emphasizes rate of responding. Information on accuracy can be easily seen. The numbers of responses involved, however, are not readily apparent unless they are written in. Two kinds of rate graphs are found: equal-interval and equal-ratio. The first shows changes in *numbers* gained or lost; the second, in how many *times* faster or slower a behavior occurs. The *daily behavior chart* is an example of the second kind of graph.

The *cumulative record* emphasizes the running total of responses. It shows rate in the slope of the curve (steeper is higher) and is useful when an ongoing record of behavior as it occurs is desired.

TABLE III   Graphs and Their Uses

When you want your graph to emphasize	The graph to use is	But remember that
1. Accuracy or Percent only	Percent	You lose information on number of times behavior occurred and on rate.
1. Number correct and incorrect 2. Trends in correct and incorrect 3. Accuracy	Frequency: a. Line graph best shows trends in correct and incorrect b. Bar shows percent correct	Frequency graphs will not show rate. For that information, the time taken must be included or rates written over each day's data.
1. Rate correct and incorrect 2. Trends in rate correct and incorrect 3. Accuracy	Rate	Rate graphs do not show number of behaviors (problems given, etc.). That information must be written in.
1. Total number of responses made 2. Rate of responding	Cumulative Record	You cannot "subtract." Once a response is counted, it is part of that record.

EXERCISES

Concept Check VIA—Kinds of Graphs (Objective A)

For each item in Figure 6.16 below write the letter(s) of the graph(s) that are examples of it.

1. Bar Graph
2. Equal-Ratio Graph
3. Daily Behavior Chart
4. Cumulative Record

5. Equal-Interval Graph
6. Percent Graph
7. Frequency Graph
8. Line Graph

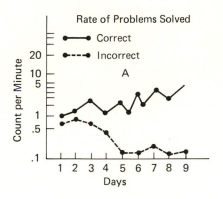

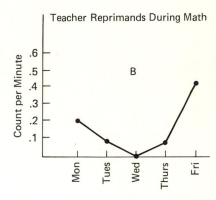

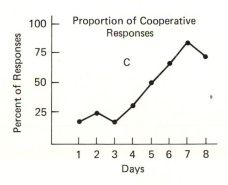

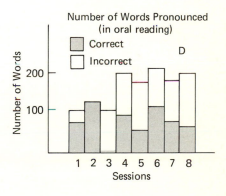

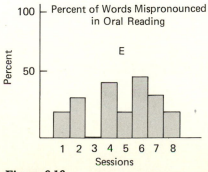

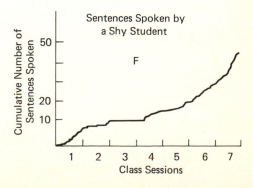

Figure 6.16

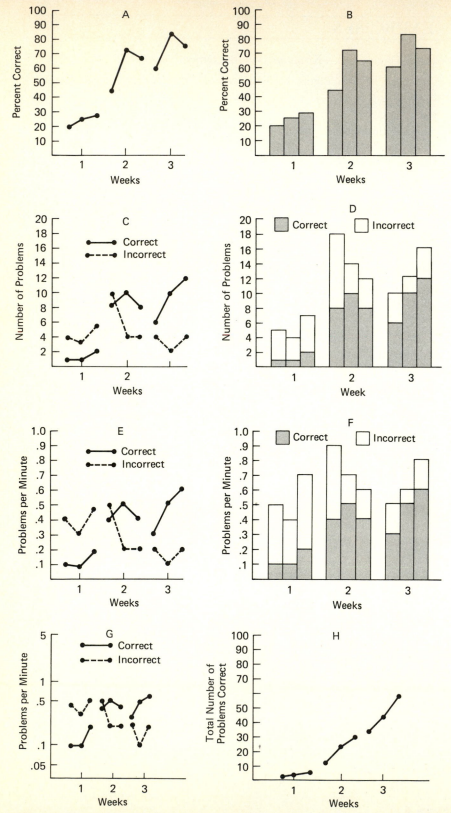

Figure 6.17 Graphs on Mike's Problem-Solving.

Answers for Concept Check VIA

1. Bar Graph: D and E
2. Equal-Ratio Graph: A
3. Daily Behavior Chart: A
4. Cumulative Record: F
5. Equal-Interval Graph: B, C, D, E, and F
6. Percent Graph: C and E
7. Frequency Graph: D (F is also correct, since it is a cumulative frequency graph)
8. Line Graph: A, B, C, and F

ANALYSIS PROBLEMS (OBJECTIVE B)

Graphs A through H in Figure 6.17 are eight ways to show the same data. Use them to answer each question below. Then write the letter of the graph or graphs you found easiest to use to answer that question.

1. About how many problems did Mike do correctly over the three weeks?
2. Which day did Mike do the greatest *number* of problems correctly?
3. Which day did Mike get the biggest *percent* of problems correct?
4. Which day did Mike solve problems correctly the fastest?
5. Which week did Mike improve in accuracy but not in rate?
6. Which graph would you use if you were Mike's teacher? Why?

Answers for Analysis Problems

The answers to the questions are in the first column. The second column lists graphs which *could* be used to answer the question. The best choices are starred because they are the graphs from which the answers can be read directly, that is, without having to add or otherwise compute. The third column lists graphs which could *not* be used to answer the questions and which therefore are incorrect graphs to choose.

I. Answer to the questions	II. Graphs which *could* be used to answer the question	III. Graphs which could *not* be used to answer the question
1. About 58	☆ H (the last dot shows the total number) C, D	A, B, E, F, G
2. The last day	☆ C, ☆ D H (the difference between two consecutive days gives the number done on the second day)	A, B, E, F, G (since E, F, and G do not specify the number done, you do not know whether the last day had a lot of problems done

			rapidly or only a few done rapidly)
3. Second day of the third week	☆A, ☆B ☆D (you can tell which bar has the greatest percent unshaded without computing) C, E, F, G (computation is required, but one can answer with these graphs)	H	

4. The last day ☆E ☆F ☆G ☆H

A, B,
C, D, (graphs C and D do not show rate; it could be that the last day Mike took longer with each problem than on previous days)

5. Week 2 ☆E ☆F ☆G

A, B,
C, D (graphs A–D do not show rate; Graph H does not show errors)

6. There is no "correct" answer here, but . . .

. . . if you feel that *number* of problems correct and incorrect is more important than how fast students work, you should have chosen graphs C or D.

. . . if you feel that the *rate* at which students can solve problems (correctly and incorrectly) is more important than how many they do on a particular day, you should have chosen graphs D, E, F, or G.

. . . if you are interested in *total number correct* and also in *rate*, you should have chosen Graph H.

. . . if you are not interested in either how many problems students do or in how fast they can do them, and thus picked graphs A or B, you are losing a lot of information. You should reconsider your choice.

The data for the eight graphs are below:

Week	Number		Percent		Rate	
	Correct	Wrong	Correct	Time	Correct	Wrong
	1	4	20		.1	.4
1	1	3	25	10 min.	.1	.3
	2	5	28		.2	.5
	8	10	44		.4	.5
2	10	4	71	20 min.	.5	.2
	8	4	67		.4	.2
	6	4	60		.3	.2
3	10	2	83	20 min.	.5	.1
	12	4	75		.6	.2

PROBLEM-SOLVING EXERCISES (OBJECTIVE C)

Each of the following problems is taken from a published study. For each problem decide how you would graph the data to best show progress and draw a graph to show your choice, fully labeling both axes.

1. Jake, a seven-year-old, tattled on other children too much. "He directed his tattling to the school secretary, two teacher aids, the principal and his classroom teacher. Jake would approach one of the above people and describe some inappropriate action of another child . . . throwing snowballs, climbing up the wrong end of a slide, hitting, playing ball where prohibited, bring a jacknife to school and similar behaviors."[4]

2. A teacher, Doris Mosier, had a problem with two 11-year-old boys. One whom she calls "S," would rile the other, "E," by calling him "Keify." Ms. Mosier decided to try to eliminate the "namecalling."

Sample Solutions for Problem-Solving Exercises

1. The graph the authors used is Graph A in Figure 6.18 below. Your graph may be different but be just as good or better. Consider your graph "correct" if you have days along the bottom axis and, on the vertical axis, either *number* (frequency) or *rate* of "tattling episodes," "tattles," "times Jake comes and tattles," or the equivalent. (Note: Baseline shows what Jake's behavior was like before anyone did anything about his tattling. Since it appeared that attention was reinforcing Jake for tattling, everyone agreed during the experimental days to say nothing to Jake when he tattled, not even "Please be quiet." They simply continued work as if he were not present. It didn't take long for Jake to stop.)

2. Graph B in Figure 6.19 below is the graph Ms. Mosier used. A more informative one is Graph C because it also shows the number of times S addressed E *appropriately*. You could also graph the *rate* of S's calling E "Keify" (Graph D) or both that rate and the rate of addressing E by his name (Graph E). Whatever your method, you should have days along the bottom axis and number or rate of S's responses along the vertical axis. (Note: During the "baseline" days, E responded as usual to being called Keify. He replied, "Cut that out," "Quit it," and so on. During the four "experimental" days he did two things. First, he completely ignored all "Keify's," often walking away. Second, when S called him by his name, he responded by saying something like "I'm glad you didn't call me "Keify." Unfortunately, the number of these appropriate responses is not included in the article.)

---

[4]John H. Wright and Robert P. Hawkins, "The Elimination of Tattling Behavior Through the Use of an Operant Conditioning Technique," *School Applications of Learning Theory* 2, no. 1 (February 1970), pp. 9–13.

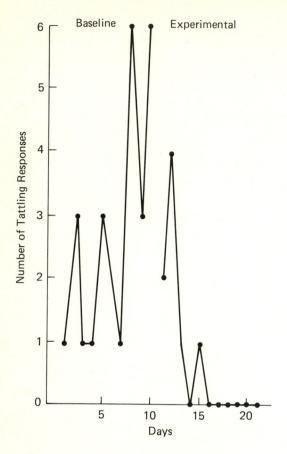

Figure 6.18 The Elimination of Tattling Behavior. (After Figure in "The Elimination of Tattling Behavior Through the Use of an Operant Conditioning Technique," *School Application of Learning Theory* 2, no. 1 (February 1970) by John H. Wright and Robert P. Hawkins.

SELF-PROJECT—CHANGING YOUR OWN BEHAVIOR (PART II)

Using the suggestions in this chapter, design a graph for your behavior-change project and graph your data so far. Make sure that you can easily see the kind of change you are interested in so that a big change would show up well on your graph.

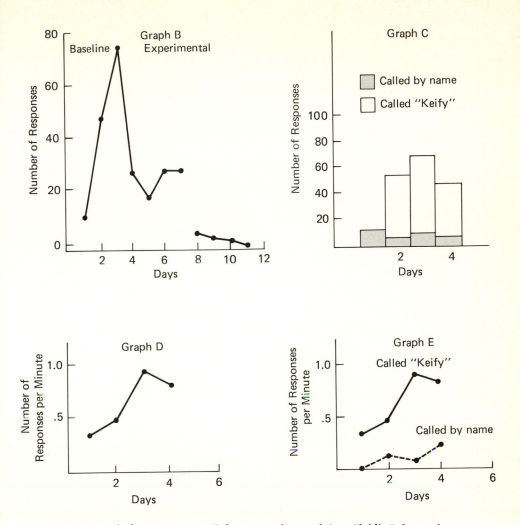

Figure 6.19 (After Figure 1 in "The Manipulation of One Child's Behavior by Another Child in a School Adjustment Classroom," *School Applications of Learning Theory* 2, no. 2 (April 1970), pp. 25–27 by Doris Mosier.)[5]

[5]Doris Mosier, "The Manipulation of One Child's Behavior by Another Child in a School Adjustment Classroom" *School Applications of Learning Theory* 2, no. 2 (April 1970), pp. 25–27.

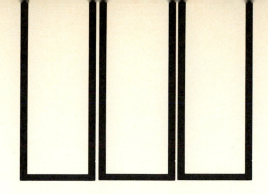

Techniques
for change

OVERVIEW

Part III is designed to teach you how to analyze the factors in the environment which are responsible for behavior and how to change them in order to change behavior.

Kinds of consequences— some definitions

OVERVIEW

Of the three terms in a contingency, we have discussed only the "response" at length (how to pinpoint, measure, and graph it). In this chapter we will look at consequences.

OBJECTIVES

By the end of the chapter you should be able to:

A. Define and give (or identify) examples of:
   1. Reinforcement
   2. Extinction
   3. Punishment
B. Describe (and/or identify) a typical pattern of behavior during extinction.
C. Tell (or tell how to determine), what kind of consequence a particular event is for a given student.

DEFINING CONSEQUENCES BY THEIR EFFECT ON BEHAVIOR

Operant behavior is behavior maintained by its consequences. So once we have specified what we wish to change, all we need to do is to reward good behavior and disapprove of bad, right? Unfortunately, it is not so simple. "Reward" and "disapprove" are words for what *we* like or dislike. What kinds of consequences they are for others depends not on our opinion but on how they work. We define consequences by their effects on behavior.

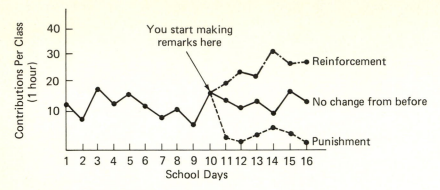

Figure 7.1 Kinds of Consequences.

Suppose you have a student, Sandra, who speaks up during your discussion period about once very five minutes. For three weeks she continues at about the same rate. Something must be maintaining her behavior (since without any consequence, behavior dies out in what is

Figure 7.2 Two Ways to Reinforce.

called *extinction*), but you cannot tell offhand what it is. One day you decide to try something. Every time she speaks up you say, "Good point, Sandra," or make some similar remark. What effect might you have on Sandra's behavior? There are three possibilities (shown in Figure 7.1). You might increase her rate, in which case your statements are *reinforcement;* you might decrease it, in which case you have used *punishment;* or you might have no effect at all.

REINFORCEMENT

To reinforce is to strengthen. Reinforcement is any event which strengthens the operant it follows. There are two ways we can reinforce a student (see Figure 7.2). We can give something or take something away.[1]

For most students such things as approval, grades, gold stars, free time, library passes, and so on are reinforcing, and for those students, we strengthen behavior by giving them. But we can also strengthen behavior by *removing* something. When we *take away* things a student avoids, such as a penalty, a required test, or our disapproval, we also strengthen behavior.

Reinforcement

is any event which maintains or increases the probability of the response it follows.

Reinforcement is an individual thing. We cannot say of a particular thing or event, "That's reinforcement!" It may be reinforcing for one student but not for another. Tammy may work toward a football ticket but Carl may not. Sometimes an event will reinforce a student today but not tomorrow. Susan may work for extra recess on Monday but not on Tuesday. The better you know your students the better you can guess what will reinforce them, but you can never be sure without trying.

When you guess wrong, you may be tempted to say that reinforcement isn't working, as in the example in the following cartoon (Figure 7.3).

Why isn't the teacher being effective? The teacher guessed wrong. "That's excellent" is *not* a reinforcer for Sarah.

The Criticism Trap. What we think should be a reinforcer may not be. In addition, what we think should *not* be reinforcing may be so. Teachers often reinforce behavior they do not intend to strengthen. If,

---

[1] In *Science and Human Behavior,* B. F. Skinner defined reinforcement and punishment a bit differently than they are defined here. See "reinforcement" and "punishment" in the glossary for details. (B. F. Skinner, *Science and Human Behavior,* New York, Macmillan, 1953, pp. 72, 185.)

Figure 7.3 "Why Doesn't My 'Reinforcement' Work?"

for example, we scold Pat for "talking out of turn," we expect Pat to talk out less often in the future. We assume we are correcting Pat's behavior and that our scolding is a mild kind of punishment. But by scolding we are giving attention, and attention is reinforcing for most students. Perhaps, for Pat, getting a scolding is better than no attention at all. In that case, we may be *increasing* the very behavior we are criticizing.

The example of Pat is fictional, but the reinforcing effect of criticism is real. It was demonstrated beautifully in a study by Becker, Engelmann, and Thomas, where they reported the following:

It was 9:20 A.M. The team-taught first grade had forty-eight children in it. Two rooms were available for the class, with a movable divider between them. The children's desks were grouped into six tables of eight children each. They had been assigned work to do at their seats, while the two young teachers taught reading in small groups. Two observers entered the room, sat down, and for the next 20 minutes they recorded the number of children out of their seats during each ten second period. The observers also recorded how often the teacher told the children to sit down, or to get back to their seats. During these first six days about three children were out of their seats every ten seconds. The teachers would say "sit down" about seven times in a 20 minute period.

Then some very strange events began to occur. The teachers were asked to tell the children to sit down more often. During the next 12 days, the teachers said "sit down" 27.5 times each 20 minutes. *The children stood up more*—on an average of 4.5 times in ten seconds.

The sequence was tried again. For the next eight days, the teachers went back to saying "sit down" only 7 times in twenty minutes. Out-of-seat behavior declined to an average of 3 times every ten seconds. Again the teachers were asked to tell the children to sit down more often (28 times in twenty minutes). Again the children stood up more—4 times every ten seconds.

Finally the teachers were asked to quit telling the children to sit down, but rather to praise sitting and working. They did this, and fewer than two children stood every ten seconds, the lowest standing observed.

What can be going on? How do we explain such happenings? There is one further perplexing piece of information. The children actually did sit down when asked by the teacher to do so, so the result wasn't just due to a few children standing a lot.

A beautiful trap! Imagine, the teacher thought that telling the children to sit down worked, because they did sit down, but that was only the immediate effect. The effect on standing was not seen until later and might have been missed altogether by the teacher if careful observations had not been made. Her words were in fact having exactly the opposite effect on standing from what she desired. [See Figure 7.4].[2]

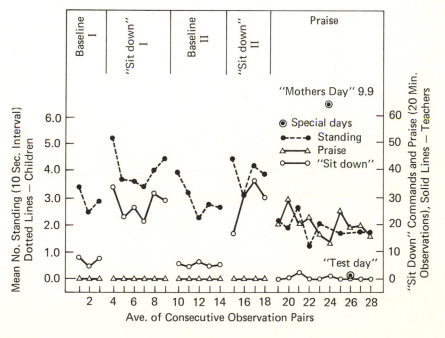

Figure 7.4   Standing-up by First Graders as a Function of "Sit-Down" Commands and Praise Given by Teachers. (Figure from *Readings in Educational Psychology* edited by R. K. Parker, Allyn and Bacon, Inc.)

[2]Wesley C. Becker, Siegfried Engelmann, and Don R. Thomas, *Teaching 1: Classroom Management*, Chicago, Science Research Associates, 1975, pp. 67–68. Copyright © 1975, Science Research Associates, Inc. Reprinted by permission of the publisher.

If telling the children to sit down increased their standing up, then the teacher was reinforcing standing up, not punishing it. Whenever we criticize sloppy writing, dawdling, talking out, looking out the window, or any undesirable behavior, there is a good chance we may be reinforcing just what we want to weaken. If so, we are caught in the criticism trap.

The Criticism Trap

is a situation in which criticizing a behavior you dislike seems to work because it temporarily stops the behavior, but actually, criticizing reinforces the behavior so that it occurs more often in the future, not less.

Another example of a consequence which was misclassified is reported by Silverman and Silverman. Their problem was general disturbance. They describe their problem as follows:

The situation in our inner city junior high school had deteriorated to such a point that groups of students roamed the hallways, disrupting classes. Some pupils in classrooms created disturbances so that learning could not take place, etc.

The teachers in the school got together and decided to use Room 205 as a detention room for those students who were causing disturbances. The intent was, first, to remove the problem students so that the other students could learn, and second, to decrease the frequency of the problem students' disruptions. The results were a surprise:

As it turned out, the "detention room" proved to be a failure. During the first few weeks of its existence, only a few "customers" were brought in. Shortly thereafter, however, the ranks began to swell. It was not unusual to see 40 people (ten more than the room was built to hold) at any given time! Many of these youngsters, as a matter of fact, would ask their teachers if they could be sent to the "detention room." It was obvious that being sent to Room 205 was not a deterrent to misbehavior; *it was a reinforcer.*[3]

There is only one way to determine for certain whether or not something is reinforcing and that is to try it. Make the event contingent on some behavior and note the results. If the person behaves more and more often or with more and more vigor, then you are reinforcing that response. In order to see the results objectively and quickly, you must record behavior daily. If you also *graph* daily, any changes become immediately obvious so that you are likely to catch your own mistakes before they become serious.

[3]Helene Silverman and Stuart Silverman, "Report of a Failure—'The Detention Room,'" *School Applications of Learning Theory* 6, no. 1 (October 1973), pp. 41–42.

NO CHANGE IN CONTINGENCIES

If we do something each time a student makes a response and nothing happens (see Figure 7.1), then we have not changed the relevant contingencies at all. Whatever was maintaining the response is still maintaining it at the same rate. We have not reinforced the behavior and we have not added punishment.

EXTINCTION

Extinction is a process in which a response is repeated without reinforcement and eventually dies out. In everyday language we say there is no longer any payoff for responding. A student, for example, who has received approval for bringing in short stories or poems that he or she has written may one day get a homeroom teacher who hardly bothers to look at them. If teacher attention was maintaining the operant of "showing compositions to your homeroom teacher," then when the attention stops, the student's behavior will undergo extinction. After a few tries, and a few days of trying, the student will eventually stop showing compositions to the teacher and may not bring them to school at all.

Extinction

is a process in which a response is repeated without reinforcement and eventually dies out. When we *extinguish* a behavior, we withhold the reinforcement which has maintained that behavior in the past so that the responses go unreinforced.

In extinction the unreinforced response must repeatedly occur. It is not the same thing as *forgetting*, in which passage of time with *no* responding results in deterioration of performance. A Spanish-speaking student might speak Spanish in school less and less if it went unreinforced (the response was extinguished because no one understood or reacted), but the student might still *remember* how to speak it. The arrival of another Spanish-speaking student (a "cue" that speaking will now be reinforced) would bring out the response in full strength. In contrast, a person could *forget* Spanish by not using it over a period of time. Even the arrival of another Spanish-speaking student would fail to bring forth the words and phrases which the student had previously used.

Behavior during extinction does not decrease smoothly or gradually. Usually the first result of not receiving the usual reinforcement is an increase in strength and speed of responding. Let's assume, for example, that you have a student, Tammy, who shouts out answers when you have called on someone else and that this behavior is maintained by your attention. If one day you decide to ignore Tammy when she calls out answers without raising her hand, you must be prepared at first for

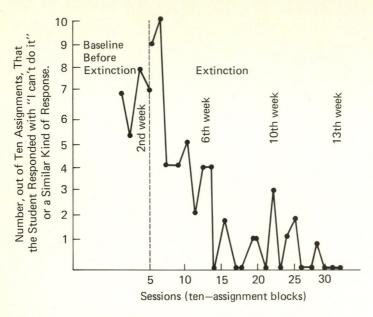

Figure 7.5 Typical Pattern of Responding During Extinction. Each point represents the number of times, out of ten assignments given, that a fifth grade boy responded with "I can't do it" or some similar statement. During the "extinction" phase all such responses were ignored. In addition to extinction, the teacher tried to reinforce the student for working, by looking at him, smiling, giving help or encouragement, and so on, whenever she caught him working.

Tammy to call out louder and more often. If you can withstand this "extinction burst" and continue to ignore her, she will eventually stop. During extinction an individual usually alternates between responding and pausing. The bursts gradually become fewer, less vigorous, and farther apart, until responding stops altogether. A typical pattern is shown in the preceding graph of a student's saying "I can't do it" when given assignments (Figure 7.5). The teacher decided to ignore all such protestations by becoming occupied with another student.[4]

PUNISHMENT

Few teachers (or parents) like to punish. It is usually a last resort, done when they "can't stand it any longer." To punish, one must hurt another in some way; either by inflicting physical or mental pain or by removing desired objects or privileges. Like reinforcement, what is pun-

[4]Robert Dietiker, "Decreasing a Fifth Grade Boy's 'I Can't Do It' Responses to Written Assignments," *School Applications of Learning Theory* 3, no. 1 (October 1970), p. 30.

ishing for one student may not be for another (for example, staying after school), but there are things which punish nearly everyone: a slap across the face, insults in front of others, removal of privileges—the list is long and all too familiar.

Punishment

is any event that decreases the probability of the response it follows. If we punish for something that occurs often, that behavior then has two consequences: whatever is reinforcing the behavior and our punishment.

Both punishment and extinction are used in order to reduce or eliminate some persistent behavior. If the behavior is persistent, it is being maintained by reinforcement from somewhere. Extinction refers to the process by which that reinforcement is discontinued. In punishment, on the other hand, a second consequence is added. Then the behavior is both reinforced (by whatever was maintaining the behavior in the first place) *and* punished.

Punishment and extinction have different effects on behavior. For example, take a student who makes wisecracks and is reinforced by peer laughter. If one day the students stop laughing completely—every remark goes over like a lead balloon—we have extinction. The customary reinforcement no longer occurs and the student will show the usual pattern in extinction, at first making more and louder jokes and then pausing, trying again, and eventually quitting altogether. If, on the other hand, the students still laugh but in addition the teacher punishes the student who makes the wisecracks, the case becomes more complex. One consequence is strengthening and one is weakening the same behavior. So long as the teacher is present (the student can "get caught"), the student will make fewer wisecracks, or at least will make them in such a way to avoid getting caught. The behavior is "suppressed." When the teacher leaves, however, and the threat of punishment is removed, the behavior will occur again at its original rate, or sometimes at an even higher rate.

In addition to being complex because of conflicting consequences, punishment also produces more than one effect on the person punished. To take another example: suppose Sandra likes to open the teacher's desk to see the grades and notes the teacher leaves there. Now suppose the teacher catches her and punishes her severely. "Opening the drawer" is weakened, but emotional responses are also produced. The next time Sandra starts toward the drawer to open it (say, when she's alone in the room), her own action will generate some of the anxiety and fear originally produced by the punishment. She may look furtively about or jump at a noise. Emotional responses of fear are by-products of punishment which usually occur in addition to the weakening effect on the act which was punished.

In contrast, suppose the teacher simply removes the reinforcement by taking everything out of the desk drawer so that Sandra repeatedly finds the drawer empty. There is no reinforcement for looking in the teacher's desk, so the "opening-drawer" behavior will die out. Sandra won't even want to open the drawer. She also will not feel anxiety, fear, or hostility. (Which treatment will help Sandra learn not to snoop is not at issue here. The example is used only to illustrate some of the problems associated with the use of punishment. The chapter on punishment explores these problems in more depth.)

SUMMARY

Consequences are classified by their effect on behavior. If a procedure strengthens behavior or maintains it, it is reinforcement. In extinction, a person responds repeatedly *without* reinforcement. Punishment is complex. It is an added consequence which reduces the strength of behavior. It does not remove the reinforcement responsible for maintaining the behavior and it often creates undesirable emotional responses which can be remarkably persistent.

EXERCISES

Concept Check VIIA—Reinforcement, Extinction, and Punishment (Objective A)

Assuming that attention, jokes, field trips, being first in line, and good grades are *reinforcing*, and classwork, homework, tests, whining, and paddling are *punishing*, classify each consequence below, using:

R   for "Reinforcement" (or "reinforcing")
E   for "Extinction" (or "extinguishing")
P   for "Punishment" (or "punishing")

1. Paddling a student.
2. Saying, "Good point."
3. Ignoring a student's interruptions.
4. Telling a student he or she will not have to take a test.
5. Stopping whining.
6. Making a student go to the end of the line.
7. By *not* calling on students who say "Oooh" while raising their hands to answer, you are _____ "saying Oooh."
8. By giving extra homework to students who say "Oooh," you are _____ "saying Oooh."
9. By telling a joke to get three yawning students to pay attention, you are _____ "yawning."

10. By dismissing class a bit early because students are starting to put on their coats, you are _____ "putting on coats when it's getting near to the end of the period."

Answers for Concept Check VIIA

1. P
2. R
3. E
4. R (This is a case in which reinforcement is the *removal* of a punishing stimulus—the threat of a test.)
5. (Since whining is that tone of voice which others find offensive, its termination reinforces whatever response ended it.)
6. P
7. E (extinguishing)
8. P (punishing) Note the contrast with Number 7.
9. R (reinforcing)
10. R (reinforcing) In both 9 and 10 you would be reinforcing *undesirable* behavior.

Concept Check VIIB—Reinforcement, Extinction, and Punishment (Objectives A and C)

For each problem, tell whether the teacher's action (underlined) is reinforcing, punishing, or extinguishing the behavior circled:

1. Sarah keeps (holding her pencil incorrectly.) Each time Ms. Ming catches her, she reminds Sarah to hold it correctly. Sarah then corrects her grip, but it isn't long before the teacher notices she is again holding her pencil incorrectly. The problem has become worse as the school year has progressed, not better.
2. Sam has trouble (drawing elevations correctly) in his landscape architecture class. Each time he must do one, he draws the elevation very quickly, so that it is sloppy and inaccurate. The instructor notices and comes over to tell him he'll have to do it again, showing him how it should be done. Sam's elevations are getting more sloppy, not less.
3. Petra is supposed to be writing a report on American Indians but, as usual, she is just copying out of her social studies book instead of (writing down her own ideas.) The teacher, Mr. Marsh goes to the student next to Petra and reads quietly, "I bet it was noisy in the longhouses." Then he comments, "You know, I hadn't thought of that, I bet it *was* noisy. You've really put in a lot of your own ideas." Petra stops copying and starts a sentence of her own. Mr. Marsh turns to her and makes a comment about enjoying her composition. Petra continues to write without copying.
4. Sasha talks up readily in Spanish class but she is behind the others usually and answers only in short, "safe" sentences. The teacher has recorded the number of (sentences Sasha says which are at least five words long and which use negatives or tenses other than the present indicative.) Usually the

number runs to about two per period. One day when Sasha has just given a long, complicated answer, the teacher really <u>lays on the praise</u>. The rest of the period Sasha doesn't answer at all.

5. (Tom always asks the teacher for some extra homework.) Ms. Davis, pleased, excuses herself from the other students and takes about five minutes to look through her books with him, picking out suitable work. But Tom never does the extra work. One day the teacher decides she has had enough of Tom's behavior. When he asks her for extra homework she replies, "Certainly, Tom," <u>but then talks to another student</u>. Tom asks again a few times, but then leaves. After three days, Tom still comes up after class, but he no longer asks for extra work.

Answers for Concept Check VIIB

1. Reinforcing — The teacher is actually reinforcing Sarah for holding her pencil incorrectly! This is a classical example of the criticism trap.

2. Reinforcing — Since Sam's drawings are getting sloppier, the teacher must be reinforcing sloppiness. This, too, is a case of the criticism trap.

3. Reinforcing — In addition to reinforcing Petra for writing down her own ideas, the teacher also set up a situation *preceding* Petra's desirable response by letting her overhear the comment to the student next to her.

4. Punishing — Praise, in this case, was punishing. It is tempting to speculate *why* praise might be punishing—but the important thing is the effect, *not* one's interpretation of it.

5. Extinguishing — One might argue that the teacher's "turning to another student" is a punishing snub, but in that case, Tom's response should drop off immediately. Since he asked again right away but then eventually quit, the teacher is more likely extinguishing his behavior than punishing it.

ANALYSIS PROBLEMS (OBJECTIVES A AND C)

Tell why the underlined consequence in each of the three descriptions below is misnamed, and tell what kind of consequence it was.

Example

SAMPLE DESCRIPTION: Mr. Haus decided to <u>extinguish</u> Jimmy's gum-chewing by paying no attention to it. Jimmy, however, continued to chew gum at about the same rate.

SAMPLE ANSWER: Mr. Haus's treatment was <u>not</u> extinction. It was no consequence at all because Jimmy's behavior did not change. Evi-

Example *(Continued)*

dently, Mr. Haus's attention was not the reinforcement which was maintaining gum chewing, so withholding it was <u>not</u> extinction. (Probably Jimmy was reinforced by the taste and feel of the gum.)

1. Ms. Homer had two students in the back of the room who were incessant talkers. She tried to <u>extinguish</u> their behavior by ignoring them, but their talking continued at about the same level.
2. Mr. Parsons "corrected" John's incorrect spelling. He found that in spite of this mild <u>punishment</u>, John's spelling got worse, not better.
3. Ms. Carlyle had always answered students' questions herself. One day she decided to <u>reinforce</u> students for asking questions by letting them answer themselves. Every time a question was asked she would respond with some variation of "<u>Good</u> question. What do *you* think?" At first the student who had asked the question would say, "I don't know," and then repeat the question, but after a few periods, everyone stopped asking questions altogether.

Sample Answers For Analysis Problems

Sample answers are below. You should have included each underlined point, even though you said it in different words.

1. Ignoring the students was not extinction. Since the students <u>continued talking at about the same rate</u>, Ms. Homer's ignoring them was <u>no consequence at all</u>.
2. "Correcting" John's spelling was <u>reinforcement</u>, not punishment, because John's <u>spelling got worse</u>, not better. (The rate of incorrectly spelling words increased when they were "corrected.")
3. Ms. Carlyle is <u>extinguishing</u> asking questions, not reinforcing it. She had given the answers herself. It seems that students were reinforced by having their questions answered. Then she withheld the answers. Since the students at first <u>repeated the questions, and then eventually quit altogether</u>, the withholding of answers was extinction, not punishment. (If Ms. Carlyle had used punishment—say, by commenting in a nasty tone, "Boy that was the stupidest question I have ever heard"—one would get an immediate drop in behavior: the student would not repeat the question right away.)

How to change behavior by changing contingencies

OVERVIEW

Chapter Eight presents principles and rules of thumb for changing behavior by changing the contingencies under which reinforcers are given.

OBJECTIVES

By the end of the chapter you should be able to:

A. Name the reinforcement which is probably maintaining a given behavior.

B. Describe how you could change behavior by changing the contingencies for a given behavior, using the following principles:
1. Reinforce immediately.
2. Reinforce often with small amounts rather than infrequently with large amounts.
3. Reinforce small improvements, don't hold out for perfection right away.

In order to strengthen desirable behavior, we must reinforce it when it occurs. We need, then, to know what we do and what we have in our classroom that is reinforcing for our students.

HOW TO FIND REINFORCERS

Although one cannot be certain that something will reinforce behavior without trying it, there are ways to make pretty good guesses. Some things, like attention, reinforce almost everyone. Other things vary from individual to individual or from age to age. The opportunity to play "Ring Around the Rosie" will not reinforce college students but it works beautifully with most kindergarten children. Conversely, books or articles which reinforce college students are of little value for reinforcing kindergarten children. The best way to find out what will reinforce a particular student or group of students is to look and listen.

What Do Your Students Ask For? Students who say, "May I go get a drink?" are telling you that a drink is a reinforcer for them. Paper, books, new pencils, being line leader, extensions on due dates for assignments, all are reinforcers for students who ask for them. You can also ask your students what they would like. In one school, fourth, fifth, and sixth graders were asked to list what they would like to work for. Among other things, they requested "taking a hike, skipping one book report, getting out of a paddling, eating on the playground, and wearing a hat for one hour." Some other reinforcers that have been used successfully are listed in Table I.

What Do Your Students Do? If you watch students before and after class you will see a variety of behaviors. Whatever your students do —whether it be talking, running around, looking at bulletin boards, writing letters, or flipping through magazines—can be used to spot reinforcers.

You can find reinforcers in the learning activities in any subject or field. If students prefer doing an experiment to completing written exercises, the teacher can make "opportunity to do the experiment" a reinforcer for completing exercises. Teachers whose students come to discussions unprepared may realize that discussions are more reinforcing than "reading assignments." When they design a unit, then, they can set up a contingency: if students pass a simple quiz on the reading, they get to join a discussion on the material.

In What Ways Are Your Students Progressing? One of the greatest reinforcers in any field is to see progress. It is reinforcing to see that you can do something today that you could not do yesterday. The improvement itself will not be reinforcing unless it is noticed. Any signs of progress a teacher introduces are likely to be reinforcers. Individual charts showing quizzes passed, pages of exercises satisfactorily completed, objectives mastered, or any record which lets students see their progress will do.

In using records, however, you must be careful that the slower as well as the faster students see progress. If slower students compare

TABLE I   Some Reinforcers Teachers Have Used

FOR ALL AGES
teacher attention
peer attention
free time
grades and points toward grades
marks of progress, honors, or
    certificates of accomplishment
preferred foods
snacks and drinks (or breaks to
    get them)
crossword puzzles or other games

Opportunity to:
use equipment (typewriter,
    filmstrip machine, etc.)
be with or talk with friends
work in a group
watch favorite TV program
see or hear self
get works published in news-
    paper or booklet
sit next to friend

PARTICULARY FOR ELEMENTARY SCHOOL
"good" stars
"smileys"
trinkets
stickers of all sorts
glue
play dough

Opportunity to:
play games
lead line
wash blackboard
wear hat in class
chew gum in class
give tests (spelling or other
    orally presented tests)
be inspector or checker for the
    work of other students

PARTICULARLY FOR SECONDARY SCHOOL
music
trinkets
decorations for notebooks, etc.
colorful folders
no homework
parties
snacks

Opportunity to:
attend sports event or other
    entertainment
wear preferred clothing
go on field trip
be first to lunch
groom (comb hair, etc.)
do project of choice

COLLEGE
(for smokers) cigarettes (and
    smoking breaks)
field trips
books and reprints of articles
coupons or passes for restaurants,
    theaters, sports events

Opportunity to:
talk with peers
teach others
leave class early
have coffee breaks
watch TV
do demonstrations, experiments
talk with professor
go to professor's home
meet famous people

their performance with their own previous record rather than with the progress of faster students, they will see what they achieve as success, not failure.

What Follows Persistent Undesirable Behavior? The students who create the most distress for teachers are those who disrupt the classroom. The "disciplinary problems" may not seem to seek any of the usual reinforcers such as grades, teacher approval, and so on. The teacher as a result may feel that there are no consequences strong enough to change such students' behavior. "Disciplinary problems," however, are students who engage in undesirable behavior day in and day out. They repeatedly make unwelcome comments, walk around the room, hit others, grab, throw things, fiddle with their belongings, or whatever. In short, they show remarkably persistent behavior. Any operant these individuals repeat day after day must be getting reinforced at least some of the time or it would eventually die out. Something in the school setting, therefore, must be maintaining the "disciplinary problems'" misbehavior. The chances are that the stimulus change following the misbehavior is reinforcing the students, even if it doesn't appear to be desirable. The consequences of persistent misbehavior are, then, likely to be reinforcers.

CHANGING CONTINGENCIES

If the consequence of student misbehavior is something we, as teachers, are providing (and usually we have some control over it), we need only change *when* it occurs to change our students' behavior. For example, if we are criticizing, we might change the timing of our attention. Instead of reacting to the misbehavior, we might try attending to the students when they are behaving well. To extinguish misbehavior we might also try to stop criticizing the students for undesirable behavior.

Suppose, for example, we have a student, Joe, who always procrastinates. On a typical day we announce cleanup time after labs and most of the students start getting ready to go, but not Joe. Knowing that he is likely to be last, we go to him and warn, "Joe, you'll have to start now if you want to be ready on time." Joe starts to clean up, and we turn to attend to others. Later, noticing that he hasn't progressed, we remind him again. Finally, about one minute before classes change and another group of students comes into the room, we end up putting the equipment away and gathering up the trash for Joe, giving a mini-lecture on how he can see he hasn't started early enough, etc., etc. The pattern has become habitual.

Using the principle of finding reinforcers by looking at consequences, we might suspect that teacher attention is reinforcing for Joe. If so, we couldn't have arranged consequences better to build the very behavior we want to eliminate. In the example, Joe gets attention (or "reminders") only when he is *not* getting ready. The one time he starts to clean up, the teacher leaves. And finally, the teacher cleans up for him.

We need to change the contingencies. While we may be unable to resist reminding Joe once (rationalizing that otherwise he'd never start), we should stick around and give our help while he *is* cleaning up, leaving when he slows down or stops. We need to watch like a hawk (out of the corner of our eye) for Joe to do anything close to getting ready and to speak to him then, giving as little attention as possible otherwise. Finally, if we *must* help at the end, we can at least do so in a routine, matter-of-fact way, without saying anything one way or another.

Each of the following case histories demonstrates how a problem was eliminated by changing contingencies. Before reading the teachers' solutions, you might outline what you would have done. First you will need to identify what is maintaining the undesirable behavior, and then describe how you would change the contingencies to produce desirable behavior instead.

Case History I: Dee—A Nursery School Child

The Problem. Imagine that you are one of two teachers at a university nursery school. You have cleaned out the cupboards, ordered supplies, and organized the rooms in preparation for the first day when 12 three-year-olds, six boys and six girls, will arrive. For the first week parents will stay for the two and one-half hour sessions, but by the end of the second week, you and your aid will have the children to yourselves.

On the first day, parents and children arrive, hand in hand. Most of the children are shy at the beginning, but they start playing after a few minutes. One little girl named Dee, however, remains crouched on the floor. When anyone approaches her, she turns her head away or hides her face in her arms. She does not stay close to her mother but crawls from indoors to outdoors and from place to place as school activities shift, remaining, however, always on the floor.

By the end of the second week of school, Dee is still avoiding others and is spending over 90 percent of her day sitting crouched on her hands and knees. She does not speak, except once in a while, when she softly says "Yes" or "No" to a teacher at snack time.

You speak to Dee's parents, a pleasant young couple. Dee's father has begun a professional career and Dee's mother seems warm and family oriented, having two other children, a boy of 18 months and one 8 months old. The mother is very much concerned about Dee and says that at home she is gentle, sweet, and cooperative but that she shows the same crouching behavior when visitors come to her home or when she takes Dee out. She had felt that perhaps nursery school would help Dee get over her shyness. The problem, then, is yours. How would you get Dee to stay on her feet?

One Solution. This problem is exactly what confronted two kindergarten teachers in a school in Washington in 1963. They decided to try using principles of operant conditioning to get Dee on her feet. Noticing that Dee got teacher attention for being *off* her feet, they decided to use attention as a reinforcer. They describe their procedures as follows:

It was decided that the teachers should attempt to weaken Dee's off-feet behavior by withholding attention (giving neutral stimulation) when Dee was off her feet. An exception to this might occur at group times, when attention was to be a minimum consonant with courtesy. The withdrawal-of-attention procedure was to be casually implemented by a teacher simply by becoming fully occupied with any one of the many immediate requirements always confronting nursery school teachers. In other words, teacher attention was to show no obvious relationship to Dee's off-feet behavior. Teachers were also to avoid displaying any behavior that might suggest anger, disappointment, disgust, shame, or dislike. There was to be nothing punitive about their behavior.

Concurrent with the above procedure, on-feet behavior was to be immediately positively reinforced. That is, Dee was to be given attention whenever she displayed standing behavior. Since she stood up so infrequently, and so briefly, the behaviors closely approximating standing were also to be reinforced during initial days. That is, when she rose even partially to her feet, as well as when she stood, a teacher was to give her attention. Such attention was to consist of going immediately to her and making appropriate interested comments about what she was doing. Sample comments might be, "You hung that up all by yourself. You know just where it goes," and, "It's fun to let water slide over your fingers. It feels nice and warm, doesn't it?" A teacher's attention behavior was to convey to Dee that she was liked, appreciated, and considered capable.

In order for a reinforcer to be most effective, it must immediately follow the behavior to be changed. Therefore, to insure that Dee received immediate positive reinforcement for standing positions, one teacher was assigned to remain within range of her at all times, carrying major responsibility for this aspect of the guidance program. The other teacher was to carry major responsibility for the program of the rest of the children in the group. The teacher assigned the role of giving positive reinforcement every time Dee got on her feet was selected because she seemed to have a good relationship with the child. For example, Dee usually crawled to her group at snack time.[1]

It took one week to get Dee standing most of the time [see Figure 8.1], and by the end of two weeks (one month after entering school), she was also talking readily to the staff member assigned near her, using all of the outdoor play equipment and working at the easels, playing house, and working with clay. She was not making direct responses to the other children nor initiating contacts with them or with the other teacher, but otherwise acted like the other children. Her mother also reported marked improvement at home.

[1]Florence R. Harris, K. Johnston, D. S. Kelley, and Montrose M. Wolf, "Effects of Positive Social Reinforcement on Regressed Crawling of a Nursery School Child," *Journal of Educational Psychology* I (1964), pp. 35–41.

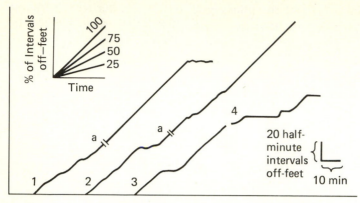

Figure 8.1 Subject's off-feet behavior on four different mornings: the first (Curve 1) and second (Curve 2) mornings of giving attention during off-feet and ignoring on-feet behavior, and the third (Curve 3) and fourth (Curve 4) mornings of giving attention during on-feet and ignoring off-feet behavior. Breaks at points "a'" indicate snack times averaging 12 minutes duration, which were not included in the data.

It was by noting that Dee's crouching usually brought her the attention of her teachers that the project staff realized that teacher attention was a reinforcer for Dee, even though the child seemed to *avoid* it. Similarly, any student's current behavior and its consequences can tell you what the reinforcer is if you take time to read it.

A similar analysis of contingencies can be used with an entire class.

Case History II: The Case of the Disappearing Pencils

The Problem. A fourth grade teacher we will call Ms. Michaels, who was in her second month of teaching, had a problem with disappearing pencils. She calculated (by new math, of course) that at the current rate, the entire year's supply of pencils would be gone by the end of November. She had passed out new pencils about every week, with the students' names neatly scotch-taped on the ends, but still the students were losing them, breaking them, or taking them home. Then, whenever she started written work, the class would be interrupted by students saying they had no pencils, and she would have to go get them new pencils. By then the momentum of the period would be lost. It was not a serious problem, but it was a constant irritation to the teacher involved. What would you say was reinforcing the students for saying they had no pencils? How could you use that reinforcer to reinforce the students for hanging on to their pencils?

One solution. Ms. Michaels asked herself, "Why can't the kids hang on to their pencils?" Then, knowing a little bit about behavioral psychology, she rephrased the question: "What is maintaining the behavior of losing pencils?" In analyzing the contingencies, the reason became perfectly clear: the students were getting new pencils by losing the old ones. The teacher needed to change the contingencies so the students got new pencils by *hanging on to* their old pencils. At the same time they should *not* receive a new pencil if they did lose an old one. One Monday, then, the teacher announced something like the following: "Sometime this week I will pass out new pencils. To get one you have to turn in your old pencil. From now on I will not tell you when I will pass out pencils, but you can get a new one only by passing in your old one."

The problem was solved within a week. Only a few students misplaced pencils, and they had to use other students' old chewed-up pencils (the turned-in ones). Several students became proud of not losing their pencils and even refused to exchange them for new.

By December, a few students were using two-inch-long stubs, all that remained of the original pencils which had been labeled with their names. Other students brought extra pencils from home so they'd be sure to have a pencil in hand in case it was new-pencil day.

In solving the pencil problem, no new reinforcers were added; in fact, the teacher gave out fewer pencils than she had before. In addition, it took less of Ms. Michael's time to work the new system than to handle the previous situation. A simple change in contingencies was all that was needed to change student behavior.

ESTABLISHING CONTINGENCIES TO GET GOOD BEHAVIOR STARTED

Once we know what reinforces our students, we still have to decide how to give reinforcement to best produce change.

We can strengthen a weak behavior best by reinforcing it immediately every time it happens. Three things are critical in getting behavior started:

Reinforce Immediately. You should give reinforcement *while* the student is still doing what you want to strengthen. If you wait too long, you may be reinforcing stopping or pausing, rather than behaving appropriately.

Immediate Reinforcement

is reinforcement which occurs while the reinforced person is still responding, or at least before he or she has a chance to make another response.

Suppose you wish Tom to work on written assignments. When you see him writing, that's the time to go to him even if you have to interrupt him to show approval. If you wait, saying to yourself, "Well, he's finally working; I won't disturb him," you are losing a chance to reinforce. Eventually he will look around the room or start picking on a neighbor. Then if you go and encourage him, saying, "You were working so well," you are reinforcing undesirable behavior, not what you want.

Reinforce Often with Small Amounts Rather Than Infrequently with Large Amounts. Since each time you reinforce you strengthen behavior, it follows that the more often you reinforce, the more you change behavior. The size or quality of reinforcement is not particularly important; look at what an elephant will do for one peanut or how a person will struggle to open the last pistachio in a bag, breaking fingernails or risking cracked teeth. The teacher need not overdo reinforcement. In giving attention, a single smile, nod, or word usually has as much effect on behavior as a ten-minute-long compliment. In fact, the smaller reinforcement will probably be more effective. Individuals tire of any reinforcement when given too much at one time. In addition, students compare their performance with that of other students. Praise which is out of keeping with their own assessment of their accomplishment may be taken as "not genuine"; that is, it may actually be punishment, not reinforcement.

The key to changing behavior is *frequency* of reinforcement. It is not impossible to attend in some small way to a particular student once every couple of minutes. When starting to work on a problem, then, you can reinforce 10 or 20 times in a half hour, or 20 to 30 times in a 50-minute period. Later, when the student is behaving appropriately most of the time, you can reinforce less often until only a normal amount of reinforcement will maintain the behavior.

Frequency of Reinforcement

is how often reinforcement occurs. It can refer to the number of reinforcements per unit of time or to the number of responses that are reinforced out of the number made.

Reinforce Small Improvements—Don't Hold Out for Perfection Right Away. If you want to reinforce often, you cannot wait until the student behaves perfectly. While you may feel that the student can and should do better, at first you must strengthen the best of what he or she does now. Once a student routinely does better (so that there is little danger of reverting to the previous level), you can raise your standards. When working with problems or exercises, a rule of thumb is that each student should get nine out of ten correct. Even at the college level, students get discouraged when they make more than one error in about ten tries.

SHAPING BEHAVIOR

Shaping is the process of building an operant by reinforcing those responses that are closest to the final performance. If you follow the three rules above, you will be shaping behavior. At first, the best ap-

---

Shaping

is the process of building an operant by reinforcing only those responses that are closest to it.

---

proximations that you reinforce may barely resemble the final behavior desired. When Dee's teachers, for example, wanted to get her on her feet, joining in nursery school activities, they had to start with the best of what she already did. To shape standing and walking, they had to start by reinforcing Dee when she pulled herself up to the sink or coatrack because that was the best approximation they had to work with. They reinforced immediately with small amounts (of attention) rather than infrequently with large. As Dee stood more often, they continued to reinforce the best of her behavior and no longer reinforced what had been the best before.

Another example of shaping occurs in the game in which a person tries to find a hidden object, guided by the clapping of peers who know where the object is. The person's movement in the room is shaped by the clappers, who reinforce only for responses which are increasingly closer to whatever movements will reveal the hidden object. The criteria for reinforcement shift as the person gets closer and closer. Responses which at first were reinforced (by clapping) are no longer reinforced when they are no longer the closest responses that have been made.

Similarly, when we teach a student to solve algebraic equations, form a sculpture, write a paper, work independently, and so on, we start by reinforcing behaviors which *eventually* lead to the final complex operant. (See Chapter Thirteen for suggestions on how best to do this.) We shape behavior slowly, step by step.

SOURCES OF REINFORCEMENT

For effective shaping of behavior, students must be reinforced frequently and immediately with small amounts. If you are one teacher in a classroom full of students, it is physically impossible to dispense reinforcement to each student at the exact moments necessary for effective shaping. While you may be able to concentrate on one student at a time when you have problems like Dee, you cannot possibly *personally* dispense reinforcement for a number of students with anything like the timing and frequency needed. You must arrange it, then, so that they get reinforced for behaving but so that you don't personally need to deliver each reinforcement. You need to set up a system, in other words, in which the students' reinforcement depends, not on your behavior, but on theirs.

NATURAL CONSEQUENCES

So far, the kinds of consequences we have considered have been provided by people. Much of what we do, however, is reinforced by the natural consequences of the behavior itself. When we walk, for example, we are normally reinforced by the progress we make rather than by the attention of other people. When we doodle, we may be reinforced solely by the marks we produce. We read to find out what happens next. In each case our own behavior creates the stimuli which reinforce us. When we are reinforced by natural consequences, we may also be reinforced by others, as when supervisors or peers comment on, or otherwise reinforce, our walking, doodling, or reading.

Natural (or Intrinsic) Consequences

are stimulus changes which are produced by (and are dependent on) the behavior of the individual who experiences them. Natural consequences are contrasted with "artificial" or "extrinsic" consequences, which are provided by (and are dependent on) the behavior of others.

When behavior is automatically or naturally reinforced we say that the person "enjoys" behaving or "has an interest" in what he or she is doing. When we teach reading or math we want students to read "for the love of it" or to "enjoy" tackling mathematical problems. We want, in other words, to bring our students' behavior under the control of natural consequences so that they will be reinforced automatically by the stimuli their *own* behavior generates.

For much behavior, natural consequences are conspicuous. When we walk, for example, it is clear when we are behaving effectively and ineffectively. A step which bumps us into a wall has a consequence which is conspicuously different from a step which moves us out a door. For walking, nature provides clear stimuli to control our behavior.

Other behaviors, however, do not *naturally* produce stimuli which enable us to behave effectively. In flying an airplane, for example, we must be able to respond to differences in altitude and speed which we cannot detect with our unaided senses. To behave effectively, we need to bring our behavior under the control of those differences—and we do so by designing meters and dials which provide the necessary stimuli. The behavior of the pilot, then, comes under control of the dials.[2] He or she is reinforced for flying well by what the dials show. Reinforcement depends on his or her own behavior.

The changes in stimuli which occur from effective learning are another example of stimuli which are difficult to detect with the un-aided senses. We cannot easily "see" our progress in understanding a concept, or in thinking creatively, or in learning to effectively solve problems. There are few conspicuous consequences which naturally follow effective learning in those areas. As teachers, we need to create stimuli which, like the dial of an airplane, make student progress conspicuous. These stimuli, then, can reinforce the students for behaving effectively.

It is not easy to design a system which makes student progress conspicuous, but we can at least move in that direction. We can design instruction which asks for student responding at each step and some method by which students can check their own exercises. (Some of the newer materials have self-correcting exercises in which students reveal a special sign when they mark a correct answer.) We can set up objectives and check off each one each student meets. We can display creative works and compare later works with earlier ones, to show progress. We can set up point systems in which students earn points by completing academic exercises (giving different students different exercises depending on the level at which they are working). By graphing, or otherwise displaying points, we make progress conspicuous.

Points can be given more value by letting students buy privileges, "vacations," grades, or even articles with them. Some examples of point systems are shown in Figure 8.2. One word of warning, however. If *too* much rides on points, their value as an indicator of progress will be destroyed: with highly desirable things to buy, student attention (that is to say, the control of their behavior) becomes centered on what they can buy instead of on what they are learning. In general therefore it is wise to use as few "backup reinforcers" as possible. If points alone work, there is no reason to add other reinforcers. If points alone don't produce satisfactory progress, then the teacher can add backup reinforcers such as the ones in the following examples of point systems.

[2] I first heard this analogy used by Hank Pennypacker (University of Florida at Gainesville) in 1976.

Examples of Point Systems
Elementary school

After finding out each student's reading level, the teacher places him or her in a series consisting of self-instructional lessons. Students then work at their own level, and usually no two students will be doing the same lesson on the same day. The teacher checks each completed work sheet before assigning the next, in order to make sure each student progresses well. Points are earned by completing the exercises at 85 percent correct or better. Each 30 points earns the student a certificate like the one opposite. When students get their second certificate (and each even numbered certificate thereafter) the students also get a Polaroid picture of themselves holding their certificate. By working hard, students can also earn a "vacation." If they earn six points in five days, students get a pass to an area called the "Fun Center," where they can play games, read, do art projects, talk, and so on.

Examples of Point Systems
Secondary school or college level

Grading will be on a point system and you can earn points by the following activities:

	Total Possible
1. Take a test on the day it is scheduled (100 points possible—you get whatever points you score).	400
2. Write a paper on a topic agreed upon in advance by you and the instructor (100 points possible).	400
3. Do a sheet of exercises in class or as homework assignment (10 points possible).	100
4. Read a book or article and hand in a one-page critique (10 points possible).	100

NOTE: No second chances or revisions will be possible. There are enough other opportunities to earn points. Final grades will be:

    A = 450–500 points
    B = 400–449 points
    C = 350–399 points
    D = 300–349 points
    F = Fewer than 300 points

Chapter Fourteen discusses in more detail strategies for using conspicuous natural consequences. The point here is simply that we can arrange for reinforcement to depend on student behavior. We do not need to personally hand out each reinforcer.

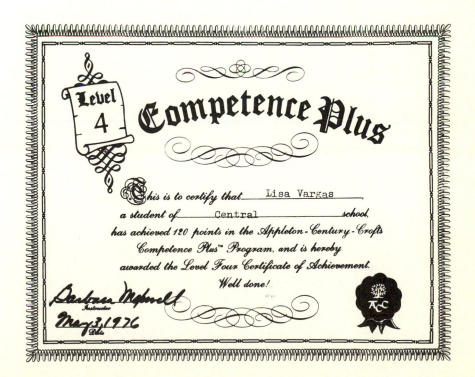

TROUBLESHOOTING

Many people have tried using reinforcement but have given up because it "didn't work." Most unsuccessful attempts at changing behavior are rather casual—the behavior desired is only vaguely defined and no good records are kept of how often it occurs. But even with these failings, nine times out of ten the main problem is failure to start with a realistic first step. Too much is required for reinforcement, which is not given frequently enough.

It is tempting to hold out for the very best a student can do. If Mary solved a difficult problem once three weeks ago, we say to ourselves, "I know she can do it. She did it before." By waiting for the exceptional behavior, however, we are missing many opportunities to reinforce. We could be changing Mary's behavior instead of waiting around. And what about Mary? Without reinforcement she is likely to become discouraged. She may even misbehave. If we *then* encourage her, we are reinforcing her for showing signs of discouragement or for misbehaving. It is better to reinforce small improvements more frequently.

By setting up unrealistic standards, we are not using reinforcement at all, but punishment. We are creating a situation in which failure is likely. The punishment that can come from using reinforcement without carefully shaping behavior can be severe. One parent, for example, set up a contract with his son for improving his grades (which on his previous report card went something like this: F, F, D, F, C, F). The student badly wanted a go-cart, so there was no problem in finding a reinforcer. The student came into school one morning jubilant, telling everyone that his father was going to buy him a go-cart for "getting all A's." Whether the father was serious or whether he was just using the opportunity to "get the kid off his back" about go-carts, the teacher never found out. But he couldn't have better programmed the adolescent for failure. In addition to not specifying the behavior well (grades are a result of many different behaviors, and they depend on other people besides the student), the father broke every rule in the book. He did not reinforce immediately or frequently. Grades were given every nine weeks. Studying now wouldn't be reinforced for weeks. And what about reinforcing small improvements? To go from F's to A's in nine weeks is an almost impossible task. Nevertheless the boy *did* try at first, but the predictable result nine weeks later was heartbreak. Not only did the student get poor grades, but he had lost the go-cart, and he had to take the humiliation of facing his friends, to whom, for nine weeks, he had talked about the go-cart he was going to get.

If the father was really prepared to buy a go-cart, he could have programmed his son for success. He might, for example, have put his son on a point system: nine hundred points for a go-cart. Homework, assignments at school, extra reading (with a report to his father) could all have been given point values. That way, reinforcement would have been immediate, frequent, and the behavior expected realistic. It is doubtful that, even with such a point system, the student would have made all A's, but he would have done much better than he did, and he would have been reinforced for academic performance—thus experiencing success where before he had met only failure.

Whenever you are not getting the behavior you want, the first thing to check is whether you are reinforcing immediately and frequently enough. You are probably asking for too much improvement. You cannot reinforce behavior often if it doesn't occur often. By trying a smaller step you make it possible to reinforce more frequently. The more frequently you reinforce a person, the greater the effect you have on behavior.

SUMMARY

Any teaching situation, from the one-room schoolhouse to the inner-city college, is full of reinforcers. Teachers use them unknowingly all the time. The contingencies under which they are given determine how students behave. Teachers maintain or create disciplinary problems or hardworking and serious students by the contingencies they set up. Getting students to learn is not a matter of discovering or buying new reinforcers; it is a matter of arranging contingencies under which students obtain, through academic progress, reinforcers which are already available in any classroom.

EXERCISES

ANALYSIS PROBLEMS (OBJECTIVE A)

For each cartoon in Figure 8.2, name: (a) the specific response which needs to be increased or decreased and (b) the reinforcement which is probably maintaining the undesirable behavior of the student.

1. BILLY

2. VIOLET

Figure 8.2

3. EMILIE

4. RICHARD

Figure 8.2 *(Continued)*

Sample Solutions for Analysis Problems

Consider yourself correct if your solutions are more like the sample Acceptable solutions than they are like the sample Unacceptable solutions.

	Responses to Increase (or Decrease)		*Probable Reinforcement*	
	Sample Acceptable Solutions	Sample Unacceptable Solutions	Sample Acceptable Solutions	Sample Unacceptable Solutions
1. Billy	Getting toys from box Requesting an object (Hitting) (Grabbing)	Being nice Sharing (Being a bully) (Bullying) (Being aggressive) (Picking on others)	Getting the object (car) Teacher attention Reaction of person hit or grabbed from (The cry or complaint of the person shoved or hit reinforces shoving, hitting, or otherwise attacking.)	Feeling powerful Praise (Billy isn't praised.)
2. Violet	Joining in games Doing what the teacher suggests Playing with others (Refusing to join games) (Walking away from others)	Cooperating (Being a wallflower) (Isolate behavior) (Withdrawing) (Being stubborn) (Being shy)	Teacher attention Avoidance of punishment from peers (such as ridicule for not doing it right or kids not wanting Violet to be next to them, etc.)	Fear (If Violet is afraid to join in, then *avoiding* the possible punishment of peers will be reinforcing, but the fear itself is not reinforcing her refusals.)
3. Emilie	Handing in assignments on time Completing assignments (Giving excuses)	Procrastinating Being irresponsible	Getting an extension Avoiding a grade-point penalty	Teacher attention (It is doubtful that Emilie would continue to give excuses if she got the atten-

Sample Acceptable Solutions	Sample Unacceptable Solutions	Sample Accepetable Solutions	Sample Unacceptable Solutions
			tion shown in the cartoon but *not* the extension.) Teacher approval (It is not approval to say O.K.)
4. Richard Writing Composing Writing pages or lines of the paper (Leaving the desk)	Getting to work (Procrastinating) (Avoiding work)	New pens Coffee Avoidance of the task of writing	Relief Getting the paper done (He's *not* getting the paper done.)

PROBLEM-SOLVING EXERCISES (OBJECTIVE B)

Take one cartoon from the preceding exercise that is like a problem you might encounter and describe how you could change the behavior using the principles below:

1. Reinforce what you want immediately.
2. Reinforce often with small amounts rather than infrequently with large amounts.
3. Reinforce small improvements, don't hold out for perfection right away.

Sample Solutions for Problem-Solving Exercises

There are, of course, an infinite number of ways to solve these problems. Some samples are given below. They are *not* to be considered the *only correct* solutions. They are simply examples of what could be done.

Problem 1: Billy

A problem such as this could be solved by two procedures. First, whenever Billy hits another child, the teacher could give attention to the child who was hit, turning her back on Billy. Second, the teacher could keep a sharp eye out for the few times that Billy plays *without* grabbing or hitting, and she could chat with him at those times, sometimes commenting on how nicely he is sharing.

Problem 2: Violet

Since it looks as though teacher attention is maintaining Violet's refusal to join in, one might try just giving attention when Violet does anything which will eventually lead to joining in. Perhaps the best first approximation would be to chat with her when she is watching the others; then, as she does this more frequently, to reinforce her when she moves toward the others. Gradually, depending on what Violet does, attention could be made contingent on playing with another child or on joining a small group. Gradually the size of the group could be increased.

Simply by changing the timing of attention, teachers have changed similar behaviors in a number of children.[3]

Problem 3: Emilie

The reaction of most people to this problem is to use punishment: fine Emilie along with the rest of the students. In order to use the three principles for shaping, however, you need to reinforce Emilie, not to punish her. You could start by giving such a simple assignment that it would be *very* likely that Emilie would do it. (You could give it to the whole class if you didn't want to single Emilie out.) Something like "Bring in a list of three topics in this subject you would like to include in the next unit" involves very little effort. It also has a potential "natural" reinforcement of influencing future course emphasis. Then, when Emilie handed in her list on time, you would reinforce her. Perhaps just conspicuously recording that she handed the assignment in on time would do, but if not, grade points, or being excused from certain assignments, or any other reinforcers could be used. The point is that by making the assignments initially so simple that they involve very little effort and by gradually building up their length as Emilie starts doing them on time, the "value" of any individual reinforcement need not be great.

Problem 4: Richard

In a sense all of us are Richards. Even successful writers find escape from writing reinforcing. If escape is reinforcing, then one can use escape as a reinforcer. To make it contingent on working, however, it must follow some productivity. One might start with a small step: "I will take a break *after* writing one paragraph" or "I'll just work on the outline for ten minutes and then take a break." Gradually the amount required before a break can be increased.

B. F. Skinner reports using a similar method on himself.[4] He sets an alarm clock to go off after two hours of writing each morning, counting only time that is productive. To prevent clock-watching he covers the face of the clock. When the clock rings he can stop working any time he feels like stopping. (A two-hour stint is, of course, not a *first* step, but such performance could be built up slowly.)

[3]See, for example, K. E. Allen, B. M. Hart, J. S. Buell, F. R. Harris, and M. M. Wolf, "Effects of Social Reinforcement on Isolate Behavior of a Nursery School Child," *Child Development* 35 (1964), pp. 511–518; or B. M. Hart, N. H. Reynolds, D. M. Baer, E. R. Brawley, and F. R. Harris, "Effect of Contingent and Non-Contingent Social Reinforcement on the Cooperative Play of a Preschool Child," *Journal of Applied Behavior Analysis* 1 (1968), pp. 73–76.

[4]B. F. Skinner, comments at an informal dinner at the annual meeting of the Midwestern Association for Behavior Analysis, Chicago, May 1976.

SELF-PROJECT—CHANGING YOUR OWN BEHAVIOR (PART III)

Suggestions for Changing Your Own Behavior

1. Analyze the contingencies which have been maintaining your behavior the way it was before the start of this project, answering the specific questions below.
2. Outline how you plan to change your behavior by establishing some new contingencies.

Questions to Answer

1a. What is the behavior you want to change?

1b. In what situation is this behavior especially likely and/or unlikely to occur?

1c. What sources of reinforcement have been maintaining your behavior the way it was at the start of the project?

2a. Can you change the situation to make it more likely that you will behave in the way you wish? If so, how?

2b. What consequences could you arrange to immediately follow behavior you would like to do more?

Comments

1a. Try to include both what you would like to do more (or less) and what you usually do instead.

1c. Consider as many sources as you can—both for your pinpointed behavior and for what you usually do instead.

2a. For example, it may be possible to agree with a roommate not to buy high-calorie snacks so that the dorm situation does not encourage overeating.

2b. Try to follow the three rules. Points might be useful so that you can earn them immediately and frequently. You should also be aware that most people violate Rule 3. They expect too big a first step and punish themselves when they fail rather than reinforcing themselves for small successful steps.

Persistence and independence:
Schedules and sources of reinforcement to maintain behavior outside the classroom

OVERVIEW

How will your students behave after they leave your classes? Will what you have taught them last? Chapter Nine discusses two things which affect the persistence of behavior outside the classroom: schedules of reinforcement and sources of reinforcement other than the teacher. Suggestions are given for teaching persistence and independence.

OBJECTIVES

By the end of the chapter you should be able to:

A. Identify examples of the following schedules of reinforcement:
   1. Contingent and noncontingent reinforcement
   2. Continuous reinforcement
   3. Intermittent reinforcement (predictable and unpredictable)
   4. Fixed-ratio and variable-ratio schedules
   5. Fixed-interval and variable-interval schedules
B. Describe the "schedule effects"on behavior from the schedules listed in A above.
C. Describe how you could phase out reinforcement to produce resistance to extinction.
D. Identify at least three possible sources of reinforcement that could maintain a given behavior outside the classroom and describe

how you could transfer control to these reinforcers while the student is still in your class.

THE GOALS OF EDUCATION—PERSISTENT BEHAVIOR

There would be little point in changing the way students behave if the minute you stopped working with them, they stopped responding. Think, for a minute, of what you would like to teach your students. Whether it is academic or social behavior, you are probably thinking of relatively permanent changes. You do not want your students to forget all they learned two days after graduating from your class. If you are to *educate* students then, you must produce behavior which lasts.

A person's behavior is continuously shaped by environment. As a teacher you can control part of the school environment for your students, but there is little you can do about the various environments they will enter later. You cannot follow each student around, dispensing reinforcers at appropriate times. Somehow you must arrange it so that your students will continue to develop after you are no longer around. In other words, you must make your students *independent* so that they no longer need your personal reinforcement. You must produce behavior which is persistent enough for other environments to maintain.

There are two ways to work on the problem. First, you can schedule reinforcement to produce behavior which is resistant to extinction. The student then responds with high frequency even when only occasionally reinforced. Resistance to extinction is seen in the suitor who pursues with little or no encouragement, the scientist who works for years without making a breakthrough, or the athlete who trains relentlessly in spite of few victories. Each behaves repeatedly with little reinforcement. The ultimate reinforcement may never occur. Second, you can arrange for the control of your students' behavior to transfer from you to the environment so that the students are reinforced "naturally" by what they produce or by the reactions of others. Students who work or read to get information or to solve problems are under the control of "natural" consequences. The products of their own efforts reinforce them. They are likely, however, also to get peer reinforcement, as when peers take an interest in the information they have read or find their solutions useful. Schedules of reinforcement and sources of reinforcement, then, are what we must consider in order to produce behavior which lasts.

SCHEDULES OF REINFORCEMENT DEFINED

A *schedule of reinforcement* is the way in which reinforcement is contingent on behavior. Is each response reinforced? Every third? Every response which occurs after five minutes have passed since the last reinforcement? These are questions about schedules of reinforcement. In all

---

A Schedule of Reinforcement

is the way in which reinforcement is contingent on behavior, or to put it another way, it is the rule that tells *which* responses are reinforced.

---

schedules, reinforcement is contingent on responding. This differs from noncontingent reinforcement in which reinforcement comes without regard to what the reinforced individual is doing (see Table I). In contingent reinforcement, the individual must respond in order to receive

TABLE I   Contingent and Noncontingent Reinforcement

Reinforcement may be either contingent or noncontingent

A. CONTINGENT REINFORCEMENT	B. NONCONTINGENT REINFORCEMENT
is reinforcement which is given or withheld depending on the behavior of those who are being reinforced.	is reinforcement whose timing is not related to the behavior of those who are reinforced.
For Example: If new pencils are given out only when a student asks for one, we say, "Getting a pencil is contingent upon asking for one."	*For Example:* If new pencils are handed out the first day of each month, regardless of what the students are doing, we say, "Pencils are given non-contingently."
Comments: In all schedules of reinforcement, reinforcement is contingent on behavior. The individual is reinforced *only* after responding. The schedule specifies *which* response is reinforced.	*Comments:* Noncontingent reinforcement will strengthen whatever each individual was doing when reinforced, but this relationship is accidental. Reinforcement does not depend on any behavior having occurred.
1. SCHEDULE OF REINFORCEMENT is the way in which reinforcement is contingent on behavior.	
For example: Pencils can be given out on different schedules such as (1) only when a week has gone by since the student's last request was reinforced by getting a pencil (an interval schedule, or (2) only when a student has asked several times (regardless of how long it has been since the student last got a pencil), and so on. (See Table II for a listing of some schedules of reinforcement.)	

reinforcement. The different schedules differ only in *which* responses are reinforced.

Contingent Reinforcement

is reinforcement which depends, in some way, on responding. Reinforcement which is contingent on speaking, for example, may not follow *every* spoken response, but it depends on speaking in that it cannot occur unless speaking occurs. (The particular relationship between responding and reinforcement is specified in the schedule of reinforcement.) Contingent reinforcement is the opposite of *noncontingent reinforcement,* in which reinforcement occurs without regard to any particular responding.

How we behave depends not only on the proportion of responses which are reinforced but on how these reinforcers have been scheduled. The same amount and the same number of reinforcements can produce very different behaviors when the contingencies under which they are given differ. The piece rate worker works differently than the hourly worker, even if in the end each receives the same pay. Similarly, if you reinforce students for the *number* of problems they complete correctly, you get very different behavior than if you reinforce "keeping working."

Teachers often unwittingly produce a "slow down" by the schedules they set up. One mother got into a discussion with her fifth grade daughter about how long it took to do spelling lessons. The daughter said something like the following:

"Oh, it only takes about ten minutes at home, but it takes 20 minutes at school."

"Why is that?" asked the mother. "I don't understand."

"Well, spelling period is 20 minutes, so you have to spread your lesson out to take the whole time because Ms. Walters likes to see you working."

CONTINUOUS REINFORCEMENT AND ITS USES

Continuous reinforcement (abbreviated crf) is the reinforcement of every response of a particular operant. Dispensing machines are set on a schedule of continuous reinforcement: every time you put in the proper coins, you are supposed to get the snack you've chosen. Other examples of continuous schedules are always getting approval for bringing in a project you've done on your own or always getting paid for doing a particular job.

The laws of nature provide many schedules which are continuous or very nearly continuous. *Every* time you put on a sweater, you feel warmer. *Every* time you move your legs in a certain way called "walking," you move. *Every* time you breathe and wiggle your vocal cords, you produce sounds. In each case the behavior is reinforced immediately every time it occurs.

Continuous reinforcement, in the beginning stages of learning, strengthens a weak or new operant better than any other schedule of reinforcement. Suppose, for example, you teach a foreign language. You will try, at first, to reinforce the student for every correct pronunciation made until the student "gets the hang of it." Similarly, you will try to reinforce every correct response of a student just beginning to operate a piece of equipment, or one starting to write poetry, to debate, to do experiments, and so on.

Continuous reinforcement is most effective for strengthening weak behavior which is undesirable too. The student who gets an extension every time he or she gives an excuse for being late with an assignment will learn to give excuses more rapidly than one whose first excuses are only occasionally reinforced by an extension of deadlines.

Although continuous reinforcement will strengthen a weak response more rapidly than any other schedule, it does not produce persistent behavior when reinforcement ends. We do not keep putting coins in a snack machine which fails to operate, even if it returns our coins. We have been on a schedule of continuous reinforcement for inserting coins, and we extinguish rapidly when reinforcement is withheld. Similarly, a student used to continuous reinforcement will extinguish rapidly if reinforcement is withheld. If a teacher compliments a student for every phrase of Russian pronounced carefully and then one day no longer pays any attention whatsoever to pronunciation, the student will rapidly get sloppier in Russian pronunciation. You can probably think of a time when continuous reinforcement for something you did abruptly ended. Maybe a boyfriend or girl friend had encouraged you at every opportunity—and then one day withheld all encouragement. Your behavior would extinguish more rapidly under such circumstances than after a schedule in which you had been encouraged sometimes but not always.

INTERMITTENT REINFORCEMENT SCHEDULES

Reinforcement which follows only some responses is called *intermittent reinforcement*. Intermittent reinforcement may be based upon the *ratio* of responses to reinforcement, or upon the *interval* of time since the last reinforced response, or upon some combination of the two. There are four main categories of intermittent schedules—fixed-ratio, variable-ratio, fixed-interval, and variable-interval schedules (see Table II). In the ratio schedules, reinforcement depends on the *number* of responses that are made. Students who are reinforced for finishing assignments of ten problems each are on a ratio schedule: they must make ten responses for each reinforcement—a ratio of 10 to 1. In the interval schedules,

TABLE II   Some Simple Schedules of Reinforcement[1]

Two Nonintermittent Schedules of Reinforcement Are:

CONTINUOUS REINFORCEMENT (crf), in which every response emitted is reinforced, and

For Example: You call on Tom every time he raises his hand. Tom's hand-raising is then on continuous reinforcement.

EXTINCTION (ext), in which no responses are reinforced.

For Example: You never call on Tom when he raises his hand. Tom's hand-raising is then under extinction.

The Four Basic Schedules of Intermittent Reinforcement Are:

A. FIXED-RATIO (FR), in which a response is reinforced upon completion of a fixed number of responses counted from the preceding reinforcement. (The word "ratio" refers to the ratio of responses to reinforcements.) A given ratio is indicated by the addition of a number to the letters FR. Thus, in FR 100, the one-hundredth response after the preceding reinforcement is reinforeed.

For Example: You call on Tom every third time he raises his hand. Tom's hand-raising is then on an FR 3 schedule.

B. VARIABLE-RATIO (VR), similar to fixed-ratio except that reinforcements are scheduled according to a random series of ratios having a given mean and lying between arbitrary values. The mean may be noted by a number, as in VR 100.

For Example: You call on Tom after he raises his hand a number of times—sometimes after one or two responses, sometimes after three or four responses. If you call on him an average of every three times, you have him on a VR 3 schedule.

C. FIXED-INTERVAL (FI), in which the first response occurring after a given interval of time measured from the preceding reinforcement is reinforced. A given interval is indicated by the addition of a number to the letters FI. (Unless otherwise noted, the number always indicates minutes.) Thus, in FI 5, the first response which occurs five minutes

For Example: You call on Tom only when he raises his hand after five minutes have passed since you last called on him for raising his hand. Tom may or may not raise his hand before the five minutes are up, but any such hand-raising is not reinforced.

[1]Except for the examples, which were added for this chapter, this table is from C. B. Ferster and B. F. Skinner, *Schedules of Reinforcement*, Englewood Cliffs, N.J., Prentice-Hall, 1957, pp. 5–7. Copyright © 1957. Reprinted by permission of Prentice-Hall, Inc., Englewood Cliffs, New Jersey.

TABLE II   (Continued)

or more after the preceding reinforcement is reinforced.

D. VARIABLE-INTERVAL (VI), similar to fixed-interval except that reinforcements are scheduled according to a random series of intervals having a given mean and lying between arbitrary values. The average interval of reinforcement (in minutes) is indicated by the addition of a number to the letters VI, for example, VI 3.

For Example: You call on Tom only when time has passed since you last called on him for raising his hand. The time you wait varies. If it averages five minutes, you have Tom on a VI 5 schedule.

reinforcement depends on the *passage of time* as well as on responding. The first response after a certain time interval is reinforced. In most classroom discussions, for example, a teacher will not call on students who have just answered. No matter how many times the students raise their hands, a certain interval of time must pass before the handraising is reinforced. This is an interval schedule: reinforcement follows the first response after so many minutes have passed since the last reinforced response.

Ratio Schedules. Suppose you are a school counselor. One day Ms. Juniper, a seventh grade teacher, comes to you and says:

"Could you *please* do something for Peter? He won't do more than one or *maybe* two problems at a time. He does a problem and then waits until I come over to check him. It's not that he can't do them, because when I stand over him, he gets all his problems correct. I tell him to finish the *section* and then I will check him, but he only does one or two problems before quitting. I have to stand there and check each problem as he completes it."

Ms. Juniper wants more persistent behavior. She is asking you to get Peter on a higher ratio schedule than the continuous reinforcement he is on. Peter must make many responses before getting reinforced. If the number of problems Ms. Juniper wants Peter to do before checking him is always the same, you have a *fixed-ratio* schedule. Let's say that the problems are grouped into sections of 20 each and the teacher wants to check after each section is completed. We then have a fixed-ratio schedule of 20 (FR 20). The teacher wants 20 responses for each reinforcement.

Let's take the student now and start working with him and his teacher. You have pinpointed your goal—completing 20 problems before reinforcement. Next, you need a record of Peter's present level of per-

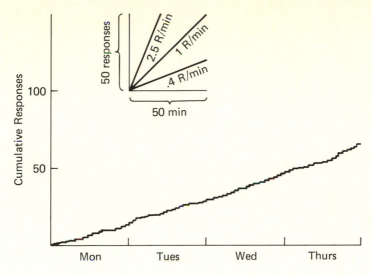

Figure 9.1 A Typical Performance on Continuous Reinforcement.

formance. With Ms. Juniper, you decide to reinforce Peter at first for each problem. To make sure that Peter isn't reinforced for *stopping* and waiting to be checked, you point out the importance of catching Peter just as he is finishing each problem. Then, while Ms. Juniper runs her class, you sit in and record the data. Because you are interested in each response and each reinforcement, you graph the data cumulatively rather than day by day (see Figure 9.1).

You note that under continuous reinforcement, Peter works relatively steadily. You talk to Ms. Juniper, who is concerned about "being fair" to the other students (who are not now getting as much attention as Peter). She says she is willing to concentrate on Peter awhile longer. For three days, Peter works steadily, doing about half of the 20 problems. His behavior seems to be well established. It is time to "stretch the ratio." To make sure that Peter doesn't revert, you plan to shape persistence slowly. The next day Ms. Juniper gives Peter easy problems with two parts. Occasionally she waits for both parts to be completed but reinforces all other responses. Again she makes sure *not* to reinforce pausing. Gradually, according to Peter's response, she reinforces less and less often. Over a period of three weeks, she gets Peter up to 20 responses per reinforcement. On an FR 20 schedule, Peter's performance should look something like the typical FR 20 cumulative record in Figure 9.2.

Just after reinforcement, we have a pause. Then Peter starts working and works more and more rapidly as reinforcement approaches.

Schedule Effects of Fixed-Ratio Schedules. Behavior on fixed-ratio schedules usually produces a high rate of responding. The rate of re-

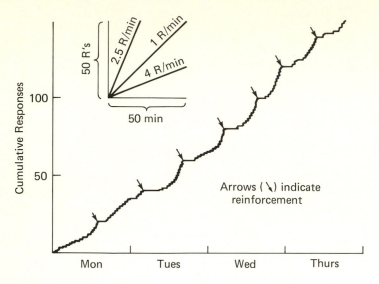

Figure 9.2 Typical Performance on an FR 20 Schedule.

sponding can reach incredible levels. A glimpse of a preunion factory in the South gives an example:

The men's underwear "factory" was a large one-room building with a roof held in place by rectangular pillars of unfinished wood. The space inside was filled with rows of old tables at which women were working frantically with pieces of light-colored cotton. Some were cutting, some packing. Most were sewing. All worked at top speed, like a movie speeded up. I stopped to watch one lady. Two foot-high piles of different shaped cloth sat to her left. She grabbed one piece from each pile as fast as she could, and, placing them together, ran them through the sewing machine in front of her, and then placed them in another pile to her right. Her speed was incredible. I listened to the rhythm and found myself saying, in time to her completing each seam, I'm sewing, I'm sewing, I'm sewing, I'm sewing.[2]

The women in the factory were paid on a fixed-ratio schedule. Every thousand seams, or pieces completed, earned them so much money. The faster they worked, the more money they made. A similar top-speed performance can be seen in the classroom. Students on a timed test whose outcome is important to them work as fast as they can. The more problems they do, the more points they earn. They are on a fixed-ratio schedule.

Behavior on a fixed-ratio schedule usually shows a "post-reinforcement pause" and "scalloped curve" like that in Figure 9.2. In the factory, for example, after a woman has completed a stack of 1000 seams, we

[2]Description of author's visit to a men's underwear factory in Alabama, June, 1956.

can expect a pause. It may be short. Perhaps she just stretches, or shifts her glasses or chair. But often it is longer. It is usually just after completing a large unit that a person takes a trip to the bathroom, gets a cup of coffee, or does something else which is a break from work. After starting again, however, behavior is steady and usually accelerates just before completing the ratio upon which reinforcement is based.

The same scalloped curve can be seen in schedules which approximate a fixed-ratio. For example, it takes a certain number of responses to finish a letter, a paper, or a section of a paper. The number of responses is not exactly the same from letter to letter or from section to section, but it does not vary widely. It is reinforcing to finish a section, so toward the end, we tend to work more rapidly and with more concentration than at the beginning. We are more likely to say, "Just let me finish this," when someone interrupts us. Just after finishing one part, however, we are likely to show the post-reinforcement pause of fixed-ratio schedules. At the end of a section, we are likely to quit for the day, to take a break, or to be easily distracted by friends. You have probably felt post-reinforcement pause when you have many papers to write. You are likely to take a break just *after* finishing a paper. You may find it difficult to get going on the next paper. Once you get started, however, it usually is not so difficult to continue working, and often the end is written in a burst of energy. This is the scallop of fixed-ratio schedules (see Figure 9.3). Of course, other factors, such as dating, deadlines, and so on, make it difficult to isolate the schedule effects, but they are there nevertheless.

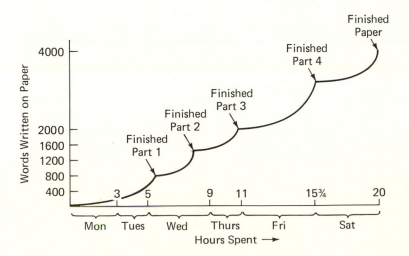

Figure 9.3 Writing a Paper: The Scallop of a Schedule That Approximates a Fixed-Ratio Schedule.

Schedule Effects

are effects on behavior which are due to the schedule of reinforcement the individual is on rather than to other factors which affect behavior, such as quantity or quality of reinforcement, deprivation level, difficulty level of the task required, and so on.

Variable-Ratio Schedules. A variable-ratio schedule is reinforcement for a number of responses—but that number varies. A teacher would be reinforcing a student on a variable-ratio schedule of 20 (VR 20) by reinforcing the student on an *average* of every 20 responses, but sometimes after fewer responses, sometimes more. Unlike fixed-ratio reinforcement, reinforcement in a variable-ratio schedule is unpredictable. You never know which response will be reinforced.

By making the variation on a variable-ratio schedule great (say, on a VR 20, having reinforcement follow as few as two or as many as 38 responses), we can eliminate (or at least reduce) postreinforcement pause. After reinforcement, the individual starts right back to work. Gambling machines are set on a variable-ratio schedule, and movies of people playing them show remarkably steady and persistent behavior. The student doing assignments of various lengths, the boy trying to get a date, the basketball player trying to make a basket, all are usually on variable-ratio schedules. If, in the beginning, they are reinforced often enough to prevent extinction, reinforcement can be gradually phased out so that they behave steadily and with high frequency for only occasional reinforcement.

Interval Schedules. Interval schedules take time into account. Instead of following each *nth* response, in *interval* schedules, reinforcement follows the first response to occur after a certain interval of time has passed *since the last reinforced response.* When the individual responds before the required time, he or she is not reinforced. Students who check a bulletin board to see whether their grades are posted, for example, are on an interval schedule. They won't be reinforced for going to look at the bulletin board until the time when grades are posted. The reinforcement is still contingent upon responding. The students must go check to see their grades. If they simply wait at home, they will *not* be reinforced. Similarly, we are on an interval schedule when telephoning a friend who is often out or when checking for a favorite magazine at the local newsstand. In school, students are on an interval schedule when volunteering for privileges which are given only so often to each student or when raising their hands in class when the teacher doesn't like any one student to answer too often. In each case, reinforcement follows the first response after a certain time period has passed since the last reinforced response. Responding before that time is not reinforced.

Like ratio schedules, interval schedules can be fixed or variable.

Fixed-Interval Schedules. In fixed-interval schedules, the intervals between reinforced response and the time when reinforcement is again available for responding are the same. A fixed-interval schedule of ten minutes (abbreviated FI 10) is one in which reinforcement is available for responding ten minutes after the previous reinforcement. If grades are posted at exactly the same time each week or if magazines are delivered weekly at the same time, we have a fixed-interval schedule of one week. (We will assume that we check as soon as possible, since an interval is measured from the last *reinforced response.* If we delayed a day in checking the next time we would have an interval of six days, not seven.) In each case, behaving before the interval is up produces no reinforcement, and failure to respond is also not reinforced.

Unlike ratio schedules, responding on an interval schedule doesn't make the reinforcement become available sooner. It does, however, make it likely that we will be reinforced as soon as reinforcement is available.

Variable-Interval Schedules. There are many more instances of variable-interval schedules in daily life than of fixed-interval. Usually, when we must wait before a response will be reinforced, the amount of time we must wait varies. Checking at the library or bookstore to see if anything new and interesting has come in, for example, is on a variable-interval schedule. Sometimes it is a short time before checking is reinforced by finding something good, but sometimes it is very long. In the classroom, the teacher may wait for a while before giving some privilege again to a student who always requests it, but the time the teacher waits is likely to vary. When we telephone a friend who is often out, we will be reinforced (by our friend's answering) on a variable-interval schedule. We will be reinforced when our friend returns, but how long that takes is likely to vary from day to day.

Behavior on Interval Schedules. Like ratio schedules, interval schedules produce persistence, but the persistence is of a different sort. Instead of extremely rapid bursts of responding, interval schedules produce a more steady, but slower, rate of responding. The difference can be seen in phone-calling. When we get no response after dialing a number, we are not likely to dial over and over again right away. Even when the call is very important, we pause between tries because the longer we wait, the more likely we are to find the person at home when we dial again. Dialing, in this case, is on an interval schedule. When phoning is on a ratio schedule, however, we behave differently. When we are reinforced for the *number* of calls made, as when calling a list of people, we dial again as soon as we hang up from the previous call. We are on a ratio schedule; the more calls we make, the sooner we complete the job.

THE VARIETY OF SCHEDULES

In daily life, contingencies are often extremely complex. We are rarely on a "pure" schedule such as those listed in Table II. For example, in a classroom discussion, a teacher may call on students according to both how many times they raise their hands (ratio schedule) and how long it has been since they last answered (interval schedule). Or the teacher may shift back and forth from one schedule to another. In addition, calling on a *particular* student depends on how many hands are raised, who the teacher thinks will answer well, and many other factors. This can produce a very complex schedule for the student.

Fortunately, complex schedules such as those given in the Table below are often good because they provide unpredictable reinforcement, and it is unpredictable reinforcement that best produces resistance to extinction once a response is established. Variable-ratio and variable-interval schedules are, therefore, the best schedules to use to maintain behavior and to make it persistent.

The Complexity of Schedules of Reinforcement

can be seen in this list of schedules taken from the book *Schedules of Reinforcement* by Ferster and Skinner.[3] The authors analyze cumulative records of key-pecking by pigeons under the schedules of reinforcement shown here and also those in Table II.

The three main schedules involving both numbers of responses and intervals of time are:

E. Alternative (alt),[4] in which reinforcement is programmed by either a ratio or an interval schedule, whichever is satisfied first. Thus, in alt FI 5 FR 300 the first response is reinforced: (1) after a period of five minutes, provided 300 responses have not been made; or (2) upon completion of 300 responses, provided five minutes have not elapsed.

F. Conjunctive (conj),[4] in which reinforcement occurs when both a ratio and an interval schedule have been satisfied. For example, a response is reinforced when at least five minutes have elapsed since the preceding reinforcement and after at least 300 responses.

G. Interlocking (interlock),[5] in which the organism is reinforced upon completion of a number of responses; but this number changes during the interval which follows the previous reinforcement. For example, the number may be set at 300 immediately after reinforcement, but it is reduced linearly, reaching one after ten minutes. If the organism responds very rapidly, it will have to emit nearly 300 responses for reinforcement. If it responds at an intermediate rate, it will be reinforced after a smaller number—say, 150. If it does not respond at all during ten minutes, the first response thereafter will be reinforced. Many different cases are possible, depending upon the way in which the number changes with time.

On two important schedules a single reinforcement is received after two conditions have been satisfied in tandem order:

H. Tandem (tand), in which a single reinforcement is programmed by two schedules, the second of which begins when the first has been completed, with no correlated change in stimuli. In tand FI 10 FR 5, for example, a reinforcement occurs upon completion of five responses, counted only after a response after expiration

---

[3]C. B. Ferster and B. F. Skinner, *Schedules of Reinforcement*, Englewood Cliffs, N.J., Prentice-Hall, 1957, pp. 5–7. Copyright © 1957. Reprinted by permission of Prentice-Hall, Inc., Englewood Cliffs, New Jersey.

[4]This schedule was first used by W. H. Morse and R. J. Herrnstein.

[5]Some early unpublished experiments on this schedule were done by Norman Guttman.

of the ten-minute fixed interval. In tand FR 300 FI 5 a response is reinforced after the lapse of five seconds, timed from the completion of 300 responses. It is often important to specify which of the two schedules is the more substantial part of the schedule. This may be done by italicizing the important member. For example, tand *FR* FI describes the case tand FR 200 FI 5 sec while tand FR *FI* describes the case FR 1 FI 10. In the first the ratio of 200 is the more important part of the schedule. In the second the ten-minute fixed interval is the major part, except that the timing begins only after the execution of a single response. (The FR 1 is by no means trivial; for example, it has a marked effect in opposing the development of a pause after reinforcement.)

I. Chained (chain), similar to tandem schedules except that a conspicuous change in stimuli occurs upon completion of the first component of the schedule. The second stimulus eventually controls the performance appropriate to the second schedule and, as a conditioned reinforcer, reinforces a response to the first stimulus. This schedule is usually studied when both contributing schedules are substantial.

The values in any schedule may be systematically changed as the experiment progresses in terms of the performances generated. We have, then, another schedule:

J. Adjusting (adj), in which the value of the interval or ratio is changed in some systematic way after reinforcement as a function of the immediately preceding performance. (In an interlocking schedule the change in value of the ratio occurs between reinforcements.) For example, a fixed ratio is increased or decreased by a small amount after each reinforcement, depending upon whether the time from the preceding reinforcement to the first response is less than or greater than arbitrary value.

A complex program may be composed of two or more of these schedules arranged in any given order. Depending upon the presence or absence of correlated stimuli, we may distinguish:

K. Multiple (mult), in which reinforcement is programmed by two or more schedules alternating usually at random. Each schedule is accompanied by a different stimulus, which is present at long as the schedule is in force. For example, in mult FI 5 FR 100 the key (which a pigeon pecks) is sometimes red (when reinforcement occurs after an interval of five minutes) and sometimes green (when reinforcement occurs after 100 responses). The key colors and their corresponding schedules may occur either at random or according to a given program in any determined proportions.

L. Mixed (mix), similar to multiple except that no stimuli are correlated with the schedules. For example, mix FI 5 FR 50 represents a schedule in which a reinforcement sometimes occurs after an interval of five minutes and sometimes after the completion of 50 responses. These possibilities occur either at random or according to a given program in any determined proportion.

A small block of reinforcements on one schedule may be introduced into a background of another schedule. Such cases are referred to as:

M. Interpolated (interpol). For example, a block of ten reinforcements on a fixed ratio of 50 is inserted into a six-hour period of reinforcement on FI 10 without change of stimulus.

PHASING OUT REINFORCEMENT

We cannot produce persistence simply by reinforcing infrequently. Persistent behavior is shaped like any other: gradually, step by step, depending on the student's response. We shift slowly from continuous reinforcement to intermittent reinforcement. If we shift too fast, we run the risk of extinguishing the behavior we want. For example, suppose we have a student, Cheri, who hardly ever completes assignments on time. If we fail to reinforce her on that rare occasion when she completes an assignment on time, we are likely to extinguish that behavior. So we reinforce her every time she does her work by the deadline until that behavior is routine.

Once we are sure that a behavior occurs routinely under continuous reinforcement, we start to build persistence. We omit a reinforcement here and there. For example, once Cheri starts completing all assignments on time, we no longer need to reinforce her for each assignment she hands in promptly. We pick a time when she is working well and the assignments are relatively short or easy. We collect one assignment without special comment—then reinforce the next as usual. Gradually, as we judge her ready, we increase the number of assignments done on time before reinforcement (ratio schedule) or let longer periods of time go by before reinforcing a response (interval schedule). Gradually we progress to the point where Cheri needs only the same occasional attention the other students receive.

SHIFTING CONTROL FROM OURSELVES TO NATURAL REINFORCERS

As we reinforce less and less, other reinforcers usually take over in maintaining behavior. When Cheri starts to meet deadlines, she can more often get the reinforcement of completing assignments. She also may start to get peer approval for finishing her work—or at least reduce the censure and ridicule that follow tardiness. She may also start to become interested in being prompt for the self-satisfaction of being on time. Or she may become interested in the assignments themselves, taking pleasure in solving problems for the reinforcement of finding out the answers. The natural results of promptness itself may thus start to gain control over her behavior. We see control by natural consequences when we see Cheri working on a problem, oblivious to others and to what is going on around her. When the control of solving a problem or finishing an assignment is strong, Cheri won't want frequent teacher reinforcement any more—it is an interruption to her concentrated efforts.

Often the transfer of control from teacher to natural consequences occurs without special planning. A student who gets a lot of reinforcement and success for any particular behavior soon comes to like doing it. But sometimes we must deliberately arrange for other sources of reinforcement besides those we personally deliver. Paul may work, but he is too dependent on *our* approval: he isn't sure of himself or constantly asks us whether his work is good enough. Or Trent may analyze problems only when asked to do so for a grade. We would like him to analyze problems at other times too. Perhaps tokens or points work well, but students won't work unless we walk around dispensing them. Or perhaps our students are enthusiastic—but only so long as we whip up their enthusiasm by our own excitement: all of these behaviors show too much dependence on the teacher. Chances are that none of them will last outside the classroom. To get behavior to last we need to plan to get students working for consequences other than those we personally provide.

These consequences come from two sources: natural consequences of behavior and the behavior of other people. When you learn a skill that enables you to gain information, to create, or to solve problems, you are likely to get both kinds of consequences. The information you find, the work of art you produce, the solutions which you produce by behaving are natural consequences. They are also likely to be reinforcers. Thus, telling time, drawing cartoons, repairing an automobile, or reading a newspaper are reinforced naturally by finding out the time, owning a cartoon you drew, having the car work properly, and finding out what's going on. You may also get consequences from the second source—other people. The attention or approval of others is not an inevitable result of your own behavior, but it is a reinforcing consequence which often occurs. For example, peers may thank you for telling them the time, they may be impressed with your cartoon, or with your mechanical ability, or they may take an interest in what you read. Or you may be paid by an employer. Both your own products and other people can be sources of reinforcement outside the classroom.

To make your students independent of your personal control, it helps to start to transfer control to the two kinds of consequences they will have outside the classroom. While you are phasing out the reinforcement *you* provide, then, you should also be looking for other sources of control. Chapter Fourteen (Motivation) discusses in detail how to design classroom exercises to bring students under the control of their own products in a field (otherwise known as getting them to "take an interest in a subject"). Suffice it to say here that the more *you* directly manage your students' learning, the less of an opportunity you give *them* to be reinforced by their own efforts or by peers. If you can get your students to do their own planning, record-keeping, even their own evaluating and setting of assignments, you make it possible for them to be reinforced by the kinds of consequences which will maintain their behavior outside the classroom.

A last example illustrates how you can combine the shift from continuous reinforcement to intermittent reinforcement with a transfer of control from your reinforcement to other reinforcers in the students' environment. Suppose you would like your students to show an interest in what you teach by doing outside reading. You don't feel that it should count toward a grade, so you don't give grade points for doing it. You do, however, encourage outside reading by suggesting particularly good articles you think would be interesting, by making sure they are available in the school library, and by talking enthusiastically to students who mention outside reading. One student, whom we shall call Judy, comes in one period and mentions, for the first time, reading an article related to the subject you teach. You respond with enthusiasm (even though the source is nearly comic-book quality). The next class, Judy again comes to you after class: another article. Again you reinforce. The following week Judy mentions two more articles. In a month, it is a routine for her to seek you out, either before class or after class. The behavior of mentioning outside reading is, in other words, well established.

To maintain Judy's outside reading, you need to do two things: first, you need to get her on an intermittent schedule of reinforcement instead of the continuous reinforcement she is on. Second, you need to bring her reading under the control of other reinforcers besides your own approval. You don't want her to read just to please you, even if you succeed in moving to an intermittent schedule.

You start phasing out your reinforcement: that is easy, since you are probably a bit tired of always spending time before or after class on Judy's latest readings anyway. You cut down slowly. One day you simply tell Judy, "Yes, that *was* a good article," and then turn to talk with another student (not rudely, but definitively). When Judy again brings up the article, you talk with her as usual. (You don't want to extinguish her behavior, after all.)

While you move to intermittent reinforcement, you also start working at transferring control. First, you make sure that Judy gets natural reinforcement from working on the subject in class. Using some of the principles we will discuss later under "motivation," you have your students working on problems during class—making sure that Judy can solve the ones she gets. You have her keep records of her day-to-day performance so that her progress and success are conspicuous.

Next, you try to get other students talking with Judy about her readings so that she can be reinforced by them instead of by you. Since how they respond to Judy may not be reinforcing, you don't try this until her behavior is strong. When Judy comes up to you after class with a new article she's discovered, you try to include other students in the discussion. Sometimes this involves some ingenuity: "Yes, I saw that article," you say. (You are racking your brains for some connection to another student's interests.) "Peter, did you read that article in *Newsweek* (Pause) "No?" (You try again). "Who was talking to me the other day about that article?" (No response). "Wasn't there a TV program where a criminal used the principle from that article?" (You are really clutching at straws now, but it works. At last, a student responds.) And so you get a discussion going between Judy and other students. You have started transferring control.

Transferring control is not easy. Sometimes you are lucky and a student like Judy starts dating someone who reinforces her for academic or social behavior you feel will benefit her. But more often you have to work at the problem. Then it helps to be aware of the schedules of reinforcement you are providing and of the various sources of control for your students' behavior.

SUMMARY

Persistence is not inborn. It is a function of schedules of reinforcement—how often and when responses have been reinforced. Any operant which is repeated without reinforcement of any kind will undergo extinction. How long it takes to extinguish depends on the schedule of reinforcement it has been under before extinction started. Unpredictable and infrequent reinforcement—that is, variable-ratio and variable-interval schedules—produce the most resistance to extinction.

We try to teach behaviors which will be useful to our students in their daily lives. Useful behavior is behavior which is reinforced either by its "natural" results or by other people. We expect, then, that our students will get reinforced, at least occasionally, for the behaviors we teach them. The problem is that after they leave us, the reinforcement they receive is likely to be infrequent. Our task, then, is first to build behavior so that it occurs routinely when continuously reinforced, and second to phase out that reinforcement, transferring control to the kinds of intermittent reinforcement that occurs in daily life. We must, then, pay attention to the schedules of reinforcement we are using and to the sources of reinforcement for our students' behavior. To put it another way, we must make our students independent. This can be difficult because it tends to be reinforcing for us as teachers to keep control in our hands. It is reinforcing for students to seek our approval, to try to please us, to follow *our* ideas about how things should be done. And it is fun to be the one who hands out the "goodies." When we encourage independence, we lose the reinforcement of this kind of control. But we gain in having had a more lasting effect on the development of our students. Our job as teachers is to produce behavior and then to withdraw. Like doctors, we are most successful in our profession when we are no longer needed.

EXERCISES

Concept Check IXA—Contingent and Noncontingent Reinforcement (Objective A)

Write the numbers of the four examples below in which the underlined reinforcement is contingent on student responding and *name the response* it is contingent on.

1. The school bell rings at 2:45, excusing students for the day.
2. Only students who hand over tickets are admitted to a sports event.

3. Sometimes you get <u>food you like</u> at lunch, sometimes not.
4. Mr. Baldwin cracked <u>good jokes</u> when he was in the mood—and his being in the mood had nothing to do with anything his students did or did not do.
5. Susan <u>has no homework</u> when she completes her daily assignments during study hall. But when she goofs off and talks during study hall, she doesn't get her work done.
6. While Pete was doing arithmetic problems the <u>weather turned beautiful.</u>
7. The teacher gives out <u>privileges</u> alphabetically. Because Ms. Welsh's name starts with a "W," she is almost always last.
8. Only by getting all assignments in on time (and done at an acceptable level) can you get an <u>A grade</u> in Mr. Lyles's class.
9. Ms. Thorne grades only on participation. The more you talk up, the <u>higher grade you</u> get.
10. The teacher <u>postponed</u> a test for which Paul wasn't prepared because the ditto machine broke down.

Answers for Concept Check IXA

The four examples (with the responses on which reinforcement is contingent) are numbers:

2. (Handing over tickets)
5. (Completing her daily assignments during study hall)
8. (Doing assignments at an acceptable level and getting them in on time)
9. (Talking up, participating)

For the rest, the reinforcement comes regardless of what students are or are not doing, and it is therefore noncontingent.

Concept Check IXB—Noncontingent Reinforcement and Schedules of Reinforcement (Objective A)

For each description below write the abbreviation for the schedule described:

NC = Noncontingent
crf = Continuous reinforcement
FR = Fixed-ratio (except FR 1, which is the same as crf)
VR = Variable-ratio
FI = Fixed-interval
VI = Variable-interval

1. Every time you do a particular thing, you get reinforced.
2. You get reinforced for each ten responses.
3. Your responses will be reinforced only after some time has passed since your last response was reinforced. (The time changes.)
4. After three hours pass you are reinforced *whether or not you respond.*
5. Sometimes you must make only five or six responses before a response is

reinforced, sometimes you must respond many more times before a response is reinforced.

6. You get reinforced on the average of once every day, but there is no relationship between what you are or are not doing and when reinforcement occurs.

7. Whether or not you are reinforced depends on someone else's behavior, not on yours.

8. After a response is reinforced, three minutes must pass before another response will be reinforced.

9. You are reinforced for each response.

10. You are continually reinforced—even when you don't respond.

Answers for Concept Check IXB

1. crf
2. FR (It is an FR 10 schedule.)
3. VI
4. NC
5. VR

6. NC
7. NC
8. FI (It is an FI 3 schedule.)
9. crf
10. NC

SELF-PROJECT—CHANGING YOUR OWN BEHAVIOR (PART IV)

Suggestions for Writing Up Your Self-Project

To summarize your project, write a brief report answering any of the questions below that are relevant. The style I prefer is informal, like that you would use for an article in a student newspaper. You may pretend you are writing an article for students who want to work on behavior like yours.

Questions to Answer (where relevant)

The Problem

1. What was the *general* behavior you wanted to change, and why did you want to change it?

2. How long have you wanted to change it?

3. Have you tried changing before? If so, how, and what were the results?

4. Specifically, what behavior did you decide to count? (Examples of what you counted and did not count would be helpful.)

Recording and Results

5. How did you record your behavior, both as it occurred and later, for your daily record?

6. How did you graph your data? (Include graph, labeled with your name, the behavior you counted, and dates. Also mark the parts of the graph that show the data "before the change" and "during the change" you tried).

7. Describe the data both "before the change" and "during the change." Was your behavior consistent? Did it vary a lot? What was an average day like? Were there any unusual days? If so, were there any special circumstances on those days? What differences (if any) were there between the periods before and after the change?

Analysis

8. What were the contingencies for your behavior as it existed before the project started and during the first days of recording? (Include situations in which it is likely to occur or not to occur, as well as reinforcers.) Note that this information can be taken directly from Part III of the project.
9. Were the procedures you tried practical in cost and effort?
10. Were you consistent with your procedures? If not, what changes could you make to improve them?
11. How would you describe in operant language what you did and why it did or did not work? (You may wish to explain some of the terminology for your readers.) Some things to consider are immediacy of reinforcement, amount of behavior required for reinforcement, and whether or not reinforcement *was* contingent (that is, did you receive it *only* when you met the requirements you set?).

Suggestions for the Future

12. Whether or not you succeeded in changing your behavior, how could you maintain desirable behavior once you succeeded in producing it? How would you phase out the reinforcers you added? How could you bring the behavior you want under the control of natural reinforcers or make the immediate natural consequences reinforcing?

Punishment and its alternatives

OVERVIEW

Chapter Ten is designed to teach you to identify short-and long-term results of using punishment and to design alternative methods of eliminating undesirable behavior in students.

OBJECTIVES

By the end of the chapter you should be able to:

A. Define punishment and give examples of it.
B. Outline immediate and long-range effects of punishment and identify advantages and disadvantages of punishment.
C. Indicate in which of several situations extinction alone would be effective in eliminating undesirable behavior.
D. Identify a desirable behavior incompatible with a given misbehavior.
E. Evaluate given methods of decreasing misbehavior in terms of their immediate and long-range effectiveness.
F. Take a classroom situation and:
   1. Identify an undesirable response, the situation in which the response occurs, and the consequences.
   2. Tell what is probably maintaining the response, and
   3. Describe a way of eliminating the misbehavior without the use of punishment.

MS. RENNIX'S STORY

It was one of those days—lunch duty, and Sybil, one of my third graders, was acting up again. A likable tomboy with pigtails, Sybil could have stepped out of a Norman Rockwell painting, except for her energy. Today, for example, Sybil would not stay sitting at her lunch table, and as if that weren't bad enough, other students were following her example. I had to take action. "Sybil, come here." No response. I got up and went after her. Sybil ducked my grab and ran around the table. As I gained on her, she disappeared under one of the tables. Try as I might, I could not catch her. Just as I would clear the kids and chairs away from one table, she would run under the next. In exasperation, I left her under a table. When all the children but my third grade had left the dining room, I finally caught Sybil. I walked her to the front of the third graders. Turning to them I asked, "What did Sybil do wrong today?"

"She crawled all under the tables. Look, she got spaghetti all over her tights."

The children giggled.

"She shouldn't be out of her seat."

"She didn't come when you said."

The accusations came thick and fast. I began to feel better. "And what shall we do about it?" I asked.

"Make her stay in for recess the rest of the year."

"Make her eat alone up in the classroom."

Sybil stopped grinning.

"Send her to the principal's office."

"She should have to do spelling all day and get no art."

"Don't let her eat lunch for a year."

I was surprised at the severity of the punishments, and from her look, so was Sybil. Turning to Sybil, I asked, "What do you think we should do, Sybil?" Sybil's face turned red. She was silent. Then—and I never thought I'd live to see that day—Sybil cried.

A COMMON METHOD OF CONTROL

Did Sybil deserve her punishment? Traditionally, the answer is clearly yes. Punishment has been a part of teaching from the very beginning. In colonial days in America, teachers were expected to use corporal punishment—to whip those who failed to perform. The Dorchester School rules of 1645 stated it this way:

The rod of correction is a rule of God necessary sometimes to be used upon children. The schoolmaster shall have full power to punish all or any of his scholars, no matter who they are. No parent or other person living in the place shall go about to hinder the master in this. But if any parent or others shall think these as just cause for complaint against the master for too much severity, they shall have liberty to tell him so in friendly and loving way.[1]

[1]Clifton Johnson, *Old-Time Schools and School-books*, New York, Dover, 1963, pp. 11–12.

TABLE I   Some of the Punishments Today's College
Students Had Seen Used When They Were
in Elementary and Secondary School[2]

Column A (Punishments listed by at least 20 of the 129 students responding)	Column B (Other punishment)
Paddling	Sit in garbage can
Lost recess	Kneel in front of class
Extra homework	Hitting with cane on head
Write word over (500 times)	Stepping on toes
Stand in corner	Put in closet or cloakroom alone and in
Stay after school	dark
Yelling to get order	Erase chalk circle with nose
Stand in hall	Tape on mouth
	Nuns beat us with rulers

By the twentieth century, corporal punishment had become the exception rather than the rule, but even today, punishment is still a common method of maintaining classroom control.

In fact, to most people the very words "classroom control" suggest techniques of punishment rather than incentives or reinforcement. At least they did to a group of undergraduate education majors who were asked to "jot down one or two techniques of classroom control your elementary or secondary teachers used." Of the 635 methods listed, 570, or 90 percent, were punishments. The most common replies (listed by 20 or more of the 129 students) are given in Column A of Table I below. Column B lists some of the other punishments the students had seen used.

The extent to which punishment has become a standard part of teaching is reflected by the techniques of control that prospective teachers plan to use when they eventually teach. Table II lists techniques students said they plan to use when *they* teach. They listed techniques of reinforcement but included also many standard punishments. It looks as if threats, writing words over and over, cuts in grades, demerits, and other common punishments will be with us for a while.

WHEN TEACHERS PUNISH

Many teachers do plan not to use punishment but find themselves punishing anyway once they start teaching. Ms. Rennix did not plan to punish. She was a new teacher, fresh from college. She genuinely liked her students and they liked her. What about you? Whether or not you

[2]From a questionnaire given to students enrolled in Educational Psychology 105 (a required course for education majors), West Virginia University, Morgantown, West Virginia, 1975.

TABLE II   Techniques of Control Education Students
Said They Plan to Use When They Teach[3]

Punishment	Reinforcement
Stay after school	Give bonus points
Demerits	Smile, and reassurance
Lecturing	Attention, encouragement
Kick out of class	Bonus points
Write each spelling word 25 times	Reinforcement
Notes to parents	Appeal to students
Grades cut in conduct	Use better examples
No recess	Reinforce good behavior
Threats	Verbal praise
Send to principal	

plan to punish when you teach, you probably do not plan to do so when your students are all working well. No one punishes when everything is going smoothly. Teachers punish when, like Ms. Rennix, they've "had it"; when they have *lost* control.

WHY TEACHERS PUNISH

When a person is in an unpleasant situation, anything which ends that situation is reinforcing. Thus we leave a bad party, turn away from unpleasant sights, and turn off obnoxious commercials. Teachers in classrooms with students they cannot control are in unpleasant situations. They punish. The immediate consequence for them is that the unpleasant situation ends. When you have "had it" with noise and inattention, for example, and you shout, "Everyone who is talking has to stay in for recess!" the immediate result is stunned peace and quiet. Everyone looks at you attentively, at least for a moment. Although the effect on the students may not last, their temporary silence will reinforce *your* behavior of punishing. The next time the class gets out of control, you are even more likely to shout.

The teacher who punishes once is likely to punish again when the situation again becomes unpleasant. So the familiar pattern: the same students misbehave and are punished time and time again. The punishing teacher may not enjoy punishing but probably feels a certain relief, like Ms. Rennix, who "felt better" once she got Sybil under control, even though the control was achieved by punishment.

Teachers punish, then, to escape from the unpleasantness caused by out-of-control students. Most teachers who punish justify their actions by citing the good it will do the student. "Jim has to learn not to interrupt," his teacher says, "or he won't have any friends. It's for his own good." Sometimes punishment is justified by saying that it benefits others

[3]*Ibid.*

in the class. "I can't just let Bobby keep picking on Susan," the teacher will say, or, "Alexander is disturbing everyone. I've got to consider the rest of the students." We rationalize punishment by saying it is a painful treatment that, like a tetanus shot, will prevent difficulties later.

The trouble with punishment is that it rarely ends the misbehavior. In addition, the "treatment" may produce worse problems than the problem it is supposed to cure. To see how and why, we will analyze punishment in detail.

WHAT PUNISHMENT IS AND HOW IT WORKS

Punishment is any consequence which weakens behavior. There are two ways to punish: by taking away something reinforcing and by presenting something distasteful.

Punishment

is any event that decreases the probability of the response it follows. We punish by adding (or applying) unpleasant stimuli or by taking away stimuli which are reinforcing.

Like reinforcement, punishment is defined not by our subjective opinion of what students like or dislike but by its effect on their behavior. A scolding, extra homework, or staying in for recess may or may not be punishing for a particular student. Students who seem to be "asking for punishment" may be asking all right, but what they are asking for may be more reinforcing for them than punishing (see the "Criticism Trap," Chapter Seven.).

When attention is a strong reinforcer, *any* attention, even a bawling out, may be better than no attention. If yelling at Johnny increases the behavior for which he is being scolded, then the yelling is reinforcement for him, not punishment. To be punishment, the yelling would have to decrease his misbehavior not only immediately, but from day to day. He would have to misbehave less in the future because the teacher yelled at him. The treatments listed under "Punishment" and "Reinforcement" in tables I and II *probably* weaken and strengthen behavior respectively, but one can never be sure without trying.

Punishment differs from extinction in that in extinction *no* conse-

---

Extinction

is a process in which a response is repeated without reinforcement. In extinction, we withhold the reinforcement which had been given in the past so that responses go unreinforced. The behavior then gets no stimulus change as a result of behaving; this is in contrast to punishment, in which behaving is followed by a stimulus change.

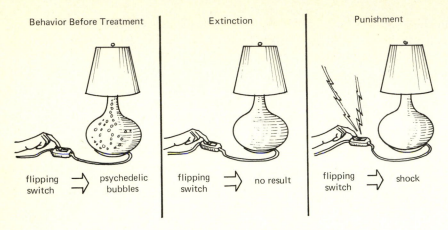

Figure 10.1   Difference Between Extinction and Punishment.

quence is forthcoming (reinforcement is withheld), where as in punishment something happens: a consequence—a stimulus change—occurs.

Suppose a teacher brings in a lamp which produces psychedelic colored bubbles when turned on. Suppose also that seeing the bubbles is reinforcing and, for the purposes of our illustration, that it only stays on for a few seconds after the switch is pushed (so students don't get satiated). You can now visualize a behavior pattern like this: when students pass the lamp, they reach out and flip the switch. Now we decide to eliminate "flipping-switch" behavior. In extinction, the behavior of flipping switch would stop producing any consequence (see Figure 10.1).

Unless the act of flipping switches itself was reinforcing, you can see that after a number of flips, students would stop trying.

For punishment, we need an unpleasant consequence for switching behavior—say, shock. Each time students flip the switch they get, in addition to the bubbles, an unpleasant shock. Like extinction, it would probably take a few tries before the students would stop reaching for the switch (depending on the severity of the shock).

In the example with the lamp, each consequence was immediate, consistent, and inevitable. In reinforcement, the switch *always* turned the bubbles on, in extinction it *never* worked, and in punishment it *always* produced shock along with the bubbles. The effects on behavior would be clear cut and rapid.

In the schoolroom the scheduling and multiplicity of consequences are rarely so pure and inevitable. When the teacher delivers consequences, some behavior may occur which the teacher doesn't see and thus doesn't reinforce or punish.

Consistency of reinforcement is not critical after behavior gets going. In fact, as we have seen, we produce more persistent behavior by reinforcing only occasionally and unpredictably rather than by reinforcing each response. When *decreasing* behavior, however, as in using extinction or punishment, lack of consistency causes serious problems. If, when we intend to extinguish a response, a reinforcement or two creeps in, we do not have extinction at all; we have intermittent reinforcement. We are then teaching the student to behave *more* persistently, not less. If, for example, we decide to reduce Tammy's interrupting by ignoring her but occasionally we forget and acknowledge her, we will not weaken interrupting. Our treatment will probably make Tammy more likely to interrupt and to do so more persistently. The problem will even be worse if we forget to ignore Tammy when she interrupts particularly forcefully. We are then differentially reinforcing *forceful* interrupting, making it more likely that she will interrupt not only more persistently but also with more force.

In punishment, lack of consistency is also serious. It is particularly serious since the behavior we punish is usually also reinforced.

Any behavior that occurs repeatedly *must* get reinforced at least some of the time or it will die out. Students' misbehaviors that occur again and again are therefore being maintained by some reinforcement in the classroom. Shoving, hitting, grabbing, writing sloppily, wisecracking, getting out of one's seat, interrupting, and all the behaviors that teachers dislike are being reinforced by something in the classroom environment. If a teacher then punishes for misbehaving the student is getting two consequences.

The two consequences can be illustrated with an example. Suppose new pencils are reinforcing for Sam and he has developed a habit of opening the teacher's drawer to get them (see "Before" in Figure 10.2 below).

BEFORE   PUNISHMENT If Caught

Behavior = open teacher's drawer   Two consequences = getting pencils (briefly)
                                                              and getting pencils and recess taken away

Figure 10.2 Punishment: Two Consequences in a Typical Classroom.

To make Sam stop opening her drawer, the teacher could, of course, extinguish the behavior by removing everything in the drawer, but let's use punishment. Sam opens the drawer, takes some pencils, and gets caught. The pencils are taken away and Sam loses recess. (We assume that both pencils and recess are reinforcing.) There are thus two consequences: Sam first got the pencils (even though only briefly) and then was punished. Since the teacher gave the punishment (in contrast to the light switch example, in which the punishment came automatically from flipping the switch), there is a chance that Sam might not get caught in the future, particularly if he is careful to open the drawer only when the teacher is not around. The consequence for repeated misbehavior is, then, uncertain. It may be reinforcement or it may be reinforcement and punishment.

The possibility of two consequences may be responsible, in part, for the kinds of behavior shown by students who have been punished. In our example, the student "wants" to open the drawer so long as reinforcement follows, but becomes "afraid" to do so because of punishment. The two behaviors show up as the vacillation in "sneaking" or in looking furtively around when opening the drawer.

Both extinction and punishment will work if they are used consistently. It is difficult, if not impossible, however, to be completely consistent. It is hard to ignore a student *every* time he or she does something undesirable. It may also be impossible to remove what is reinforcing a behavior. You cannot remove the feeling and taste of gum, for example, which reinforce chewing gum. Ignoring gum-chewing will not, then, make the student stop. Similarly, it is usually not possible to remove reinforcement when peers are providing it, as when they laugh at a student's wisecracks. It is also difficult to punish consistently. Punishing every misbehavior means catching every misbehavior, and any teacher knows how hard that is, even when students and teacher are in the same room. Since one cannot "police" students outside class, it is obviously impossible to catch all misbehavior. Even if one did, one must also contend with whatever reinforcement is maintaining behavior. It may be stronger than the punishment. We do, after all, go to the dentist and deliberately "take" pain or stand in freezing drizzle for a good show. The student who takes repeated ruler raps or humiliation again and again is getting sufficient reinforcement to maintain misbehavior in spite of being punished.

WHY NOT TO USE PUNISHMENT

We have been discussing punishment as a consequence. Severe punishment, particularly physical punishment, also produces behavior. When struck or physically threatened, a person responds with what is called respondent behavior—the reflexes said to show fear, or anger, or shame, or guilt. Later, things which have been associated with punishment produce the same kind of reflex reactions—through respondent conditioning. The student who has been hit by an angry teacher will feel some of the same reflex fears when the teacher looks angry again.

The student's own misbehavior is part of the situation associated with punishment. If Carl was whipped for stealing, he will become fearful or anxious when he steals again. He will show the effects of previous punishment by jumping at sounds, sweating, getting cold hands or knots in his stomach, flinching, and so on. The emotional reactions which punishment produces are often rather persistent; moreover, they generalize. The anxiety produced by misbehaving in a history class not only becomes associated with the misbehavior itself but with history, with teachers, or with school in general. The student may become anxious whenever called upon to perform in front of others. The anxiety associated with tests is common among students, and it is traceable to the punishment or threat of failure associated with past testing situations.

Whenever a situation creates anxiety or fear, *avoiding* or *escaping* from that situation is reinforcing. One can avoid or escape from a punishing situation by engaging in "escape behaviors" such as those in Table III or the Blondie cartoon (Figure 10.3).

Escape Behaviors

are operants which are reinforced by getting out of an unpleasant situation. *Escape* is different from *avoidance* in that in escape, we start out *in* the unpleasant situation, whereas in avoidance, we don't get into the situation in the first place. For example, we escape from rain by taking shelter after it starts to rain on us, but we avoid rain by taking shelter before it starts to rain on us.

BLONDIE   **By Dean Young and Jim Raymond**

Figure 10.3   (Courtesy of King Features Syndicate, Inc. Copyright © King Features Syndicate Inc.)

TABLE III Common Escape Behaviors of Students

Cutting class
Avoiding taking certain subjects
Daydreaming in class
Reading a newspaper instead of listening to a lecture
Procrastinating about schoolwork in general
Dropping out of school
Going shopping instead of doing homework
Rearranging papers, sharpening pencils, etc., before starting to work

Few of us progress through 12 years of school without getting some scars from punishment. We avoid taking certain subjects or put off starting assignments. Even Dagwood has trouble settling down to work. We are likely to show avoidance most in subjects in which we have experienced the most failure. Failure to achieve is, of course, punishing. When you become a teacher, the more you punish (whether or not you justify it as "good"), the more likely you are to make your students avoid you, the subject you teach, and even school in general.

You may even make your problem of classroom control worse. Punishment begets punishment. Students who are punished frequently may simply withdraw, but they may become hostile. While there are few good studies on the effects of punishment on people, experimental studies with animals show that aggression can be produced by punishment. A monkey which is calmly sitting in a cage with a life-size stuffed monkey will suddenly attack it when punished. Not only that, the monkey will learn to do something to get at the stuffed monkey in order to attack it.[4] It isn't too hard to trace hostile comments, songs such as the one in Figure 10.4, caricatures, even physical assaults on teachers or school property to punishment and failure. As a student, you have undoubtedly noticed that on "bad days" at school (that is, days full of punishment) you are more likely to lash out in anger or frustration. You have probably not physically attacked your teachers, but you may have verbally attacked them or their courses. Your students will react to you as a teacher in the same way. They too, will be likely to hit out when they fail or are punished in other ways.

Punishment not only affects the student who is punished, it also affects onlookers. Two researchers, Kounin and Gump, showed how first graders imitated their teachers when the teachers punished openly. The researchers had the teachers reprimand the students in two ways: first, by privately reminding them that "We don't do that in first grade" and,

[4]N. H. Azrin, R. R. Hutchinson, and R. McLaughlin, "The Opportunity for Aggression as an Operant Reinforcer During Aversive Stimulation," *Journal of the Experimental Analysis of Behavior* 8, 1965, pp. 171–180.

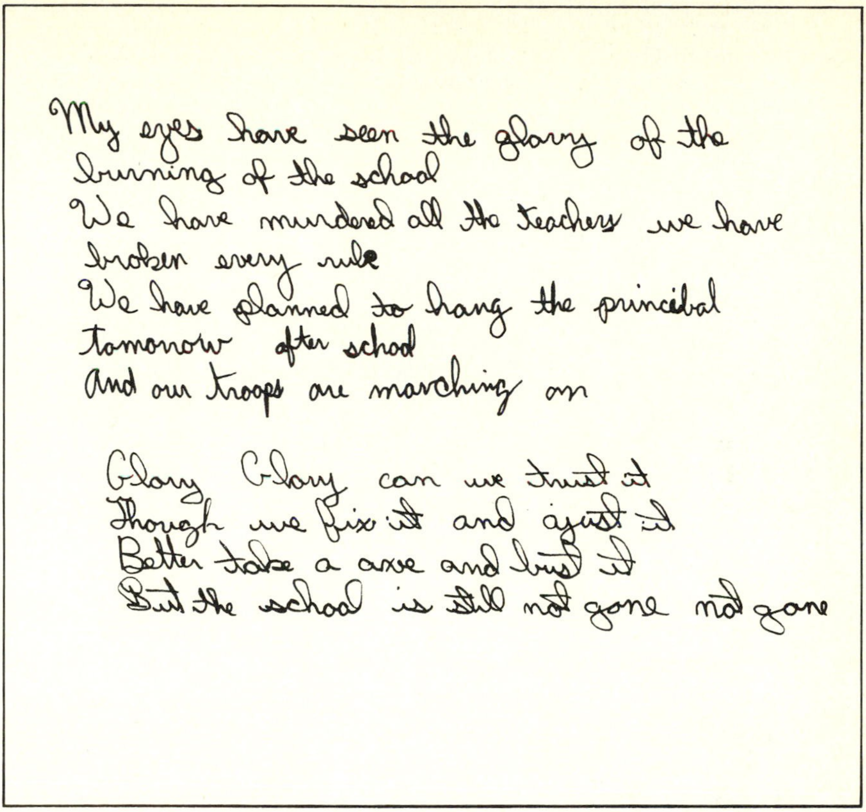

My eyes have seen the glory of the
burning of the school
We have murdered all the teachers we have
broken every rule
We have planned to hang the principal
tomorrow after school
And our troops are marching on

Glory Glory can we trust it
Though we fix it and adjust it
Better take a axe and bust it
But the school is still not gone not gone

Figure 10.4 Punishment begets punishment: students who are punished or frustrated in school may not attack back physically, but verbal attacks, like the one above, are common. The lyrics are sung to the tune of "My Eyes Have Seen the Glory of the Coming of the Lord."[6]

second, by yelling roughly at them in front of the others. When the teacher yelled, the children yelled too. They even began pushing and shoving one another. In contrast, when the teacher handled the students with courtesy, they responded by being more courteous to each other.[5]

Does punishment work? It does weaken behavior, yes, but there is usually another consequence to be taken into account. How often does it "work" in practice?

Assume for the moment that there is something Ralph does fairly frequently (such as passing notes in class) and that you punish him

[5]Jacob S. Kounin and Paul V. Gump, "The Ripple Effect in Discipline," *The Elementary School Journal* (December 1958), pp. 158–162.
[6]The Central School version of "The Burning of the School," written down by Lisa Vargas.

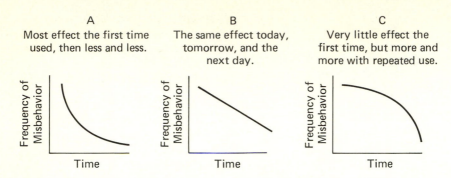

Figure 10.5   Possible Effects of Repeated Punishment in Practice.

(say, by keeping him in from physical education). What is the effect of punishing Ralph repeatedly every time you catch him? Which effect in Figure 10.5 do *you* think punishment most often has?

An analysis of more than one thousand projects using punishment showed that 84 percent followed the pattern of "A."[7] Most punishment causes behavior to decrease most the *first* time it is used. The first humiliation, the first time in from recess, the first scolding has a relatively large effect. The second punishment is less effective, and eventually the student gets used to it and reacts hardly at all.

As if all this were not bad enough, there is another major problem with punishment. If some behavior has been suppressed by punishment and then the threat of punishment is lifted, the behavior comes back— not only to its prepunishment level but often *above* it. A study with animals shows the effect quite clearly (see Figure 10.6).[8]

The first period shows the rate at which a pigeon pecked a key for food. Then, at the first broken line, he received a brief electric shock for each response. The reinforcement which had been maintaining the behavior was also continued. The bird got both food and shock. Note that the suppression effect of the shock wore off after five days. Toward the end the pigeon actually pecked *more* often than before punishment was started. At the second dotted line, punishment was discontinued. For five days the pigeon went wild. He then settled down a bit but still responded at a level *above* the one before he had been punished.

The same effect of lifted punishment is seen in the gorging done by food-lovers when they go off a diet in which eating was punished, in the

[7]Ogden Lindsley, as presented at the Second Annual Trainer's Course in Precise Behavioral Management, Kansas City, Kansas, 1969.

[8]Nathan H. Azrin, "Sequential Effects of Punishment," in *The Experimental Analysis of Behavior: Selected Readings,* ed. Thom Verhave, New York, Appleton-Century-Crofts, 1966, p. 187.

noisy exuberance of a class after a punitive teacher leaves the room, or in excess speeding after a slow police car finally turns off the highway.

If we can generalize from animal studies to students in a classroom, we should expect behavior which is punished inside school to occur at a higher rate than it did initially once the threat of punishment is removed. When the students are outside school where the teacher cannot police them, then, they should be especially inclined to do what is punished in school: to swear, to smoke, to chew gum, to destroy or mark up books, and so on. Punishment will not, then, decrease undesirable behavior where it really counts: *outside* school. It may actually *increase* it.

To summarize: Punishment has a number of drawbacks:

1. It does not remove the reinforcement which is maintaining the behavior, so that it results in two consequences producing conflict in behavioral tendencies.
2. It has undesirable side effects: hostility, aggression, fear, avoidance, and escape are common by-products.
3. It wears out with use, and when the threat is lifted, the punished behavior may not only return, it may return stronger than ever.
4. Other students may imitate a teacher who is punishing. They may also try to control other students by scolding, rough handling, humiliation, and so on.

WHEN PUNISHMENT "WORKS"

Suppose you teach in a school with a coffee machine in the teachers' lounge and that you love coffee. One day you take a sip of coffee and it tastes terrible—almost enough to make you gag. You decide not to have coffee that day, but later in the week you try again. Most of the time

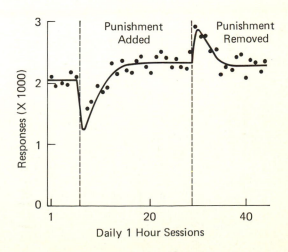

Figure 10.6 Effect of the addition and removal of punishment upon the food-reinforced responses of one subject. The punishment was a brief electric shock which followed every response on the days between those represented by the vertical dashed lines. Food reinforcement was produced according to a variable-interval schedule with a mean of 1 minute on all days. (After Figure in *Science*. Copyright © 1960, the American Association for the Advancement of Science.)

the coffee is good, but occasionally it is terrible. What would determine whether or not you continued to drink coffee?

Immediacy. Timing is crucial. If the punishing effects of the coffee did not occur until later (for example, if it occasionally gave you a stomachache ten minutes after you drank it), the punishment would be much less effective than if it occurred at the first sip.

Schedule. Punishment which is inevitable (such as getting burned for touching a hot flame) is much more effective than punishment which occurs only sometimes. If the coffee *always* tastes bad, you will quit drinking it.

Immediacy and the certainty of getting punished are more important for decreasing behavior than severity of punishment. The threat of possible sickness and even death itself are insufficient consequnces to prevent most of us from doing things we know we shouldn't: eating "heart attack" foods (such as hot dogs and ice cream), speeding on the highways, smoking, and so on. The consequences are too delayed and "might not happen to me." In contrast, even a mild consequence can suppress behavior effectively if it is *certain* we will get caught immediately every time.

Availability of Alternatives. Even more important for the effectiveness of punishment than immediacy and timing are the alternatives available. No one drinks coffee from a particular pot if there is better coffee readily available. The student who can as easily get attention or peer approval for desirable behavior will not persist in misbehaving in order to get attention.

If you *must* punish students, then you should:

1. Provide alternatives—Make sure the students know what *to do* as well as what *not* to do and that they can get at least as much reinforcement from the desirable behavior as from the undesirable.
2. Punish immediately *every* time with minor punishment rather than later or only occasionally with something severe.
3. Punish only behavior you personally see. If you rely on someone else's report, you cannot punish immediately and you may punish unjustly. If you get students to confess and then punish them, you are punishing telling the truth. It is because students often get punished when they tell the truth that they learn to lie. If sudents refuse to confess to something you are pretty sure they did, you are in a bind. If you *know* they did it, then you don't need a confession. If you don't know, you shouldn't punish.
4. Use only consequences you would like your students to use too. If you don't want students to yell at others, you shouldn't yell at them. The least harmful punishments seem to be the most natural ones, such as reparations —fixing what was broken, making up work during recess, paying for what was destroyed.

ALTERNATIVES TO PUNISHMENT

It would be very difficult never to punish a student, but in the day-to-day interaction in the classroom there are better methods of control. Rather than punishing bad behavior, these methods concentrate on building good behavior.

PREVENTION

In behavior, as with other problems, prevention is the best cure. Just as we take steps to try to prevent sickness, so we can take steps to prevent disciplinary problems. Certain situations are likely to encourage undesirable behavior. An assignment or test which students cannot readily do invites copying, avoidance (whispering, procrastinating, etc.), and even cheating. A lecture in elementary school is a situation in which you can predict that students will squirm, pass notes, and daydream. In contrast, give a timed quiz (with students working at their own level or trying to beat their own record) and you will seldom have a disciplinary problem. According to the way teachers arrange their room, they can similarly create or reduce potential problems. There is no sense in leaving around equipment you do not want handled or in expecting students to put things away if it isn't easy to find where they go.

You may wish to teach students self-discipline so they *will* sit quietly in lectures, leave equipment alone, or put things away, but that is best done by making the desirable behavior *likely* to occur. We do that by gradual steps rather than by setting up a situation in which many will fail and then be punished.

AFTER A PROBLEM EXISTS

In spite of your best plans, you will undoubtedly find that some students are doing things you feel they shouldn't. That still does not mean you must use punishment.

Punishment is intended to decrease undesirable behavior. One way to do that is to shape behavior which is incompatible with the undesirable behavior. Decide what you would like the students to do instead and build that. Rather than punishing sloppy writing, you can reinforce neat writing. Rather than punishing procrastination, reinforce the incompatible behavior of getting to work right away. Rather than punishing

---

Incompatible Behaviors

are behaviors that an individual cannot do at the same time. For example, whistling and drinking are incompatible: one cannot do both at the same time.

getting out of the seat, reinforce doing assignments. Sometimes it takes a bit of imagination. In a boarding school, one dorm had a problem with litter in the TV room. The dorm supervisor tried punishment. Of course every student denied leaving the cans and rubbish around, so the supervisor punished everyone watching TV when he entered the room and found it dirty. You can imagine the enthusiasm with which that was received! Then he decided to reinforce incompatible behavior: everyone "caught" in the room when it was *clean* got a bonus. If you get a half hour's extension of bedtime for being in a clean TV room, you make sure it's clean! At first the supervisor reinforced everyone in the room *each* time he found it clean. Then only sometimes. The room remained clean. Catching students being good succeeded where punishment had failed.[9]

SUMMARY

Because of all the problems associated with punishment, it cannot be recommended as good for the student. Undesirable behavior should be decreased; but with imagination and effort, improvement can be made without resorting to punishment. In the short run, it takes a lot of effort to shape up desirable behavior to replace misbehavior, but it is. more likely to benefit both you and your students in the long run.

EXERCISES

Concept Check XA—Punishment and Alternative Methods for Reducing Behavior (Objective A)

Write the letter for each treatment below, using:

P for "Punishment"
E for "Extinction"
R for "Reinforcement" of other (incompatible) behavior

1. You no longer give the reinforcement which has been maintaining a particular behavior.
2. You take away privileges which Kathy had already earned because of something she did.
3. You "catch the student behaving well" and show approval.
4. You give Erik a pencil because he has asked only once and not begged.
5. You take away the pencil you have just given to Jim when he asks for another one.

[9]This is based upon a program instituted by John Minor in one of the cottages at Kennedy Youth Center, Morgantown, W. Va. 1968–1969.

6. You refuse to give in any more to Jim's begging for another pencil.
7. Dolores gets burned when she lights the Bunsen burner incorrectly.
8. Dolores is unable to get a flame on the Bunsen burner because of turning the gas on too high.
9. Dolores gets a good flame on the Bunsen burner because of turning the gas to the point marked on the knob.
10. Charlie gets a stove-in finger from holding his hand at the wrong angle to catch a fly.

Answers for Concept Check XA

1. E
2. P
3. R
4. R (Asking only once is incompatible with begging.)
5. P
6. E
7. P
8. E
9. R
10. P

(Note: The consequences in numbers 7 through 10 are "natural" in that they occur automatically as a result of the behavior described rather than being provided by a teacher. Nature reinforces, extinguishes, and punishes behavior too—usually with more consistency than a teacher.)

Concept Check XB—Effects of Punishment (Objective B)

A teacher uses only punishment to reduce students' misbehavior rather than using extinction or reinforcement of incompatible behavior. Which six of the following effects would you most expect?

1. An immediate pause in misbehavior following each treatment.
2. Hostile comments about the teacher behind his or her back (and out of earshot).
3. An immediate increase in misbehavior by the students punished, but then a gradual decrease.
4. Avoidance of the subject the teacher teaches—for example, by not electing to take it when given a choice.
5. Misbehaving when the teacher can't see.
6. Increased enthusiasm for the subject taught.
7. Misbehavior decreasing less and less as the year goes on and the same treatment is used over and over.
8. An increase in the number of times the misbehaving students hit or shove others.
9. Better performance on the teachers' tests.
10. A quieter room than others in the building.

Answers for Concept Check XB

The six most predictable effects of punishment are numbers 1, 2, 4, 5, 7, and 8. Number 9 is not correct because punishment does not necessarily produce better test results. Although punishment may "frighten students into studying," it may make them revolt or withdraw—for example by being sick more often. In the latter case test results will not improve. Number 10 is not correct because punishment often produces aggression, which results in an increase, not a decrease, in noise. As in Number 9, a punitive teacher *may* produce the result mentioned in Number 10, but it is not a result you would "most expect" from what we know about punishment.

Concept Check XC—Extinction (Objective C)

In which two of the following situations could you most easily use extinction to eliminate the behavior mentioned?

1. Folding down the corners of the pages in books to mark the place.
2. Calling the teacher a name he or she dislikes.
3. Whining to get to be first in line.
4. Writing sloppily in order to finish more rapidly.
5. Smoking.

Answers for Concept Check XC

The two situations are numbers 2 and 3.

Number 1 The reinforcement for folding down corners is having the page different from the others so that it is easy to find. There is no way to remove that reinforcement, since it is the automatic result of folding down corners.

Number 4 Sloppy writing is faster than careful writing—it is reinforced by the increased amount of material produced in a given time. Like Number 1, this result is an automatic consequence and cannot therefore be withheld.

Number 5 Smoking is not normally reinforced by another person but rather by the taste and feel resulting from the behavior itself. To remove these effects would be impractical to say the least.

Concept Check XD—Incompatible Behavior (Objective D)

Which two of the following behaviors are incompatible with writing answers to chemistry questions?

1. Raising your hand
2. Drawing flowers
3. Knitting
4. Humming
5. Chewing gum

Answers for Concept Check XD

The two behaviors which are incompatible with writing answers to chemistry questions are numbers 2 and 3.

It is possible to write answers while raising your hand, or while humming, or while chewing gum, so none of these is incompatible with writing.

CHAPTER ELEVEN

Stimulus control

OVERVIEW

In chapters One through Eight we discussed two of the three terms in a contingency: the response and the following stimulus change (or consequence). In this chapter, we will look at the role of the third term in a contingency: the stimulus which precedes a response.

OBJECTIVES

By the end of the chapter you should be able to:

A. Define *stimulus control* and describe how it comes about and how a given case of stimulus control could have come about.
B. Define the following terms and identify them in descriptions of stimulus control:
   1. Generalization
   2. Discrimination
   3. Discriminative stimulus
   4. S^D
   5. S^Δ
C. Identify the defining properties of a given concept and tell which of two exercises would better teach it and why.
D. Identify whether an example of stimulus control illustrates rule-governed behavior or contingency-shaped behavior.
E. Describe the following in terms of stimulus control (identifying the operant, preceding S^D's and S^Δ's, and the prevailing consequences):
   Modeling
   Imitation
   Rule-governed behavior

F. Identify the likely source of failure in an example of faulty discrimination and suggest a remedy.

STIMULUS CONTROL—WHAT IT IS

The stimuli in our environment can serve two functions. They can reinforce (or punish) the behavior they follow and they can set the occasion for the behavior which follows them. The latter function is called *stimulus control.*

Stimulus control is the control that features of our environment acquire over the kinds of behaviors we make in their presence. When a student responds to a question, we say the question has stimulus control

> **Stimulus Control**
>
> is the control that stimuli in our environment acquire over the behavior we emit in their presence.

over the behavior of answering. When Mr. Horton notices, out of the corner of his eye, two students passing notes, his response is under the stimulus control of their behavior. Any features of our environment which set the occasion for a particular kind of response are said to have stimulus control over our behavior.

The control that particular stimuli can gain over behavior is remarkable. An extreme case is illustrated in the following story of the capture of a woman for bank robbery.

One of our officers caught a teenage girl because of a red light. Really! Her boyfriend had persuaded her to drive a getaway car for a bank robbery he had planned. On the day of the robbery, something went wrong and he got caught. He succeeded in shouting out to her to run. She took off in the car as fast as she could go. A police car followed, but it was in danger of losing her. It looked as though she might get away. But as she approached an intersection, the stoplight turned red and she slammed on her brakes. She stopped for the light. They caught her because she stopped for a red light![1]

That's stimulus control!

When we talk about stimulus control, we are talking about two things: (1) *how* we respond to particular stimuli; and (2) *which* stimuli in our environment have control over our behavior. In the above incident, for example, we are interested in what response the driver made to the red light and also in the fact that, of all the stimuli present in the getaway situation, the driver responded to the red light and not to the other stimuli. In the classroom we are interested in how students respond to

[1]The episode described is based upon an actual arrest.

given stimuli, such as questions, problems, assignments, and so on, and we are also interested in what stimuli in their environment gain control over their behavior. When we ask what they pay attention to, what they take an interest in, or what they notice, we are asking for the particular stimuli which have control over their behavior.

Stimulus control thus deals with people's sensitivity to the stimuli in their environment—with whether or not they behave appropriately in their presence. If you have ever been to a foreign country, to a wedding in an unfamiliar religion, or to a social event with procedures you have never encountered before, you know the feeling of not being able to respond appropriately to stimuli which, to others, are perfectly clear. Learning to respond appropriately on any occasion, social or academic, is what we mean by improving stimulus control.[2]

HOW STIMULI GAIN CONTROL OVER BEHAVIOR

Any feature of the environment that is correlated with reinforcement of an operant gains control over that operant. If the presence of a particular teacher is correlated with reinforcement for studying—that is, if we are usually reinforced for studying when that instructor is there—then that teacher gains control over our studying: we are likely to study in that teacher's presence. If we are successful when working in a particular subject, our tendency to respond in that subject increases. If, in the presence of people, talking aloud is reinforced but is not reinforced otherwise, we learn to talk out loud when people are present. We learn, in other words, to behave in ways which, given the stimuli present, are likely to be reinforced. The particular stimuli which are present when we are reinforced for a particular operant and which are absent when we are not, thus gain control over that operant.

Discrimination. The process in which we learn to respond differently in the presence of different stimuli is called *discrimination.* Drivers discriminate between red and green traffic lights when they stop for one but not for the other. Students discriminate between solids and liquids when they respond differently to them, for example, by calling water "liquid" and ice "solid." Racial discrimination is behaving differently toward people because of their race rather than because of their personal abilities or characteristics. We discriminate when we buy one brand of a product and not another. We discriminate when we solve problems—we write a particular answer depending on what problem is before us.

[2]Sloane et al have argued that creativity too is a particular kind of stimulus control. See Howard Sloane, Gabriel Della-Piana, and George Endo, "Creative Behaviors," paper presented at the Midwestern Association for Behavior Analysis, Chicago, May 1976.

> **Discrimination**
>
> is the process of responding differently in the presence of different stimuli.

Let's look at a simple example of how a stimulus gains control through its association with the different consequences for responding in its presence and absence.

Suppose that you teach in a school which has a dispensing machine which sells milk and that you like to drink milk. The machine is old and does not have a lot of instructions written on it. There is, however, a little light near the slot for depositing coins. The first day you put in your coins, the light is glowing faintly, and you get your milk. The next time you try the machine, the light is out. Your coins are returned. You try again, but with no success. The day after that, the light is glowing when you put in your coins and you get milk.

If the light is glowing each time you get milk but never when the machine is out of milk, the light will start to control your behavior. If it is on, you will insert your coins. If it is off, you will not. The light, a stimulus which precedes the response of inserting coins, has gained control over your behavior of inserting coins (see Figure 11.1) through its correlation with reinforcement. You discriminate between light on and light off. The example of the coin machine is simple, but it illustrates the basic process through which discriminations are formed. Stimuli gain control over behavior by their association with the consequences for responding in their presence and absence.

Discriminative Stimuli—S^D's and S^Δ's. When a stimulus has gained control over a particular response, the stimulus is called a discriminative stimulus for that response. A discriminative stimulus can be either an S^D (pronounced ess-dee), or an S^Δ (pronounced ess-delta), depending on whether a response has been reinforced or extinguished in its presence. If we have been reinforced, and thus respond when a stimulus is present, the stimulus is called an S^D for that response. If responding has been extinguished, so that we do not respond when a particular stimulus is present, the stimulus is an S^Δ for that response. In the example of the milk machine, *light on* is an S^D for inserting coins, but *light off* is an S^Δ for inserting coins when we respond according to which stimulus condition is present.

Preceding stimulus	Response	Following stimulus
Light on	Inserting coins →	Reinforcement (you get milk)
Light off	Inserting coins →	No Reinforcement (you get no milk)

Figure 11.1 An Example of how We Learn To Discriminate.

In describing the control by a particular stimulus, we must specify the response we are referring to. A stimulus can be an S^D for one operant, but an S^Δ for another. For example, a green traffic light is an S^D for going, but it is not an S^D for slamming on your brakes. It is an S^Δ for that response.

A Discriminative Stimulus (S^D or S^Δ)

is a stimulus which sets the occasion for a particular response. An S^D (pronounced ess-dee) is a stimulus in the presence of which a response is likely to be reinforced. The end of a concert performance is an S^D for clapping. An S^Δ (pronounced ess-delta), on the other hand, is a stimulus in the presence of which a response is *not* likely to be reinforced. For example, a concert *in progress* is an S^Δ for clapping. Both S^D's and S^Δ's are *discriminitive stimuli.*

Generalization. Just as an operant is a class of behaviors, a discriminative stimulus is really a class of stimuli. No two stimuli are exactly the same. Stoplights differ from one intersection to another, yet we respond similarly to them. One book is not the same as another, yet we read books we have never before been reinforced for reading. We also tend to read other printed material, such as the backs of cereal boxes, signboards along the highway, notices on bulletin boards, and so on. When we talk of the stimulus of a "red stoplight" or of "printed material" we are referring to a group of stimuli. Even the stimulus of one particular object varies from day to day. Dress, hairstyle, facial expressions, and so on, change in people, and there are slight variations in the lighting, angle of view, and so on, of objects. When we speak of a stimulus then, we really mean a variety of stimuli which share common elements.

When we are reinforced for responding in the presence of a particular stimulus on one occasion, the probability of responding increases in the presence of similar stimuli. Thus, we respond to the light of the milk machine even though it glows brightly instead of faintly. If the color of the light changed, it would probably not affect the light's control over our behavior. Other lights on other milk machines, too, will have an effect on our inserting coins although the less similar the other machines, the less the spread of effect.

The spread of effect from one stimulus to other stimuli is called *stimulus generalization,* or *induction.* If we eat an apple which is particularly delicious, the probability of eating apples which share common elements increases. The control of the properties of that apple (such as color or size) generalizes (or transfers) to other apples which have the same properties. If students are reinforced for speaking up

> **Generalization**
>
> is the spread of effect from a particular stimulus to other stimuli which share common elements.

in one setting, similar settings gain control over their behavior. They are, of course, likely to speak up again in the same class, but the effect will generalize to other settings which are in some way similar: to similar-looking teachers, to similar subjects, to other classrooms which have chairs arranged in the same way, and so on. We say their response generalizes.

The Limits of Control. Whether or not we respond the same way to two stimuli depends on our previous history of reinforcement. What we *see* as similar depends on what we have been reinforced for responding to similarly. The limits of the stimuli to which we respond are set by the differential consequences of discrimination training. The limits of control emerge when some stimuli have been accompanied by reinforcement but others have not. Where that line is drawn is where the limits of stimulus control lie. For example, when we have been reinforced for calling a wide variety of reddish colors "red," we will generalize to a wide range of reddish stimuli. If, however, the colors we have been reinforced for calling red have been restricted to a narrow range, for example by study in an art class, the limits of the colors we will call red will be narrow. We will actually see subtle differences we did not see before. The limits can become very narrow indeed:

Those who work with pigments, dyes, or other colored materials are affected by contingencies in which slight differences in color make a great deal of difference in the consequences of behavior. We say that they become "highly discriminating" with respect to color. But their behavior shows only processes of conditioning and extinction.[3]

Both discrimination and generalization describe behavioral *processes*. They are not reasons for behavior. We cannot say, "Drivers react differently to red and green lights *because* they discriminate between them," or "Drivers stop at this red light *because* they generalize from other red lights." These would be explanatory fictions because both the behavior explained and the cause describe the same set of facts. We must look instead at the past contingencies of reinforcement for our explanation.

Operant Discrimination and Reflex Behavior—A Difference in Control. When a discrimination is well established, a person responds readily

---

[3]B. F. Skinner, *Science and Human Behavior*, New York, Macmillan, 1953, p. 134.

when the S^D is presented. When a traffic light turns to red, we react right away. When a teacher calls on an eager student, the response is quick. We react almost immediately to many changes in our environment. It is easy to forget that the control of our behavior lies in the past contingencies, not solely in the stimulus preceding our response.

The control of an S^D is different from the control of a stimulus in a reflex. An operant response is "emitted," in contrast to the "elicited" response in a reflex. For example, in the eye blink reflex, a puff of air on the eyeball elicits an eye blink. To explain the eye blink, we need only to look at the stimulus which preceded it. The control of the blink lies in the puff of air. In contrast, you may respond with an eye blink when I say, "Blink," but the relationship between the discriminative stimulus "Blink" and your response is different. The control of your response does not lie in the stimulus of my word, but in the consequences of blinking when asked to do so. If you have been reinforced for following directions, you will blink. Suppose you are taking a "speed of reaction" test for a job you would really like. In that case you will blink as fast—and as predictably—as in a reflex. But the control is still different. Your behavior is operant—it is controlled by its consequences, not by the preceding stimulus. The word "blink" has control *only insofar* as it is associated with consequences. If the consequences change, your behavior to the same stimulus will change. Suppose, for example, that the test continues, but you are now told that to do well, you must *resist* blinking. Then you would stop blinking when the examiner said, "Blink." The stimulus which before was a discriminative stimulus for blinking is now an S^Δ.

The distinction between the two kinds of control exercised by stimuli is described by the words "voluntary" and "involuntary." When we blink at a puff of air, we say the response was involuntary. When, on the other hand, we blink to the word "blink," we say the response was voluntary. The word "voluntary" is misleading because it implies that control of the response lies inside the individual rather than in the contingencies which are actually responsible. For this reason, operant psychologists prefer not to use either term.

In a reflex, the strength of a stimulus determines the strength of the response. If a little puff of air elicits a little blink, a stronger puff will elicit a stronger blink. This is not the case with the response to a discriminative stimulus because the control of an operant does not lie in the preceding stimulus. In the "speed of reaction" test, for example, you would not necessarily blink harder when the examiner said, "Blink," loudly than when the word was whispered. The control does not lie in the stimulus but in its relationship with the consequences for responding in the past.

BRINGING ABOUT NEW STIMULUS CONTROL

Concepts. One kind of stimulus control we teach is called *concept formation.* A concept is a set of characteristics, or properties, of stimuli. The properties which define a concept never occur alone in nature, but

---

A Concept

is a property or set of properties shared by stimuli.

---

only in combination with other properties. Color, for example, is a concept. It is a property of stimuli, but it never occurs alone. Any particular stimulus that has color also has other properties, such as shape, texture, size, brightness, and so on.

All common nouns, verbs, adjectives, and adverbs are concepts. Each refers to a set of properties found in stimuli but not to any particular stimulus itself. The concept of "hat" refers to a set of characteristics common to all hats. No one hat is the *concept* of hat. It can only be an example of that concept. The verb "sing" is a concept. It is a behavior defined by particular characteristics. We can point to an example of "singing," but one instance of singing does not constitute the concept. Similarly, the adjective "big" refers to a property of stimuli, not to any particular large object. The adverb "angrily" is a property or combination of properties which are shared by many specific behaviors. In contrast, proper names, such as Abraham Lincoln, are *not* concepts. They do not refer to properties shared by different objects or happenings but to one specific case.

To teach a concept, we must bring students under the stimulus control of those properties which define the concept and free them from the control of the other properties which, in nature, accompany the defining properties. We say that students "understand a concept" when they respond only to the properties which define it. Students who understand the concept of color, for example, must be under the stimulus control of that property and not others. They must respond differently when that property differs between stmuli—for example, by calling a green object "green" and a red object "red"—and they must respond the same way when that property does not change, for example, by calling both a red apple and a red jacket "red." They must, in other words, both discriminate between stimuli and generalize to new stimuli on the basis of the defining property of color.

Sometimes it can be difficult to separate out just those properties which define a concept. Two examples will illustrate:

In learning the concept of number, beginning students do not discriminate between number and length. Usually, in children's experience, a longer row *does* have more in it. Young children have not encountered contingencies which teach them to discriminate between length and number, so their behavior is under the control of both properties of a row of chips. But length is not a defining characteristic of the concept "number." To free children from the control of length, we must vary length while holding number constant. Then we reinforce the student for responding to "the row that has more," when that row is the shorter of the two rows (see Figure 11.2).

Below are examples in which students failed to understand a concept. In each case, the stimulus control of the property which defines the concept has not been freed from the control of the other irrelevant properties of the stimuli presented.

Example I: The Concept of Number

Let us lay down a row of eight red (poker) chips, equally spaced about an inch apart, and ask our small subjects to take from a box of chips as many chips as there are on the table. . . . A child of five or younger, on the average, will lay out blue chips to make a row exactly as long as the red row, but he will put the blue chips close together instead of spacing them. . . . At the age of six, on the average, children will lay a blue chip opposite each red chip and obtain the correct number. But they have not necessarily acquired the concept of number itself. If we spread the red chips, spacing the row more loosely, the six-year-olds will think that the larger row now has more chips. though we have not changed the number.[4]

Example II: The Concept of Area

After describing a class in which a teacher teaches how to find the area of a parallelogram by dropping perpendiculars as in Figure 11.3, Wertheimer expresses doubts about the pupils' understanding of the concept of area, and decides to put them to the test:
I ask the teacher whether he will allow me to put a question to the class. "With pleasure," he answers, clearly proud of his class. I go to the board and draw this figure [Figure 11.4].
Some are obviously taken back. One pupil raises his hand. "Teacher, we haven't had that yet." Others are busy. They have copied the figure on paper. They draw the auxiliary lines as they were taught, dropping perpendiculars from the two upper corners and extending the baseline [Figure 11.5]. Then they look bewildered, perlexed.[5]

In the example of area (see figures 11.3-11.5), the students that Wertheimer tested were under the control of properties of shape and position of figures. Neither of these are defining properties of "area."

[4]Jean Piaget, "How Children Form Mathematical Concepts," *Scientific American*, November 1953, p. 74.
[5]M. Wertheimer, *Productive Thinking*, New York, Harper & Row, 1959, pp. 13–24.

Figure 11.2   The teacher has just asked, "Which row has more—or do they have the same number?" When Justine responds to the property "how many there are" and not to the other properties of groups of objects (such as the length of the row), we say she "understands the concept of number." (Courtesy of Robert L. Gay, The Associated Press.)

Figure 11.3

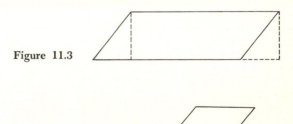

Figure 11.4

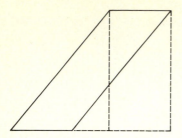

Figure 11.5

We conclude that they did not understand the concept of area because they did not respond consistently to that property of figures, and that property alone. They failed to generalize from one position of a figure to another, and they failed to discriminate between perpendiculars that would help find area and those that would not. (The dotted lines in Figure 11.5, of course, are not helpful for finding area.)

How to Teach Concepts. To teach students a concept, we must bring about a particular kind of stimulus control. The students must learn to respond to the properties which define the concept and not to others. They only way we can be sure that we teach this is to have the students respond to a *variety* of stimuli, reinforcing them for responding to the defining properties and, if necessary, extinguishing responding to irrelevent properties. To teach the concept of "red," for example, we ask our students to tell us which of two objects is red. To make sure that they are discriminating by *color,* we must free their response from the irrelevant properties of shape, size, and so on. In other words, we make sure that they cannot pick the red object by its shape or size. The red object should, therefore, not always be the round one, or the bigger of the two presented. We reinforce them for picking each red object, but not if they pick the object which is not red.

Now suppose our students can respond correctly to all the objects we have used while teaching them. Do they understand the concept of red? We cannot be sure. They may have just memorized the correct response to each object. In other words, it may be the *particular* object and not its color that is controlling their behavior. To find out, we must try them on objects they have never seen before. If they correctly respond to the objects' color—generalizing to new red stimuli and discriminating between new red stimuli and new stimuli of other colors—we say they understand the concept of red.

The more variety there is in the examples we use when teaching a concept, the more likely it is that students will response to its defining characteristics. In any concept there are certain properties which frequently accompany the defining properties but which are not part of the concept. In teaching, then, it is particularly important to vary those characteristics when having the students respond.

TABLE I   Examples of Plurals Which Share a Property Which Is
Not a Defining Property of "Plural." (Of Course,
the Examples Also Share the Defining
Property of "More Than One Thing.")

Singular	Plural
horse	horses
song	songs
ball	balls

Suppose, for example, you wanted to teach the concept "plural." What property might confuse your students because it frequently occurs in plural words although it is not a defining property of the concept? Look at the examples in Table I and see if you can pick it out.

One distinguishing property of all the plurals in the example in Table I is the final "s." Students who are just learning plurals may respond to that final "s." If so, they would make the mistakes shown in Table II when they encountered plurals like "men," which don't end in "s," or words like "bus," which do end in "s" but are not plurals.

To free students from the stimulus control of final "s," you must have them respond to a variety of plurals as well as to words ending in "s" which are not plural. It is only when the students respond to the property of "more than one thing" and not to final "s," or any other characteristics of words, that they understand the concept of plural.

The only way you can tell when a student is responding to a particular property is to vary all the others. The student must then make some fine discriminations. In teaching the concept "one-half," for example, you need to separate the defining property of "one of two equal parts" from shape, size, arrangement, number, and so on. Figure 11.6 shows how you can vary these irrelevant characteristics. The student who completes Work Sheet A correctly may think that "one-half" is a circle colored black on one side. You may think this is ridiculous, but many a student taught only on circles has had trouble with work sheets like Work Sheet B. Work Sheet B frees the student from the stimulus control of "circles" but not from other irrelevant properties. By the time a student learns to do Work Sheet D, however, the student understands the concept of one-half pretty well.

TABLE II   Mistakes Made by a Student Who Identifies
"Plurals" by Final "S"

Directions: Circle the plural words

men	shoe
(bats)	sheep
(bus)	(goes)

Work sheet: In all cases, directions are
to circle the figures that are half shaded.　　　　　　Comments

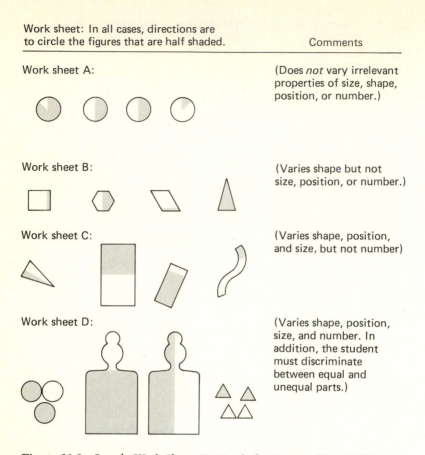

Work sheet A:　　　　　　　　　　　　　　(Does *not* vary irrelevant
　　　　　　　　　　　　　　　　　　　　properties of size, shape,
　　　　　　　　　　　　　　　　　　　　position, or number.)

Work sheet B:　　　　　　　　　　　　　　(Varies shape but not
　　　　　　　　　　　　　　　　　　　　size, position, or number.)

Work sheet C:　　　　　　　　　　　　　　(Varies shape, position,
　　　　　　　　　　　　　　　　　　　　and size, but not number)

Work sheet D:　　　　　　　　　　　　　　(Varies shape, position,
　　　　　　　　　　　　　　　　　　　　size, and number. In
　　　　　　　　　　　　　　　　　　　　addition, the student
　　　　　　　　　　　　　　　　　　　　must discriminate
　　　　　　　　　　　　　　　　　　　　between equal and
　　　　　　　　　　　　　　　　　　　　unequal parts.)

Figure 11.6　Sample Work Sheets To Teach the Concept "One-Half."

CONTINGENCY-SHAPED BEHAVIOR

All discriminations (including those required for understanding a concept) can be learned by directly encountering the contingencies for appropriate responding. In the example of the milk machine, for instance, the discrimination was learned through experiencing the consequences of inserting coins during the S^D and S^Δ conditions. No one told you the rule. The behavior of a person who has learned through direct experience with contingencies is called *contingency-shaped* to distinguish it from the behavior of following rules (called *rule-governed* behavior). Self-taught musicians who have not used instruction manuals

---

Contingency-Shaped Behavior

is behavior that is learned by directly experiencing the contingencies in behaving appropriately and inappropriately.

have been "taught" by contingencies. They repeated the kinds of re-sponses they made which were reinforced by pleasant sounds. Those responses which produced sounds which were not reinforcing were extinguished. Similarly, if you learn to do a puzzle without help, or "discover" how to operate something by fiddling with it, your behavior is contingency-shaped. To get a feeling for what it is like to learn by this method, do the program in the following Table. You will then be in the position of a student learning a totally unfamiliar concept through direct experience with contingencies.

Table showing an example of learning by directly encountering the contingencies for responding appropriately or inappropriately (also called the *discovery method*).

This is a program to teach you the concept of a "Neet."

Cover the page with a piece of paper so that you can see only what is above the first double line.

1. These are Neets: 1, 2, 3
    These are not Neets: 7, 8, 9
    Which of these are Neets? 1, 2, 9

When you have answered, move your paper cover down to the next double line. Continue by answering first, then uncovering the answer.

1a. The Neets are 1 and 2.

2. These are Neets: 12, 13, 14, 15
    These are not Neets: 16, 17, 18, 19
    Which of these is a Neet? 8, 9, 12, 19

2a. The answer is 12.

3. These are Neets: 20, 30, 40, 50
    These are not Neets: 60, 70, 80
    Which of these are Neets? 2, 10, 90

3a. The Neets are 2 and 10.

4. These are Neets: 111; 101; 2,134; 5,000
    These are not Neets: 119; 106; 8,134; 6,000
    Which of these are Neets? 202; 4,000; 9,000; 606

4a. The Neets are 202 and 4,000.

5. These are Neets: 3,412,011; 1,234,500
    These are not Neets: 3,412,061; 1,234,007
    Which of these are Neets? 3,000,090; 3,000,100; 9,876,543; 5,432,100

5a. The Neets are 3,000,100 and 5,432,100.

If you went through the exercises in the Table, you may have found yourself saying, "This is all very well, but if you want me to learn the concept of a Neet, why don't you just *tell* me what it is." You are right. By far the simplest way to teach a concept to someone with a verbal repertoire is to define the concept. If I tell you that a Neet is a numeral that has no digit larger than 5, you will learn the concept in one step. Of course, I would still ask you to pick out Neets, just to make sure that you understand, that is, that you can respond to that property of numerals. (Your behavior, however, in following the rule "Pick the numerals which have no digits larger than 5" would be rule-governed instead of contingency-shaped.)

USING EXISTING STIMULUS CONTROL

In giving a definition or rule, we are drawing on a discriminative repertoire we expect our students to possess already. The definition itself is an S^D for responding appropriately to examples to which it applies. In the classroom, we are constantly using existing stimulus control. Two of the discriminative stimuli we use most are demonstrations and rules.

Imitation and Modeling of Behavior. The stimulus of an action by another person is often a discriminative stimulus for doing the same thing. We are frequently reinforced for imitating others. Imitation learning starts early. Babies are reinforced by others for imitating motions (patty cake), sounds (say 'Mama"), facial expressions (smiles), and so on. They are also reinforced by natural consequences for imitating. What Mama or Brother eats is more likely to taste good than other things in the babies' environment, such as soap or glue. They are thus reinforced naturally for eating what others eat. Children are reinforced for acting grown-up, for imitating characters on TV, and for all the things we tell them to do "like this." By the time a child enters school, the behavior of others is a pretty strong S^D for imitating.

We are particularly likely to be reinforced for imitating others who are receiving social or material reinforcement, such as people with status or authority. A high school student, for example, is more likely to be reinforced for acting like a popular singer or athlete than for acting like a child. Those we tend to imitate—those who are getting reinforcers *we* would like to receive—are called *models*.

When we teach, we are in a position of authority over our students. Teachers, in our society, also have status. Whether we like it or not, we are models for our students. The ways in which we behave as teachers are discriminative stimuli for imitation by our students. If we treat others with consideration, talk rather than shout, and deal calmly with problems, we set the occasion for similar behavior from our students.

If, on the other hand, we deal punitively with others (perhaps being polite only to superiors), or make sarcastic remarks, brag about "bending or breaking rules," or engage in other undesirable behavior, we create an atmosphere for similar behavior by our students. How we behave is an S^D for students to imitate what we do.

The behavior of a model doesn't *cause* imitation. It is only an S^D. It sets the occasion for similar responding. What consequences students receive for imitating determine how they will continue to behave, as in any operant. It is easier, however, to set up a situation in which students are likely to behave well and then to reinforce them, than to have to deal with a lot of unwanted behavior.

Demonstrating How to Do Something as an S^D. In demonstrating how to do something, you are intentionally modeling behavior. A demonstration is particularly effective when students imitate right away. In that way, they can continue to be reinforced for imitating, and demonstrations continue to be S^D's for imitation. If students do *not* have a chance to behave like the demonstrator—or if the opportunity is too delayed—then the demonstration ceases to be an S^D. It loses control over the students' behavior. In everyday language, we say they "lose interest." It is no accident that students pay more attention to a demonstration when they will have to do it themselves immediately afterward than when they will be tested on the "content" weeks later.

Demonstrating "Thinking" and "Problem-Solving." Just as you can demonstrate (or model) physical skills, such as how to operate equipment, you can demonstrate some of what we call "thinking." Normally, when you are teaching, you solve many problems while students are watching and listening. But often you are likely to omit the steps you go through. If you teach math, for example, you can look at an equation and solve it without writing down the steps you take. To your students it looks as though you just "came up with" an answer. Similarly, when an apparent inconsistency arises in a discussion or a student asks a particularly difficult question, you are likely to tell the students only your solution. They do not see the thinking you did to arrive at your answer. In both cases, however, you are probably more interested in teaching the *process* of finding answers than the answers themselves. You want to teach students to think the way you did. To model "thinking," you can think out loud. Instead of giving just answers, you can talk to yourself. In working out an equation, you can say, "Let's see. First I have to get rid of the fractions. How can I do that? Well, if I multiply by x — 1. . . . Yes, that would do it . . . ," and so on. For a contradiction raised by a student you might begin, "You're right. That *doesn't* make sense. Something is wrong somewhere. Let's take it step by step. First, what do we know? We know that the government report on nuclear power stated that . . . ," and so on. By reasoning *out loud* you are demonstrating "thinking." You are providing an S^D for students to think when *they* encounter a problem. They are then less likely to guess at answers or to jump to conclusions and more likely to think problems through step by step.

Following Directions. Like "imitation," "following directions" is an operant which is well established by the time a person enters school. When we tell a student, "Please sit down," we are presenting a stimulus which already has some control over the student's behavior.

The amount of control any directions have depends, like the control of any S^D, on the consequences students have received for obeying and not obeying in the past. How well students will continue to follow your directions depends upon the consequences they receive for doing so in your presence.

Some consequences are provided naturally from behavior itself. Some are provided by teachers. A student who is having trouble finding a word in a dictionary will be reinforced for following your directions on how to find words by finding the word. The student who, by following directions, is able to solve a problem that he or she couldn't do before is likewise reinforced by the natural consequences of the behavior of following directions. As a teacher, you may reinforce the student also with comments like "Yes, that's it. You've got it now."

When there is no natural consequence for following directions, students will stop following them unless *you* consistently provide consequences. If you tell students to do things and then do not follow up by reinforcing when they comply, you will find the stimulus control of your instructions weakening. In such cases, you will find yourself giving the same instructions over and over again, a sure sign that there was no consequence for responding the first time.

Teaching Rules and Principles. Rules and principles are special cases of directions. Like all directions, they tell how to behave. In addition, however, they imply consequences. The rule "No running in the halls" implies that there will be consequences for running—at the very least being asked to stop. The principle "It is better to reinforce behavior you want than to punish behavior you do not want" tells how to behave if you wish to change behavior. The implied consequence is success.

Just as your statement of a rule or principle can be a discriminative stimulus for your students, their own verbal behavior can be a discriminative stimulus. When you have students memorize a rule, you are teaching them to make a verbal response which can later serve as a discriminative stimulus for them. You then have a chain (see Figure 11.7). The first stimulus is an unsolved problem. The students respond to this stimulus by reciting the rule to themselves. The rule which they say to

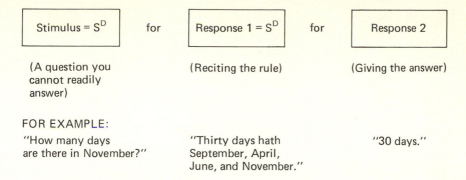

Stimulus = S^D	for	Response 1 = S^D	for	Response 2
(A question you cannot readily answer)		(Reciting the rule)		(Giving the answer)

FOR EXAMPLE:

| "How many days are there in November?" | "Thirty days hath September, April, June, and November." | "30 days." |

Figure 11.7 Diagram Showing How Our Response of Reciting a Rule can Be an S^D for a Second Response.

themselves, is a discriminative stimulus for the behavior which will solve the problem. They are then able to emit the behavior they could not emit before. With the rule, they solve the problem. Suppose, for example, you cannot remember whether a word is spelled with "ie" or "ei." You have a problem in that you cannot emit the appropriate behavior. So you recite the rule to yourself, " 'i' before 'e,' when sounding like 'e,' except after 'c,' " With the rule, you can spell the word correctly. Or, to take another example, answer this question. "How many days are there in November?" Most people do not know off hand. To answer, they recite, "Thirty days hath September, April, June, and November." *Then* they have the answer. These examples are extremely simple, but the chain involved is the same whether we are solving problems in urban design, in history, even in writing a poem. When we come to an impasse—a situation to which we do not readily respond—we engage in "thinking," which is largely the verbal behavior of reciting to ourselves the rules, principles, or verbal directions which have helped us solve problems in the past.

Rule-Governed Behavior. We teach rules and principles because it is a quick way to build appropriate responding in our students. It is easier to teach students to use the " 'i' before 'e' " rule than to teach them how to spell all the "ie" and "ei" words in the English language. It is quicker to teach a student to follow an auto repair manual (which is nothing more than a series of directions) than to teach how to repair all the problems in all the existing makes of cars. It is easier to teach the one rule, "Do what your hostess does," than to teach all the appropriate actions for all possible social functions.

We behave differently, however, when we are following rules than when we have been shaped directly the contingencies themselves. The person who has already learned how to spell the word "receive" behaves differently from one who is "applying the rule." You behave differently when fixing your car if you are following directions in a manual than when you have learned to fix cars by tinkering around. The person who grows up in "society" behaves differently from those who have been told how to behave. In each case, the person who has learned through direct experience behaves more readily and more smoothly. Contingency-shaped behavior is usually more effective than rule-governed behavior.

Rule-Governed Behavior

is behavior which is under the control of rules, in contrast to behavior which has been shaped through direct experience, which is called *contingency-shaped behavior.*

Teaching rules, then, is not enough to get competent behavior. Reciting a rule is *not* the same as doing what the rule says. Students must also follow (apply) the rule if they are to learn the behaviors it specifies. As they follow the rule, they come under the contingencies of responding itself. Their behavior becomes smoother and less hesitant as control by the rule diminishes. After spelling enough words, you no longer need to say the "ie" rule to yourself. The correct behavior seems to come naturally. The same is true of fixing a car, interacting in a social group, or of problem-solving in general.

FACTORS AFFECTING STIMULUS CONTROL— PRINCIPLES FOR TEACHING

If I wanted to bring your behavior under the stimulus control of the light on the milk machine so that you would respond appropriately, what would I do? What factors would affect how rapidly and how thoroughly you learned? First, it would help to tell you the rule, "Light on means you'll get milk." You would learn to respond to the light, however, only if you inserted coins yourself. Even if you did memorize the rule to my satisfaction, you would be likely to forget it if you never went near the milk machine. You have probably forgotten many things you memorized for tests because you never used them. Next, it would be important that the stimulus vary. Without being told the rule, there is no way you could learn to discriminate between light on and light off unless you experienced both conditions. Even with the rule, if you always found the light on, you would stop paying attention to it. You would insert coins "without thinking." The consistency of consequences you received for inserting coins in the S^D and S^Δ conditions would be critical too. If the light had a faulty connection and sometimes was off when it was supposed to be on (or on when it was supposed to be off), you could become "confused." If the inconsistency was great, the light might never gain control over your behavior. You would ignore the light, insert your coins and "take your chances." (If the light had *no* connection with the likelihood of getting milk, it would not be an S^D, and your "try and see" response would then be the appropriate response to make.) Lastly, the brightness of the light would make a difference in how fast you learned. If the light was very faint, so that it was not clear whether it was on or off, you would learn more slowly than if the difference was very noticeable at first.

These, then, are the things to keep in mind when trying to bring about stimulus control—including all the kinds of stimulus control discussed in this chapter:

Principle I: Use Existing Stimulus Control Where Possible. Rules, definitions, and principles enable beginning students to learn more rapidly than they would otherwise. Similarly, by demonstrating or modeling a response, you provide an S^D which increases the students' chance of success. However, learning rules or principles, or watching demonstrations or models is not a substitute for direct experience: we would never expect a student to learn to swim by memorizing rules or watching Olympic swimmers. Similarly, students will not learn problem-solving, creativity, scientific procedures, or any other academic behaviors simply by memorizing rules or by watching someone else perform.

Principle II: Have Students Respond as Frequently as Possible to Stimuli as Varied as Possible. It is only through responding in the presence of different stimuli that the limits of stimulus control are set. The more the students respond to the full range of possible stimuli, the more they learn where those limits lie. The more ways we vary the problems we give our students, then, the more likely they are to respond to the important characteristics and to be free from "giveaway" clues that are useful only in the classroom. Suppose, for example, we want to teach the concept of addition. Our students will need to know when to add and when not to add in order to solve problems in their daily lives. To find out such things as how much several articles will cost, they must add (not subtract, multiply, or divide). They must also learn when not to add, for example, in deciding how many eight-ounce cups a 32-ounce can will fill. The stimuli to which we must make our students respond are the *operations* involved: putting together, splitting into equal parts, and so on.

In the classroom we attempt through word problems to bring students under the kinds of stimulus control they will encounter in daily life. We want students to respond to the *processes* described in the word problems, not to specific "giveaway" clues. If, however, every addition problem has the sentence "How many are there all together?" students will soon respond not to the characteristic of "combining," but to those specific words. Whenever they see "How many are there all together?" they will add, and if they don't see those words they will not add. Or, if a work sheet announces a page of word problems with the heading, "Word Problems in Addition," students need only hunt for numbers and add in order to get the right answers. They do not need to "think," that is, to discriminate between different processes. While they may get their classroom problems correct, students who respond to specific words are under the wrong stimulus control for understanding addition. They will not be able to function effectively in daily life, where their problems will not come with giveaway phrases. To bring students under control of the *processes* involved, we must give them problems with as different wording as possible. That way we can reduce the control of giveaway clues and make it more likely that students will respond to the defining properties of the concepts (or processes) we are trying to teach.

Principle III: Make Sure That Consequences Are Consistent for Responding in the Different Stimulus Conditions. It is not difficult to reinforce only responses in the presence of the discriminative stimulus when working with academic behavior. Most teachers are consistent in what they call "correct" and "incorrect." But consistency is a big problem in nonacademic discriminations. You may wish students to speak only when another student is not speaking (that is, not to interrupt). Someone else talking *should* be an S^Δ for talking; it is the stimulus in the presence of which a response should not be reinforced. However, if you are not consistent and occasionally reinforce someone who interrupts— say, by picking up on his or her point or by listening to the interrupter instead of to the person who was interrupted—no discrimination will occur. Instead of extinction during "someone else's talking," you have intermittent reinforcement. That makes interrupting more persistent, not less.

The same problem is found with all rules. Students are supposed to learn when to talk, when to be silent; where they may and may not smoke; when it is appropriate to criticize, when it is not; and so on. If the consequences are not consistent with the contingencies stated in the rules, students will not follow them.

Principle IV: Make Differences Conspicuous at First. It is easier to teach the difference between a noun and a verb with clear, obvious examples than with examples which are subtle. Students who have been taught that a noun is "the name of an object or thing" and a verb is "a word that shows action or being" will more quickly come under those properties of words if they are first asked to respond to clear examples. They will learn to discrimiate sooner between words like "dog" (clearly a "thing") and "run" (clearly an "action") than between words like "life" and "live," which are more difficult to tell apart.

SUMMARY

A large part of education consists of trying to increase students' sensitivity to their environment. To function effectively in our society, a person must be under the control of many kinds of stimuli—for example, words, numbers, social cues, and so on. Students learn to respond to certain stimuli and not to others and to discriminate among them—responding one way when one stimulus is present but another way when it is absent or another stimulus is present.

The way in which we respond in the presence of a particular stimulus, that is, *what* properties of the stimulus control our behavior, depends on our past history of contingencies of reinforcement. We learn to respond both to properties of stimuli and to particular objects through differential reinforcement for responding in their presence and absence. Properties, or combinations of properties, are called concepts. We do not literally "form" concepts. What happens is that our behavior comes under the control of certain properties of objects and not others. We discriminate between objects which have a particular property and those which do not, and we generalize to objects we have never before encountered—still responding to those properties which define the concept.

In teaching, we create new forms of stimulus control, but we also use the existing control of demonstrations, verbal instructions, and rules. The behavior of imitating and following rules is, however, only a step in the teaching process. Eventually students must come under the control of stimuli as they occur in their environment. They must, in other words, come under the kind of stimulus control which will enable them to deal effectively with their world.

EXERCISES

Concept Check XIA—Discrimination and Generalization (Objective B)

Identify the one main process best illustrated by each example below, using:

D for "Discrimination"
G for "Generalization"
N when neither process is specified

1. You respond the same way to two similar stimuli.
2. You respond one way in the presence of one stimulus but a different way in the presence of a second stimulus.
3. You tell the difference between two objects.
4. A student runs rapidly.
5. Students make a response like one they made before in similar situations.
6. In geometry, Sam uses the Pythagorean Theorem no matter what problem he gets.
7. Judy drinks only soft drinks. She turns down all others.

8. A student correctly operates a machine because of familiarity with a similar machine.
9. A student avoids taking further chemistry courses because of failure in a previous chemistry course.
10. Alice works when the teacher is watching her but stops when the teacher's back is turned.

Answers for Concept Check XIA

1. G
2. D
3. D (In "telling the difference betwen two objects" you are responding differently to them.)
4. N (No stimuli are specified. No doubt the student is both generalizing and discriminating—for example, by running on a path rather than into a thornbush—but since no stimuli are specified, this example does not illustrate either process well.)
5. G
6. G (Sam is making the same response (namely, "using the Pythagorean Theorem"), when given the different stimuli of different problems. He is also, no doubt, discriminating between problems in geometry and other exercises, but the *main* process illustrated by the example is generalization.)
7. D
8. G
9. G (Note that undesirable generalizations can occur.)
10. D (The stimuli to which Alice is responding differently are "teacher watching" and "teacher's back turned.")

Concept Check XIB—Discriminative Stimuli, S^D's and S^Δ's (Objective B)

Write the words which correctly complete each item below.

1. A student answers "64" when asked, "What is the square of 8?" The question is an _____ for the response of _____, but an S^Δ for the response "73."
2. "What does C-A-T spell?" is an S^D for the response _____, but an S^Δ for the response _____.
3. Ms. Maxim allows students to sharpen pencils only if the points are so bad that the pencils won't write, but not if the points are just dull. For the response of sharpening pencils, having a pencil that won't write is an _____, but having a dull pencil which will write is an _____.
4. Mr. Williams is upset that his students cannot tell the difference between factual articles and propaganda. He wants them to use only factual references in papers. One S^D for citing something as a reference, he feels, should be an article which is _____. A propagandistic article should be an _____ for citation.
5. In imitation, the behavior of one person (the model) is an _____ for others to do the _____ thing.

Answers for Concept Check XIB

1. S^D, 64
2. cat, dog (or any other response *except* "cat")
3. S^D, S$^\Delta$
4. factual (or equivalent), S$^\Delta$
5. S^D, same (identical, or equivalent)

Concept Check XIC (Objective D)

Which four examples below illustrate rule-governed behavior (as opposed to contingency-shaped behavior)?

1. You get to a friend's apartment by following written directions.
2. You start to go a new way to classes one day, after discovering that you arrive earlier that way.
3. You have learned by experience.
4. You can tell by the sound and feel that a tennis shot is going to be a good one.
5. You think as you write a paragraph, making sure that it contains only one main idea.
6. You have written enough sentences so that you no longer need to check to make sure that each one contains both a subject and a verb.
7. As you start each step in dissecting your frog, you wait for the student tutor to tell you how to proceed and you find the suggestions helpful.
8. You have drawn so many horses that your pencil seems to guide itself.
9. You are such a good speller that you never have to think about how to spell words.
10. In learning to play the violin, you are careful to imitate your teacher.

Answers for Concept Check XIC

The four examples of rule-governed behavior are numbers 1, 5, 7, and 10. In each, your behavior is under the control of rules: written directions in Number 1, a rule you memorized in Number 5, a tutor's statements in Number 7, and a teacher's demonstration (with the implied rule "Do it like this") in Number 10.

In all of the others, your behavior has been shaped by the natural results of your actions.

PROBLEM-SOLVING EXERCISES (OBJECTIVE C)

For each concept below: *first,* write down the letter of the exercise that would teach the concept better, and *second,* name a property of the examples in the other exercise that needs to be varied in order for students to learn that it is not a defining property of the concept.

Example

1. Concept = ONE-HALF

Directions for both exercises: Circle the figure which is half shaded.

SAMPLE ANSWER: Exercise A teaches the concept of one-half better. Exercise B needs to have the characteristics of shape and size varied since these are not defining properties of "one-half."

---

1. Concept = GREATER NUMBER
   Directions for both exercises: In each box, circle the set that has the greater number.

Exercise A   **Exercise B**

2. Concept = RHYME (the ending *sounds* of words)

   Directions for both exercises: In each row circle the word that rhymes with the first word.

Exercise A

hate	weight	star	eating
say	slight	out	neigh
do	Sue	go	cat

Exercise B

hate	mate	star	eating
say	slight	out	play
due	Sue	go	eat

3. Concept = EXPLANATORY FICTIONS

Directions for both exercises: Which of the statements below is *not* an explanatory fiction?

Exercise A

a. Sue writes well because of high motivation.
b. Tom shoots baskets well because in previous environments he has been reinforced for accuracy in shooting baskets.
c. Sam doesn't progress well because he isn't motivated.
d. Richard works hard because he is very motivated.

Exercise B

a. Sue writes well because of high motivation.
b. Tom shoots baskets well because he is tall.
c. Sam's lack of progress is due to his lack of readiness.
d. Richard works hard because he has a high need to achieve.

Answers for Problem-Solving Exercises

(Note: You may have thought of other properties besides the ones listed here. If you mentioned any of the properties listed or any other one that should be varied, consider yourself correct).

1. Exercise B teaches the concept better.
   Exercise A fails to vary the following properties:
   —spacing or length. (Exercise A always has the longer row contain the greater number so that students cannot learn to discriminate between length and number.)
   —size. (The greater number doesn't necesssarily mean the greater size. To free students from that property of sets, Exercise B has one example in which the set with the greater number [of boxes] has *smaller* boxes. Students must respond to number and *not* to size to get that item correct.)
   —arrangement. (The number of things in a group of objects is independent of how they are arranged. In daily life things are not usually as neatly lined up as in Exercise A.)
2. Exercise A teaches the concept better.
   Exercise B fails to vary the following property:
   —ending spelling. (All of the rhyming words in Exercise B end with the same letters. Students can get all of the correct answers by responding to the ending letters and not to the ending sounds of the words. To make sure that students do not go by looks, Exercise A varies spelling and has a wrong choice ("go"), which looks like the first word ("do"). To get this item correct, the student must respond to sound and *not* to looks.
3. Exercise B teaches the concept better.
   Exercise A fails to vary the following properties (that is, students can get the right answer for the following wrong reasons):
   —length of sentence. (Length is not a defining property of explanatory

fictions. In Exercise A, however, the explanatory fiction stands out by being the longest.)

—kind of language. (Explanatory fictions are not necessarily more technical than other statements, yet the right choice in Exercise A is more technical than the others. Students selecting that answer may be discriminating on technicality of language rather than on the defining properties of explanatory fictions.)

—"give-away" words. (Every choice in Exercise A except the correct one has some form of the word "motivation" in it. Students quickly pick up cues such as this. Explanatory fictions in magazines, texts, and so on, often do not use that word, which is not a defining property of explanatory fictions. To get students to identify explanatory fictions in their daily lives, then, their wording should be as varied as possible.)

IV

Planning ahead

OVERVIEW

The previous chapters of this book have concentrated on what to do when a behavior problem occurs. The following chapters discuss how to plan ahead to prevent problems. Of course, you cannot prevent all possible problems, but you *can* design courses in which students will learn more and will enjoy learning more than in the traditional lecture-discussion class. Part IV discusses how.

Setting objectives— what should your students learn?

OVERVIEW

Chapter Twelve looks at how you as a teacher determine what students should learn.

OBJECTIVES

By the end of the chapter you should be able to:

A. Define student needs in behavioral terms.
B. Define relevance in terms of generalization, both to immediate and long-term situations.
C. Give one reason for each principle below for selecting what to teach:

Principle 1. Teach a few skills well.
Principle 2. Have students apply, rather than just repeat, rules or facts.
Principle 3. Include objectives you feel are important even if they are hard to specify.

D. Tell which of several objectives are most behavioral, using the following criteria:

1. The objective is stated in terms of student behavior.
2. It specifies measurable behavior.
3. It indicates a criteria for acceptable performance.

You are going to teach. Soon 20 or 30 or more students will enter your classroom. How do you determine what will most benefit each of those individuals in the subject areas for which you are responsible? What does each of them most need?

Needs are those behaviors which a person lacks which make or will make life difficult. Our society expects a person to be able to do a wide variety of things. A person who cannot read or write, or hold a job, or interact in socially approved ways will have a difficult time. He or she will be dependent on others for practically every aspect of existence, from getting information to the basic necessities of life. It is the school's

---

Needs

are behaviors which a person lacks which are necessary in order to function effectively and independently both in the present and in the future.

---

job to identify the skills which will enable individuals to function as independent adults and to make sure that they learn them.

WHO SHOULD SET OBJECTIVES?

In deciding what to teach, we must consider not only the students' present but their future. What will benefit them most—not only today, but later, when they grow up? The first grader does not need to be able to read to get along in a first grader's world. The only thing gained by being able to read "Run, Dick, Run" is the approval of the teacher or of peers. Reading is not relevant until later. Similarly, being able to write complete sentences may not be relevant to a particular high school student's *present* daily existence, but it will be crucial in determining the possibilities that will open up in the future.

Although students are in the best position to know what is most relevant for their present lives, they may not be able to see what will be relevant later. Teenagers, especially, are known for being rather short-sighted because of the certainty with which they predict their futures —often wrongly. For example, many young people choose a marriage partner they expect to stay with "until death do us part." No matter how certain they are of their futures, divorce statistics show that for some, at least, life turns out in a way they did not anticipate. When life changes, all the things they were so sure they would never need suddenly may become very important.

No one would question the wisdom of including "driving on hills" in a driver-education course taught in a flat section of Ohio, even if students say it isn't relevant because they don't drive on hills. But we do question the teacher of English or history who makes similar judgments. No teachers *know* what a student will need later in life, but they are probably in a better position to guess than the students. Part of the task of helping someone to learn is selecting what is and is not important. Because a teacher possesses a more objective viewpoint and greater knowledge about a field, the final responsibility for setting objectives is the teacher's.

RELEVANCE

The question of relevance in education today has been raised for good reason. Much of what is taught is not very useful—either for the present or for the future. We all can remember having to memorize names, or dates, or facts, or phrases which we never have used and probably never will. To make learning relevant, some teachers try to use only content which is already familiar to their students. But relevance is not achieved by substituting popular songwriters for state governors or ghetto language for French. Relevance depends on how well whatever is learned generalizes to new situations.

Relevance is a matter of future needs as well as present ones. It is impossible in today's changing world to tell what specific information will be useful in the future. Certain kinds of skills, however, will transfer widely. The "three R's" (reading, writing, and arithmetic) are useful tools for almost any field. So are less tangible skills such as problem-solving strategies, thinking crictically, creating, or working long periods without supervision. And what about the increasing leisure in our society? We might want to teach students to use spare time constructively. Some of these skills can be built into any course, using any content. Any subject, in other words, can be made relevant by teaching basic skills and tools of thinking, creativity, and self-management. It is what students learn to *do* in a course, as much as the particular information they use, that is critical. Some facts are important, too, since one cannot develop skills or apply principles without them, but facts are to *use*, not to memorize. By setting specific objectives for whatever skills the teacher sees as critical for the students' future lives as well as their present preferences, the teacher makes the course relevant. Your students will need to solve problems, think critically, create, work independently, cooperate, and so on, so you should include those skills in your objectives.

Relevance

is the usefulness of skills learned—both for a student's immediate life and for the life he or she may lead many years later.

BEHAVIORAL, OR PERFORMANCE, OBJECTIVES

To determine what any individual student needs, you must be able to tell what he or she can and cannot already do. You must, in other words, be able to *measure* performance in the skills you consider critical. Your objectives, then, must be stated in a way which allows you to tell whether or not your students have reached them. Since the only thing you can measure is behavior, your objectives should be stated behaviorally, that is, in terms of what students should be able to do. The importance of clarifying the behaviors students should exhibit is particularly important for general goals. It is frustrating for students to be told a paper does not show "critical thinking" or that they should try to "get along with others better." What you communicate to your students is that you are not pleased with them, but you have given them little help on how to improve. If, on the other hand, you specify the behaviors required, you let them know how to change. They know what is expected if they hear "You need to state at least two points of view," or, "tell others what they do well, not just what they have done wrong."

Behavioral objectives (also called "performance objectives") are statements of what students should be able to do by the end of a unit of study. Behavioral objectives make it possible to determine what each

---

Behavioral Objectives

are statements of what students should be able to do at the end of a unit of study. They are also called *performance objectives.*

---

student needs and to communicate it. In addition, behavioral objectives encourage the teacher to get students actively involved. With an objective in hand requiring student behavior, it makes sense to have students behave. If an objective states, "The student should be able to write a story conveying at least two different viewpoints about the same event," the teacher is likely to get students writing and then provide help where needed. In contrast, with a nonbehavioral objective such as "to further the understanding of the creative process in short stories," no clear-cut learning activity is suggested. With the latter objective, many teachers will fall back on the lecture method—the one method of teaching in which the teacher gets *no* information on what each student can do or what each student needs.

Sometimes you may have an activity which you feel is valuable for your students but you are not quite sure why. Perhaps you find a "good" article they would benefit by reading, or you have read about an activity which generates tremendous enthusiasm in students and you think it would be fun to try it. There is usually some benefit from an activity you feel is worthwhile. If students cannot do anything better as a result of the experience, then the activity is "busywork" or "entertainment." If the students learn something from the activity, then it is worthwhile taking the time to determine what that is. By pinpoining what behaviors are desired, you can help every student get more out of the experience.

Besides helping you to plan learning experiences, behavioral objectives guide student studying. It is impossible to remember everything one reads or experiences. Some students will concentrate on what is important, some will not. The range of what different individuals consider important is shown in Table I. Nine students in a course for practicing teachers were asked to study *one* page of text for a quiz. After five minutes, instead of a quiz, they were asked to turn over the paper and write a test question themselves. Table I shows the page of text and some of the questions they wrote.

TABLE I   The Variety of Test Items Written for One Page of Text[1]

The so called "teaching machine movement" is not a new development unless the stress is placed on the word movement. The first teaching machine was patented in 1866, although the device did not include all of features that present day auto-instructional devices incorporate. Sidney Pressey, a psychologist, developed a machine shortly prior to 1920 that could produce measurable amounts of learning in students, but after experimenting and publishing his results, he found little enthusiasm among either educators or psychologists.

Pressey's machines were essentially multiple choice testing devices. They differed from pencil-and-paper tests in that the student was informed of the correctness or incorrectness of each answer as soon as it was given. A question appeared in a small window in the front of the machine along with three or four possible answers to the question, and the student selected an answer from those listed by pressing a corresponding button. If he pressed the incorrect button the question remained in the window, an error was tallied on a counter, and the student had to try again. The machine adequately performed its testing function, but what is more important is that students learned to discriminate between right and wrong answers by using the machines, and that they were able to transfer their knowledge to other questions dealing with similar principles. Pressey believed that the use of this sort of device could produce significant changes in the effectiveness of instruction, but in 1932 he wrote,

> The writer has found from bitter experience that one person alone can accomplish relatively little, and he is regretfully dropping further work on these problems. But he hopes that enough may have been done to stimulate other workers, that this fascinating field may be developed.

The impetus that was lacking in the 1920's was ultimately developed by B. F. Skinner, an experimental psychologist who is primarily responsible for the current industry and interest in teaching machines. Skinner (1968) attributes the lack of enthusiasm for Pressey's machines to cultural inertia

[1]From a class for practicing teachers, West Virginia University, Morgantown, West Virginia, 1971.

TABLE I   (Continued)

and the inadequacy of the principles of learning as they were understood in the 1920s. According to Skinner, Pressey and his associates had to work against a background of research and theory in the psychology of learning that was not adequate. This is not to say that psychologists now completely understand the learning processes, but the importance of the concept of learning as one of the cores of psychology has resulted in the development of many effective laboratory techniques for the study of learning both in humans and in less complex organisms. The conditions under which learning does or does not occur are better understood and are more readily defined now than they were forty years ago. It was partly as a result of his extensive research experience that Skinner was able to apply the laboratory methods of producing learning to the development of a teaching machine very different from that developed by Pressey over forty years before.[2]

Five of the nine test items on the text above were:
1. The reason why Pressey failed when he introduced his teaching machine was . . .
   a. lack of financial support
   b. lack of enthusiasm among educators
2. What are the different ways Pressey and Skinner developed their teaching methods?
3. Briefly discuss the principle of Pressey's first "teaching machine," including (1) the method of obtaining the question, (2) the method of giving the answer, (3) the method of obtaining the correct result, (4) the method of scoring.
4. List two reasons for Pressey's abandonment of his study with his teaching machine and explain how these reasons might not apply today.
5. Who continued the work on the teaching machine which was started by Pressey in 1920?

There is quite a variety in the questions. How would you feel if you prepared for Question 1 but got Question 2? If there is this much difference in what nine people can select out of *one* page of text, imagine how much variation there is in a whole chapter or a whole book! Students who do not know what the teacher considers important will waste valuable time trying to remember unimportant sections or they may expend considerable effort trying to find out what the teacher wants (see Figure 12.1). They may look up old tests or talk with other students. If teaching is helping students learn, then *you* should let your students know what to study.

[2]William A. Deterline, *An Introduction to Programed Instruction*, New Jersey, Prentice-Hall, 1962, pp. 9–10.

Figure 12.1 If you don't specify your objectives behaviorally, then tests become a guessing game for students, as in this "Peanuts" cartoon. (Note that the cartoon also shows that specifying objectives doesn't necessarily make them worthwhile or relevant.) Copyright © 1975 United Feature Syndicate, Inc.

HOW TO GO ABOUT SETTING OBJECTIVES

Different teachers have different ways of arriving at behavioral objectives (see Figure 12.2). Some find it easiest to start with general objectives, some prefer to start with texts and materials they will be using or with old tests they have filed away. Some start with general skills such as critical thinking and with central concepts and then try to imagine how they could spot an excellent student. The kinds of things good students can do are their behavioral objectives. Some teachers believe that students should learn how to decide what is important. One of their objectives, then, is for the students to be able to set their own objectives for a unit or for the term, or even for their own future lives.

Whatever method you find easiest for you, the following suggestions should help you to keep your objectives relevant and help you avoid the kind of teaching in which students are "exposed" to a lot but learn to *do* very little.

Principle I—Teach a Few Skills Well. In order for students to apply what they learn to their lives outside school, to future courses, or to their adult lives, their behavior must be fairly well established by the time they leave a course. Students who can add only with great effort

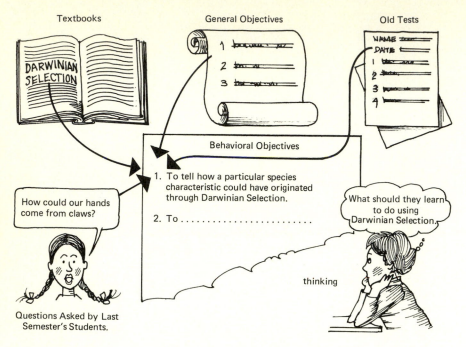

Figure 12.2   Different Ways of Arriving at Behavioral Objectives for a Course.

will hestitate to use math even when it is appropriate for some problem they encounter outside school. To be useful, a skill must be learned well. It is also more reinforcing to really master something you could not do before than to feel shaky about a lot of things. It is tempting for teachers to "cover" a lot of content, but it is better to teach students fewer skills well than many skills poorly. Students should go on to Step 2 not only when they can do Step 1 but when they can do it easily.

Principle 2—Have Students Apply Rather Than Just Memorize. In any subject area there are one or two concepts or principles which occur over and over again. Because of their broad use, concepts and principles are likely to generalize to new situations the students may encounter. Facts and details, in contrast, refer to only one situation. Unless the need for that particular information occurs over and over again, memorized facts will not be useful in new situations. While it is important to learn that 8 times 7 is 56 because you can use the fact for many problems, reciting the Bill of Rights has little general utility. You might rather have your students learn the principles in the Bill of Rights so they can judge which articles apply to problems they may encounter or read about.

It is easy to find basic concepts by flipping through textbooks. You

TABLE II   Some Things Students Can Do to
Show "Concept Formation"

1. Define (preferably in their own words)
2. Give examples
3. Identify things that are examples and things that are not examples of the concept
4. Apply the concepts to given problems and to current life
5. Create problems
6. Design demonstrations to illustrate the concept
7. Illustrate the concept

---

can ask yourself, "What terms occur as chapter headings or are printed in bold type?" In physics you might find "force" stressed in one unit. "Overpopulation" might be a key concept in an ecology class. Muliplication—the process of combining equal groups—is a basic concept in mathematics.

Once you have identified a few key concepts, you can write objectives which ask students to use them in a variety of ways. Some suggestions are given in Table II.

The more students are asked to use principles or concepts in a variety of ways, the more they learn to apply their learning to new situations.

Principle 3—Include Important Objectives Even if They Are Hard to Specify. Many teachers oppose behavioral objectives because they do not appear to consider the broad, but important, outcomes of learning such as feelings, attitudes, cooperation, self-knowledge, and so on. This concern is justified, because it is hard to write behavioral objectives for these areas. If one does *not* specify the behaviors involved, however, neither teachers or students can tell whether or not students have reached these broad goals and which areas need to be pursued further. What happens is that "teaching" in critical areas tends to be sporadic. If cooperation or self-knowledge is important, we should include it in our curriculum. We can start by setting some behavioral objectives we feel are relevant. Perhaps we feel students should learn to set long-term plans or to describe their own strengths and weaknesses. As we go along, we can add others. If we do not look at the behaviors involved in "important areas," how can we teach them? The fact that our schools are so notably weak in producing behavioral change in exactly the areas instructors say are critical may be due to the fact that teachers literally do not know *what* to teach. By specifying at least some of the behaviors which make up seemingly intangible objectives, we can at least start to work on them.

STATING OBJECTIVES BEHAVIORALLY[3]

A good behavioral objective meets three criteria: (1) it is stated in terms of the student; (2) it specifies measurable behavior; and (3) it indicates a criteria for acceptable performance.

Stating Objectives in Terms of the Student. To write a behavioral objective we first state the objective as student behavior. Instead of, "This course covers the basic of . . . ," we need to write, "In this course the students will learn to . . . ." Instead of, "The goal of the language arts program is to expose students to . . . ," we write, "The goal of the language arts program is for students to be able to . . . ."

Activities are sometimes confused with behavioral objectives. Activities describe what students will do *during* instruction but not what they should be able to do as a result of their experiences. A statement such as "The students will read four Hemingway novels," for example, tells what the students will do, but it is not an objective because it does not tell what the students will get *out* of their experience. An objective, in contrast, would state what the students should learn to do as a result of their reading, such as "to describe Hemingway's view of women, using specific scenes from at least two of his novels to illustrate your view." The objective is the final behavior, not what one does to get there.

Many teachers find it helpful to start writing behavioral objectives by using a lead-in phrase such as "By the end of this unit (course), the student will be able to . . . ." In completing that sentence one is set to write objectives in terms of the student. The lead-in can be written once at the top, with the objectives listed below, as is done for each of the chapters in this book.

Specifying Measurable Behavior. To get the students' behavior in measurable terms (Criteria 2 for a behavioral objective) is a bit more difficult. Words like "understand," "know," and "appreciate" creep in. One cannot see or hear students "understanding," "knowing," or "appreciating." We must decide what students *do* that makes us conclude they "have understanding." Like pinpoints in precision teaching, we need to state goals so we can tell when students have met them. We can see many behaviors, such as describing, putting together, writing, defining, defending a position, solving a problem, creating a work of art, and so on. They are what we use as evidence of "understanding," "knowing," or "appreciating," and they are our behavioral objectives.

Setting Criteria for Acceptable Performance. Usually the most difficult part of writing objectives is establishing criteria for acceptable perform-

---

[3]For a more extensive discussion of objectives and for exercises on writing objectives, see J. S. Vargas, *Writing Worthwhile Behavioral Objectives*, New York, Harper & Row, 1972. (Paperback)

ance. It is easy to decide that students should be able to write a story, or create a work of art, or set their own objectives. But how will you and the students tell what characteristics the students' products need in order to meet your objectives? As students put it, "Is this good enough?" You may find that it becomes easier to set criteria if you pretend that you are grading the students' final performance. What would you look for in their works? What kinds of differences would there probably be between what your best student and what your worst student would produce? We all grade on *some* basis. We have to set criteria in order to hand in grades. It is too bad when we delay setting standards until final grade time and only then discover what our criteria in fact were. We may think, "No, no. That's not it at all. A direct comparison should have been included." For a work of art, we may say "That's fantastic— such a novel use of materials! Their unique characteristics were really used to advantage." By final grade time, it is too late to help students. How much more helpful it would have been to tell the students at the beginning. "You should be able to make direct comparisons . . . ," or "The objective is to stretch your imagination—by that I mean to use materials in novel ways, but ones which utilize the particular characteristics of the materials."

It is obviously impossible to determine all the criteria when asking students to create or design, but the more you can tell them, the better it will be. You can at least outline some of what makes an effective product or the kinds of things last semester's students did well or badly in order to help this semester's students do better. Setting criteria is a continual process. We all gain more and more ideas of what misconceptions students are likely to have and we learn what to say to help them produce more original and more effective work.

INDIVIDUALIZING INSTRUCTION

To individualize you must treat each student differently. You must have each person work on what he or she most needs and skip what is already mastered. How can you keep in mind how each student does on each of the skills you feel he or she will need? You can't. But if you have a list of behavioral objectives for your courses, you can keep records relatively easily. Behavioral objectives become a kind of checklist—a kind of insurance that no student is missing something just because he or she is quiet or looks attentive, or because you forgot to check to see whether or not the person could do it.

Objectives can be used in many ways to individualize. In some programs each student progresses through a curriculum of behavioral objectives at his or her own rate. When students master one skill they move on to the next. In order to let each student progress at an individual rate, the teacher needs to organize materials so that everyone can be on a different lesson. Those teachers who find it too difficult to keep track of 30 students all doing different tasks *can* individualize even though they keep all students on the same unit at the same time. One way is to hand out a unit guide with behavioral objectives written on it, such as those at the beginning of each chapter in this book. Students are tested to find out which skills they already have, and they work on those areas in which they are weakest. After studying, they take a test to see whether they have learned all the skills, and if not, they are sent back to work more on those areas which they've not yet mastered, perhaps using the more advanced students as peer tutors.

With a standard set of objectives you can individualize not only what skills students work on but also learning experiences. There are many different ways of achieving any final objective. Students who are asked to "be able to diagram the thematic structure of a piece of music and note all key modulations" can learn equally well on Mozart or Bob Dylan. One way to individualize, then, is to give students the objectives and let them select examples for the learning they will do to meet them.

In most educational programs there are essential skills and optional skills. Behavioral objectives can include both. The list of objectives can then be used as a kind of shopping list. Certain staples are needed first, but then other things can be added according to the students' tastes.

SUMMARY

Checking each student's progress on a list of behavioral objectives makes the teacher aware of what each student needs and of each student's progress from week to week. It alerts the teacher to basic problems which are often overlooked.

Whenever a teacher says "I thought you knew that," or, "Didn't you cover this last year?" the teacher is revealing a lack of specific knowledge of what the students can and cannot do. That information is essential for determining individual needs and it is too important to just try to remember. We make shopping lists so we won't forget what groceries we need. Surely our students are important enough for us to note their needs in writing too. Behavioral objectives remind us what to look for so we won't leave out any critical skill. They can give the teacher freedom to let students go off in their own directions without losing track of what each student is accomplishing and what he or she still needs to learn in order to have a successful future.

EXERCISES

Concept Check XIIA—Behavioral Objectives (Objective D)

Which six of the following objectives are most behavioral?

1. The students will demonstrate proficiency in fourth grade handwriting.
2. The teacher will show how three major wrestling holds are performed.
3. The student will be able to use the principles of experimental control in the work he or she does in connection with science labs.
4. The student will be able to correctly assemble the plastic model of the human ear given only the parts.
5. The students will list any ten of the basic elements in order of mass (using the periodic table of the elements).
6. To be able to run one mile in less than eight minutes.
7. To have a working knowledge of the amendments of the Constitution.
8. To write one original paragraph of at least six complete sentences.
9. To classify any of the foods you eat into one of the four basic food groups.
10. To tell in your own words how Radical Behaviorism differs from Methodological Behaviorism on the issues of scientific method and the subject matter of psychology.

Answers for Concept Check XIIA

The six most behavioral objectives are numbers 4, 5, 6, 8, 9, and 10.

Number 1 does not specify what the student must do to "demonstrate proficiency." Those behaviors need to be specified.

Number 2 is written in terms of what the *teacher* will do. It should be rewritten to specify what the *students* are expected to do.

Number 3 does not specify behavior. It needs to be rewritten to say what the student who is "using the principles of experimental control" is doing. Is he or she following written lab procedures, designing experiments which have features of experimental control, analyzing what parts of an experimental procedure provide control, or what? The objective does not help you visualize the behavior which is wanted.

Number 7 "having a working knowledge" does not specify behavior. The objective needs to be rewritten to specify what a person "with a working knowledge" can do that a person without that "knowledge" cannot do.

Designing learning sequences to shape complex behavior

OVERVIEW

Chapter Thirteen discusses how to design learning sequences—activities, exercises and work sheets—to teach complex skills, using the principles for shaping behavior.

OBJECTIVES

By the end of the chapter you should be able to:

A. Identify the strengths and weaknesses of given teaching procedures according to the principles of shaping:
    1. Active responding by the student
    2. Immediate reinforcement (or feedback)
    3. Successive approximation: small steps; lower error rate
    4. Progression depends on mastery
B. Identify examples of the following successive approximation techniques:
    1. Ask the student to select before asking him or her to produce.
    2. Go from simple to complex and from part to whole.
    3. Withdraw prompts and help as soon as possible.
    4. Go from easy to fine discriminations.
C. Select the best instructional step for given situations using the principles in Objective B above.

PRINCIPLES OF SHAPING

Thanksgiving was over and the harvest was done. Time for reading.
Mama took us one by one after supper to a corner away from distractions.
She handed us the Bible and, with a serious face made more solemn still
by the flickering candle, had us read. The little ones started with "In the
beginning God created the Heavens and the Earth." They had to point
to the words as they read them, so Mama could be sure they hadn't just
memorized the passage. Mama encouraged us, helping along, until finally
we began to recognize some words. Gradually as the winter months
passed, more and more words became familiar.

Such is how the teaching of reading in pioneer days might have
been described. In many ways it was good teaching. Mother usually
worked with one child at a time and had her child read rather than
listen to her as she read. She let the child know whether each word
read was right or wrong, and when the child finally got a difficult
word right, she would reward him or her with a nod, or say "good for
you," or make some other encouraging comment. When a word was too
difficult, she would give a hint or read it herself if she thought her child
couldn't guess it. In fact, there is only one real difference between the
way the pioneer woman taught reading and the way you would tutor a
child today if you were given that job, and that is what you would
choose as reading materials. You would probably not start your five-
year-old out on the Bible.

The trouble with the Bible as a beginning reader is that it's too
hard. The sentences are too long and there are too many big words
for a five-year-old. To teach beginning reading you would look for a
book with easy words and short sentences so that your student could
more easily experience success.

Success is what shaping is all about. You shape behavior by reinforcing the best of what the students already do. You selectively
reinforce not just what you think they can do but what you *see* them do
at a high rate. Your students, therefore, get reinforced frequently; they
are right most of the time and they feel success.

Shaping

is the process of building an operant by reinforcing only those
responses that are closest to it. When the operant we want is a
response to a certain kind of stimulus (such as answers to a question or solutions to problems) shaping also requires a "building"
in the stimuli to be presented. The first questions or problems
given to students are not as complex as those we expect them to
solve later. This breaking down of stimulus materials is a major
part of the design of instructional materials.

The behavior you start reinforcing may not look much like the behavior you are after. Take reading, for example. You want the students to read sentences, but you will probably start by having them tell the names or sounds of letters, or perhaps read simple words. Saying "ah" for the letter "a" is a long way from reading a passage such as the one you are reading now. A few more examples may help.

Nursery School. In Chapter eight we looked at a three-year-old nursery school child called Dee. Dee, you remember, wouldn't walk at school; she crawled from place to place and, of course, didn't join in any of the games the other children played. The teachers decided to try to get Dee walking by reinforcement, but they couldn't reinforce walking because she didn't walk at all. They had to shape walking "step by step" so to speak. They attended to Dee when she was *close* to walking. The closest she got was when she pulled herself up to a sink or table, so they started by reinforcing that. Whenever Dee pulled herself up, a teacher would go to her and chat briefly. The rest of the time, when she crawled or sat on the floor, the teachers left her alone. The first morning of this reinforcement procedure, Dee began pulling herself up more and more often. As she got close to standing, the teachers continued to reinforce Dee's "best"—the closest thing Dee did to walking. At the same time they stopped reinforcing Dee's "worst"—what had been her best before. The final performance, walking and running around like the other children, was very different from what they had to start reinforcing.

College. Dr. Hedstrom, college counselor, used shaping too. His problem: James Newworth came in one day very upset because he couldn't get himself to study.

"What's the closest thing you do to studying?" asked Dr. Hedstrom.

James answered, "I go to the library, sit down, open my books, and then—I don't know. . . . Well, you know, maybe a pretty girl walks by, or I can't decide which subject to study. I'm behind in chemistry and in French and I'm *three* assignments behind in. . . ."

"You *do* go to the library, though," Dr. Hedstrom interrupted, cutting off the chain of complaints. "Do you think you could study for just ten minutes?"

"Yes, I guess so."

Dr. Hedstrom and James worked out a program. James bought a kitchen timer and took it to the library after class the next day. When he sat down to study, he set it to ten minutes, opened the book on the top of the pile of books he'd carried in, and worked until the timer rang. Then, feeling very silly, he stopped and left. Dr. Hedstrom had insisted he stop no matter whether he felt like working more or not.

"You see, leaving the library is reinforcement," Dr. Hedstrom had said. "If you feel like studying more when it's time to leave, good. By leaving then, you make 'feeling like studying' more likely to occur again." Each day James carried out the program. By the end of the week, it was almost hard to leave. He returned to Dr. Hedstrom and reported his success.

"Do you think you could set the timer for 20 minutes each day next week?" asked Dr. Hedstrom.

"Oh, I get it," replied James. "Then it'll be 40 minutes, then an hour. That's it, isn't it? How simple!"

The two examples may seem different but they both use the following four principles of shaping:

1. *Active Responding by the Student:* It is the student who takes each step of improved behavior, not the teacher or counselor.
2. *Immediate Reinforcement:* Each time the student does his or her "best," he or she is reinforced immediately. In a sense, the reinforcement interrupts the good behavior.
3. *Successive Approximation:* The student is reinforced at first for what he or she *already* does. Steps requiring improvement are broken down into small enough units that the student has a high rate of success. (For problems or exercises, the student should be right nine times out of ten tries.)
4. *Progression Depends on Mastery:* The student goes on to a more difficult step as soon as the previous one is mastered and only when it is mastered.

As James said, "How simple!" The principles seem like common sense. Almost all of us would follow them without thinking about it if we were tutoring someone. If we had to teach Robert to read or to write complete sentences, to describe the major social movements in England in the nineteenth century, to serve correctly in tennis, or to plan a nutritionally sound menu, we would get him actively responding by reading, writing, describing, serving, or planning. We would give him immediate feedback after each response by telling him whether or not he was right. If he made a lot of mistakes, we would back up to an easier task and we would progress only when Robert was ready; that is, when he had mastered the previous step. If you think of what you would do if you had to tutor a student in your own subject area, you will probably think of strategies using the same four principles.

But something happens when we go from tutoring an individual to teaching a group. Common sense goes out the window and we "teach" as we have been "taught." We lecture or give demonstrations, thus eliminating active responding. We take home papers to grade overnight, thus depriving the students of immediate reinforcement. We give the same work sheet to a whole class regardless of what John and Judy can or can't do, thus insuring that at least half of the students get something too hard or too easy. Where is the successive approximation? And finally, in a triumph of administrative convenience over reason, we progress not when the *students* are ready but when a predetermined school calendar says to progress. We are supposed to assign Chapter 7 on November 10 regardless of whether the students have mastered Chapter 6, or for that matter, whether or not they can *already* do everything taught in Chapter 7.

It is difficult, but not impossible, to use the principles of shaping in a regular classroom with, say, 30 students. Some suggestions follow.

Active Responding. How active is active responding? The more you can get students to respond, the better. If you were tutoring *one* student, how many times would he or she respond during one 50-minute class

---

Active Responding

is *student* behavior rather than teacher behavior. Lessons in which *each* student talks, writes, solves problems, or otherwise responds at a high rate are said to require *active responding.*

---

period? In math, it might be 100 times or more. In history, perhaps 30. There you have your standard. You should aim for 100 responses a period from *each* student in math, about 30 a period from each student in history, if that is what you'd get if you were tutoring.

When we look at the number of responses each student makes in a class, some techniques that look full of active responding come up short. I once was talking to a teacher just outside her classroom when I noticed she was looking over my shoulder into her classroom with obvious pride. I turned and looked too. It was a tenth grade English class. A student teacher was leading a discussion. The desks had been pushed back and students sat on chairs arranged in two large rows along the long walls, with a circle of seven chairs in the middle. The student teacher was part of the circle, sitting on a desk with her feet on a chair. She was leaning forward, listening intently while two of the students in the circle argued vehemently. Three or four others jumped into the conversation and the volume picked up as emotions increased.

The teacher beside me was getting excited too. "Look at that," she said. "Look at that involvement. What a discussion!"

It was true. It was an excellent discussion. The seven or eight students were talking at a great rate. But what about the others? There were two long rows of six or seven students who were not talking. How profitable was the discussion for them? I looked along the rows. The students near the circle were sitting leaning toward the group. One was contributing to the argument—the others, watching. As you moved away from the circle, the students sat farther and farther back in their seats, like a wave falling back from its crest. At the far end, a couple of students sat slouched back in their chairs, feet outstretched, only half listening.

I did a rough calculation. Twenty-two students in the class—seven I had seen talk, three of whom were talking at a high rate. That meant that two-thirds of the students hadn't said one word, although I guessed that half of them were at least listening. And it was a *good* discussion as classroom discussions go!

If you had 22 of your friends standing around at a cocktail party and only seven did any talking at all, would you be happy with the "active involvement"? No, you would hustle around trying to get *everyone* involved. You would probably start by splitting up the large group into smaller ones. It is physically impossible to have everyone talking up in a circle of ten or more people. A classroom is no different. If you really want discussion, you should arrange for everyone to talk at a high rate with as much effort as if you were hosting a party. You can start by breaking a large group into small ones (see Figures 13.1 and 13.2).

Figure 13.1   Even a *good* class discussion fails to get a high rate of responding from every student. While one student is talking, others must sit and listen, or, like the two girls at the table in the back, wait for their turn to respond. (Central Elementary School, Morgantown, W. Va. Courtesy of Robert L. Gay, The Associated Press.)

Figure 13.2 In contrast, by breaking the class into small discussion groups you can get more responding per student. This picture shows a continuation of the discussion pictured in Figure 13.1 after students were told to work out their ideas in small groups. Note how much more actively these four students are participating. (Central Elementary School, Morgantown, W. Va. Courtesy of Robert L. Gay, The Associated Press.)

But perhaps it is not discussion you want. Perhaps you wish to present some content, and rather than lecture, you want some class participation:

"Today we're going to talk about adjectives. I'm going to write three sentences on the board and underline the adjectives. You see if you can tell what adjectives *do*." Mr. Monstrate writes. . . .

The boy hit the <u>red</u> ball.
The <u>old</u> shirt hung on the nail.
I ate my <u>first</u> egg.

"Can you figure out what an adjective does? (pause) "Suzi."
Suzi: "It describes something."
Mr. Monstrate: "Good. It describes something. An adjective describes

something. What does 'red' describe?" "Frank."

Frank: "Ball."

Mr. Monstrate: "That's right. Red describes ball." He points to the words as he says them. "<u>Old</u> describes <u>shirt</u>, <u>first</u> describes <u>egg</u>. So we can say that an adjective is a word that describes something. What kind of a word does an adjective describe? Sam."

There is a pause. Sam looks uncomfortable.

"Joe."

Joe: "It describes a noun."

Mr. Monstrate: "Right. An adjective describes a noun. We say it modifies a noun. Sometimes it tells which one we're talking about. The boy didn't hit any old ball; he hit the red one."

"See if you can pick out the adjectives in the sentences I write on the board." He writes three sentences. The students watch. "Jo Ellen, you try the first one."

This is a typical question-and-answer presentation. In perhaps three minutes, the teacher asked for four answers—not a bad rate—but how many questions did *each* student answer? Except for Suzi, Frank, Joe, and Jo Ellen (who each responded once), we can't even be sure that other students answered any questions correctly, even if they raised their hands to be called on.

If Mr. Monstrate had asked each student to write the answers to each question, he could have had everyone responding. By looking quickly around the class, he could then have seen how each student was doing. If Mr. Monstrate had a free period before his grammar class, he could even have run off a "fill-in" sheet like the following (see Chapter Fourteen for another example):

Sample Fill-in Sheet on Grammar

(1) An adjective _____ something.

(2) In the sentence on the board, "red" describes _____.

(3) An adjective describes a _____.

(4) Write the adjectives in the sentences on the board.

   Sentence #1_____ Sentence #2_____ Sentence #3_____

The fill-in sheet provides for active responding in a lecture or question-and-answer presentation. It is not perfect shaping, however, because each student can't progress when ready but must keep pace with the instructor. Once all the students are responding at a high rate, however, teachers become more aware of differences between students. More than one class which started off as a lecture with fill-in sheets has broken up into peer tutoring, small groups, or self-instruction when differences in student behavior made it clear that not everyone needed the same thing at the same time.

Immediate Feedback

One stereotype of a teacher found in television shows or G-rated movies is of an attractive, young, but somewhat shabbily dressed person carrying a stack of papers to correct.

Like most stereotypes, the picture isn't very accurate, but it does contain a bit of truth. Many teachers do spend a lot of time grading papers. Most consider it a chore—a necessary evil. The exercises that are the most boring are the ones with one right answer, like spelling, grammar, or math. With all their training and intelligence, many teachers can be found, day in and day out, checking lists of answers against an answer key: "27—27 right, 18—18 right, 28—35 wrong." And so on.

Why grade papers? We grade papers to give feedback and to evaluate performance. But the feedback from graded papers is too late to help learning. By the time Sandra sees that 28 is wrong, she has forgotten why she wrote 28 in the first place. Students needs to know *right away* whether or not they are on the right track.

IMMEDIATE FEEDBACK

is a consequence that occurs as a response is being completed or just after it has been completed. To be immediate, the consequence must occur before a second response is made. Immediate feedback may occur naturally or it may be added. The high jumper gets natural immediate feedback for each jump from whether or not the bar falls down. He or she may also get immediate feedback which is added by a coach commenting on form as each jump is completed. In the classroom, feedback is often a mark indicating whether a response is right or wrong.

It's easy for a tutor to give immediate reinforcement, but how do you do it with 30 active students? You can't—at least not directly. So you must arrange for students to get feedback from some other source. First, you can use materials which give immediate feedback, such as programmed instruction or exercises with answers in the back of the book. Better still, some of the newer materials use a chemical process and a magic pen: you mark a choice, and if you are correct, a stripe, or the word "RIGHT," or some other mark appears (see Figure 13.3). If you have chosen incorrectly, you get a solid gray line, or the words "TRY AGAIN," or some other indicator. Such materials are good, too, to prevent peeking ahead to the answer. You can't find out the right answer without committing yourself to one choice or another. Special sheets for use with ditto masters are also available so that you can make your own work sheets with invisible print which a special pen reveals.

Second, use other students. Students working in pairs can function

Figure 13.3 Many materials now have immediate feedback built into them, like these work sheets which reveal a stripe when the correct answer is marked. (Courtesy of Robert L. Gay, The Associated Press.)

like tutors for each other. Advanced students can take less advanced students. Or you can check the first ones finished with some unit and have them become checkers for the next students coming through.

Third, you can increase the amount of immediate feedback by setting criteria and letting students evaluate themselves. This is particularly effective in high school or college, where there is no single right answer. For a test or paper done in class, you can make up a model "good" paper for students to use as a standard for judging their own. Often a good paper from a past semester makes a good model. Students pick up the model paper when they hand in one copy of their paper. In class, they grade a second copy of their paper and revise, if necessary. You, the teacher, can grade only a few papers chosen at random. If you grade them during class time, you can compare your evaluation with your students' and discuss differences and similarities on the spot.

SUCCESSIVE APPROXIMATION

The heart of shaping lies in *successive approximation*—the method of progression. It is the art in teaching: the sensitivity to students' needs.

Successive Approximations

are the steps the *student* takes as his or her behavior slowly progresses from its initial level to the final level desired.

Students should progress as fast as possible, but not so fast that they get difficult tasks so soon that they become discouraged. If a student is having problems, we must find a step that is small enough for the student to take successfully but that is still large enough for progress.

Although only experience can give a teacher a feel for how to break down learning steps, there are some rules of thumb which may help you when planning learning steps or when faced with a student who can't seem to do a particular problem.

Rules of Thumb for Breaking Down Instruction into Successive Approximations

Rule 1—Ask the student to select before asking him or her to produce.
Rule 2—Go from simple to complex and from part to whole.
Rule 3—Give the student only as much help as he or she needs to be successful and withdraw prompts and cues as soon as possible.
Rule 4—Go from easy to fine discriminations.

Rule 1. Ask the student to select before asking him or her to produce. It is easier to recognize a correct answer than to produce one from memory. Try it yourself. Which question below would be easier for you to answer right now?

QUESTION *A*—Select the four characteristics of shaping from the list
below (without looking back):

1. Active responding
2. Immediate feedback
3. Spontaneous recovery
4. Successive approximation
5. Progression depends on mastery

QUESTION *B*—Write the four characteristics of shaping (without looking
back): _____

_____

_____

If you are like most people, Question A is easier than Question B.
For Question A you need only select among choices, but in Question B
you must produce or recall the characteristics from memory.

When you are teaching, all of the terms, concepts, formulas, principles, and so on, which are familiar to you are likely to be new to your
students. They are in the same boat as you are when presented with
Question B or when you've been introduced to several new people at a
party. It's not so easy to *recall* (produce) an unfamiliar definition, or
list, or name, but if someone says, "Was it Markle Q. Svezinski?" you
can say, "Yes," or, "No."

Almost a century ago, a teacher named Segun realized that "select"
is a step which comes before "produce." He wrote three steps for teaching which are quoted in Maria Montessori's book, *The Montessori
Method*. See if you can find the "select" and "produce" steps in their
method.

FIRST PERIOD. The association of the sensory perception with the name.
For example, we present to the child, two colours, red and blue. Presenting
the red, we say simply, "This is red," and presenting the blue, "This is
blue." Then, we lay the spools upon the table under the eyes of the child.
SECOND PERIOD. Recognition of the object corresponding to the name. We
say to the child, "Give me the red,' and then "Give me the blue."
THIRD PERIOD. The remembering of the name corresponding to the object.
We ask the child, showing him the object, "What is this?" and he should
respond, "Red."[1]

The second period is a "select" step. "Give me the red" is a multiple-
choice question with two choices, red and blue. In the third period, the
student must "produce" the correct color name. Whenever you have a
student who cannot answer a recall question, such as "What is the name
of a four-sided figure with only two parallel sides?" or "What is the name
of this?" when you are pointing to a particular part under the hood of a

[1]Maria Montessori, *The Montessori Method*, New York, Schocken, 1964, pp.
177–178.

car, you needn't give the answer. You can have the student *select*: "Well, is it a parallelogram or a trapezoid?" or "Is it the carburetor or the radiator?" When you are planning a lesson, you can build in steps in which students select the correct part, term, concept, or whatever, before you ask them to produce it themselves.

Rule 2. Go from simple to complex and from part to whole. The beginning student of computer programming will be more successful tackling a simple problem than a complex one and a part of a large program rather than the whole thing. The student who cannot pronounce a whole word may be able to get it by reading it syllable by syllable. We are proceeding from simple to complex when we learn to add one-digit numbers before two-digit ones, to drive in a quiet area before we drive downtown in rush hour, to play "Pop Goes the Weasel" on the clarinet before "The Flight of the Bumble Bee," and to analyze a simple poem before *Paradise Lost*.

We proceed from part to whole when we learn a swim stroke by practicing using our hands and our breathing (standing waist deep in water) separately from our kick and then later combining them. Similarly, in learning first nouns and verbs, then adding pronouns, adjectives and adverbs, then other parts of speech, we are going from part to whole.

Rule 3. Give the student only as much help as he or she needs to be successful and withdraw prompts and cues as soon as possible. Suppose you were going to learn to fly an airplane. Using Rule 2 (simple to complex), you would probably start with a small single engine propellor plane (simple) rather than with a Boeing 747.

Your instructor would have you sit in the left-hand seat in the cockpit, and after you were airborne the instructor would have you make some turns. Your instructor would probably have you use the steering wheel only, teaching you to use your feet to control a rudder later (Rule 2—part to whole). Other than that, there's no way to make the task simpler—you can't learn to turn one wing, then the other, then the whole plane. So the instructor demonstrates first, and now it's your turn. You turn the wheel left and the plane obediently tilts. Your instructor talks: "As soon as you are in the turn, straighten the wheel. The plane will continue by itself." You feel your wheel straighten out as the instructor works the dual control. The plane remains tilted and turning. "Apply a little back pressure. The plane will tend to descend in a turn, so you need to pull back." You pull back and the plane rises. "That's right. Not too much now," your instructor says. Now *you* are flying the airplane (making the *whole* response) but you are getting verbal help. Your instructor will continue to give you "crutches"—instructions and, if needed, physical help—until you can finally make the response unaided.

Then, going from part to whole, you will learn to ascend and descend, to take off and land—each time following Rule 3: "Let the student respond with help at first, and withdraw that help as soon as possible." Finally the day comes when help is withdrawn altogether. You go home with your shirttail cut off—the sign of a successful first solo flight.

Probably the most common help that teachers first give and then gradually withdraw is verbal instructions or rules. When teaching children to tie their shoes, teenagers to use a balance scale, education majors to operate a movie projector, it is helpful to "talk" them through the procedure first. Printed instructions are also verbal crutches. At first learners follow the instructions at every step. Their behavior is rule governed. But as they behave, their behavior becomes contingency shaped as they "get the feel" of assembling, operating, or whatever the instructions are about.[2]

A good teacher should likewise fade out of the picture, giving help only *as needed*, not taking over. A sign in a nursery school for three- and four-year-olds read: DO NOT DO ANYTHING FOR THE STUDENT THAT HE CAN DO FOR HIMSELF. It's good advice for any level.

It is hard not to interfere with learning by giving too much help. It is easier to put a child's boots on for the youngster than to have the child do it while you give encouragement and guidance. It takes more patience to watch students struggle with a long division problem or fit a part into a machine than to do it for them. But they must do it themselves in order to learn. Similarly, when elementary school students ask how to solve a word problem, high school students have difficulty dissecting a frog, or college students can't seem to translate a sentence into Russian, the temptation is to show them by doing the task yourself. Students will learn more, however, if you let them do things themselves, giving only as many hints as necessary: "Do you remember the rule you used last time?" "Can you think of another problem like it?" and so on. As the students are successful, you give less and less help until they perform alone.

Rule 4. Go from easy to fine discriminations. Everything we learn involves discriminating. From flying to naming tools to reading, we learn to respond differently to different stimuli or tasks. The pilot discriminates between a runway and a mountain top, a handyman discriminates among different tools, and the reader discriminates between words. Whenever we call something by a name, we are discriminating between it and other objects or concepts.

Some discriminations are more obvious than others. Students new to a woodworking shop might have difficulty discriminating between types

[2]See pages 199–200 for a discussion of the distinction between rule-goverend and contingency-shaped behavior.

of lumber. Faced with a stack of boards, they might not be able to tell the spruce apart from the white pine or balsam or oak. If the instructor gives them different woods to learn which have a similar color and grain, the students are bound for failure. Instead, to start with, the learners would have more success with very different woods; with very easy discriminations. For example, even a beginner can tell redwood (which is reddish, as its name would suggest) from knotty pine (which is whitish with knots in it).

What looks like inborn *in*ability to discriminate may be simply inadequate successive approximation, or starting with too fine a discrimination. Even people who call themselves tone deaf, for example, can tell the difference between a high note sung by a soprano and a low note sung by a man with a deep voice. That is the first approximation for telling pitches apart. By having the tone deaf student tell which note is higher and slowly decreasing the distance between tones—with, of course, immediate reinforcement for correct responding—good pitch discrimination can be taught. For the very young, the mentally retarded, or the physically handicapped, the steps must be smaller and progress slower, but anyone who can respond at all can learn to discriminate *better* if given easy enough discriminations to start with. (See Table I for examples of easy and fine discriminations). Once students have learned to make the more obvious discriminations, they can progress to examples which are more difficult to discriminate between.

What may be an obvious difference to you as a teacher may not be obvious to the beginner. To the woodshop instructor, the woods are as different as peas and beans are to you and me. To the dentist, the dark areas on dental X-rays which indicate cavities are clearly different from other dark spots; to you and me they all look alike. To the classical music expert, it is difficult to see how anyone could mistake Mozart for Beethoven. To others, Mozart, Haydn, and Beethoven all sound the same.

For Sandy who is learning to read dental X-rays or to identify composers, or for any student who is starting out to learn any discrimination, one way to insure success is to gather very clear or obvious examples for a first successive approximation, introducing subtleties later. The student then progresses from easy to fine discriminations.

WHEN TO USE THESE PRINCIPLES

The chances are that you have used these methods already. You may have used them in helping your niece or your roommate with homework. At the very least, you used them in studying for tests yourself. You may ask, "Why bother with all these fine discriminations between ways of breaking down material when I do them already without thinking about it?"

TABLE I   Examples of Easy and Fine Discriminations

Directions for the Student: "Name the letters."
An EASY Discrimination:
   O I B
A FINE Discrimination:
   O C G

Directions for the Student: "Circle the nouns."
An EASY Discrimination:
   The dog ran.
A FINE Discrimination:
   Seeing is believing.

Directions for the Student: "Mark X in front of the objective which is more behavioral."
An EASY Discrimination:
   ☐ To understand Beethoven and Mozart and their styles.
   ☐ To tell whether Beethoven or Mozart wrote a piece from hearing it.
A FINE Discrimination:
   ☐ To demonstrate ability in doing math word problems at fifth grade level.
   ☐ To solve math word problems at fifth grade level.

Directions for the Student: "Which teacher, X or Y, progresses from easy to fine discriminations?"
An EASY Discrimination:
   —Teacher X has kindergarten students learn to name the colors red, blue, and yellow before introducing the more confusing colors of pink and orange.
   —Teacher Y has kindergarten students learn to name the similar colors pink, red, and orange before introducing blue and yellow.
A FINE Discrimination:
   —Teacher X has kindergarten students learn to name "circle," "triangle," and "square" drawn on paper before naming the shapes of objects around the room.
   —Teacher Y has kindergarten students learn to name the shapes of objects around the room (circle, square, or triangle) before progressing to shapes on paper.

The examples under EASY discriminations are easier for the beginner to tell apart than those under FINE discriminations.

Have you as a student ever had difficulty grasping something you were supposed to learn? You read it over and over again, and it just didn't make sense. Perhaps you asked someone else—a classmate or teacher—to explain, but it still wasn't clear. Now put yourself in the teacher's shoes for a moment. Here is a student who doesn't seem to be getting the point, no matter how many times he or she goes over the material. You've explained it ten times to no avail. That's when it's time to run home, scrounge around in your bottom drawer and emerge triumphant with principles of successive approximation. It's fine to follow your impulses or to teach "by instinct" until you have a problem, then try breaking down the steps to be taken by one or more of the methods suggested here.

SUMMARY

I took French in the ninth grade. It was in a private school so proud of its reputation that it charged student teachers money for the privilege of working full time for a semester there. In French we weren't so lucky as to have a student teacher. Our "professor," Monsieur Dupié, pronounced "Du"—with a French "u" sound, "pié" with—oh, never mind, taught in the traditional manner: he gave weekly assignments and we were supposed to learn everything by Friday. Except for one Thursday afternoon when my friend and I discovered an old spring mattress in her attic and practiced vocabulary, one word per jump, I found little motivation to study. The threat of the Friday test didn't motivate more than ten minutes of homework until Thursday evening, and by then I decided it would be better to get a good night's sleep than to study so late that I'd be too tired for the test.

Class time was spent by the instructor asking questions in French and calling on students to answer. Class time was spent by the students —or by me at least—in figuring out ways *not* to be called upon. I discovered that M'sieur Dupié rarely called on students who looked attentive but that he invariably called on students who were daydreaming. He called on hand-wavers more than those who held up their hands quietly, and he tried to call on everyone approximately the same number of times. My strategy, therefore, was as follows: for the first part of the period, when M'sieur Dupié asked easy review questions, I waved my hand and gave two or three answers. That got my average up and took the heat off me for the day's lesson which would follow. Then when M'sier Dupié asked questions I couldn't answer, I would look attentive, sometimes even raising my hand (but not waving). When the rare question that I could answer came along, I started drawing large flowers on the margin of my notepaper and did my best to look as if I were thinking of summer vacation. The final touch was to pretend I hadn't heard and ask, looking guilty, *"Encore, s'il vous plait"* (Could you repeat that please?). Then, of course, I'd come out with the flowing full answer I'd silently rehearsed.

That is how I passed French. Unfortunately French also passed me. I remember only my creative effort of the year, a poem to the tune of "Dites-moi pourquoi" from *South Pacific,* written in French, which attests, I fear, to the quality of my learning.

Poem

Dites-moi pourquoi	Tell we why
Cette class malade	This sick class
Est dormi toujour	Is always sleeping
En a l'ecole	While in school
Dites-moi pourquoi	Tell me why
L'elève est triste	The student is unhappy
Esce que parce que	Is it because of
M'sieur Dupié	Mr. Dupié

I later met M'sieur Dupié as a person and discovered him to be a nice, quiet man, and a dedicated teacher. What a shame he didn't use the principles of shaping:

ACTIVE RESPONDING—Many (say 60 or so) responses per hours, not three or four.

IMMEDIATE REINFORCEMENT—For each correct response—some reason to speak correctly, not just acknowledgment by asking another question of another student.

SUCCESSIVE APPROXIMATION—So the student is right nine times out of ten.

Suppose, for drill, M'sieur Dupié had put the words we had translated on Friday's tests on to index cards and we'd kept a daily chart of our rate of correct translation—say, by using a daily behavior chart with a line drawn at 60 words per minute. Each day we'd try to get over the line, to beat our record of the day before. Those who did could go on to new vocabulary cards—or maybe could write a skit in French. For conversation, suppose M'sieur Dupié had split us into pairs or small groups according to our performance in French and had had us make up French conversations which, after practicing and checking out with M'sieur Dupié, we would present to the rest of the class.

Just those two procedures—which would not have involved extra materials, or equipment, or any more preparation time—would have increased active responding to a respectable rate, provided more feedback and the reinforcement of creating, and they would have permitted successive approximation. I've no doubt that I not only would have learned more French—I might even have *liked* it.

EXERCISES

Concept Check XIIIA—Successive Approximation (Objective A)

Which three of the following descriptions best illustrate successive approximation?

1. Ms. Marx has students who cannot find words in dictionaries look up only the guide words first (found on the tops of the pages). When the students can find the guide words without hesitation, then she has them find words that are not guide words.
2. Mr. Parsons has all of his second graders first do work sheets on which they put the missing numbers on a clockface. The second week, he has them all draw the hour hand in on clockfaces to show even hours. The third week, he has them circle the correct time from three choices (using whole and half hours only).
3. Students in English 120 learn to write research reports by first writing the conclusion of an incomplete report. As soon as each one can write acceptable conclusions, he or she is given a report to complete, with the analysis and conclusion missing. At each step the students must write more of the report, until finally they are researching and writing entire reports completely on their own.
4. Ms. White has each first grader read aloud from a Level One lesson until he or she can read readily without errors. Then the student is given a Level Two lesson to read aloud.
5. The algebra teacher explains how to solve linear equations, starting with simple examples and progressing to increasingly more difficult ones.

Answers for Concept Check XIIIA

The three best illustrations of successive approximation are numbers 1, 3, and 4.

Number 2 is not good successive approximation because each student does not progress according to his or her performance but according to what week it is. All are given the same materials, no matter what their ability to tell time. Some of the students might be able to tell time perfectly at the beginning.

Number 5 is not good successive approximation because it is the *teacher* who is behaving, not each student.

Concept Check XIIIB—Successive Approximation Techniques (Objective B)

For each item below, write down the main technique of successive approximation it illustrates, using:

A. for "Ask the student to select before asking him or her to produce."
B. for "Go from simple to complex and part to whole."
C. for "Start with prompts and withdraw them as soon as possible."
D. for "Go from easy to fine discriminations."

1. At first you help the student by telling him or her how to do something as he or she performs, but later the student must perform without your verbal help.
2. You have a multiple-choice item for students to do before asking them to supply technical terms from memory.
3. You ask students to tell which of two rocks is volcanic, starting with examples in which the differences are marked and then using examples which are increasingly more difficult to tell apart.
4. To teach writing sonnets, you first give students some models of sonnets, with phrases they can incorporate into their own poems. Then as they continue to write more and more sonnets, they rely on the models less and less, until they can write a complete sonnet without using the models at all.
5. In woodworking, the teacher has students first learn how to make joints, then has them make a complete box.
6. In learning to classify schools of modern art, the students are first given relatively pure examples of each style and then later are given works whose distinguishing features are more subtle.

Answers for Concept Check XIIIB

1. C. The prompts which are withdrawn are verbal directions. The student is making the whole response even at the beginning, but he or she gets help at first, then the help is withdrawn.
2. A. Answering multiple-choice items is "selecting." It is a different behavior than supplying from memory, which is "producing."
3. D. In each step, the students are asked to pick out the volcanic rock, but the discrimination required in the first steps (examples with marked differences) are easier than the discriminations required in later steps (examples which are increasingly more difficult to tell apart).
4. C. In each step the students write a whole sonnet—but at first they have the prompts of models. Later the prompts are withdrawn.
5. B. The students first make part of the box (the joints) and then make the whole box.
6. D. It is easier to discriminate between "pure" examples of schools of art than between "subtle" ones. The latter require finer discriminations.

Motivation

OVERVIEW

Teachers are always talking about motivation. Chapter Fourteen
looks at what we mean by motivation in terms of student behavior
and what controls that behavior. Suggestions are given on how to
motivate in two senses of the term: (1) to increase the effectiveness
of existing reinforcers and (2) to make other stimuli become
reinforcing so that students enjoy working in a subject area.

OBJECTIVES

By the end of the chapter you should be able to:

A. Identify statements which describe motivation as something to be
produced rather than as a cause for behavior (the latter statements
being explanatory fictions).
B. Define "to motivate" as
1. To set up contingencies for responding—to provide reasons for
working.
2. To increase the effectiveness of existing reinforcers.
3. To make the stimuli from working in an area become conditioned
reinforcers so that students will enjoy working in a field.
C. Tell how to increase the effectiveness of given reinforcers through:
1. Deprivation
2. Providing for variety
3. Use of sampling for group activities
D. Identify procedures which will and will not motivate
effectively (in the sense of B2 above) including:
1. Ways to get students to "pay attention."

2. Various systems of grading, such as grading on a curve and point systems.

E. Describe how you would apply the following principles to improve motivation in a given unit of instruction:
   1. Make sure the students are likely to be successful by adapting the learning task to their current level of achievement.
   2. Reinforce as immediately and as often as possible and make improvement conspicuous.
   3. Have each learner actively participating so he or she gets natural consequences.
   4. Use the natural reinforcers in a subject area—work them into the learning situation.

WHAT MOTIVATION IS, AND ISN'T

"I know he can do it if only he would try."
"She would do well if she paid attention."
"He just isn't interested in the subject."

Getting students to do what they "can" do is an age-old problem. It is different from shaping up a particular operant. The teacher may state the difference this way: "Sam knows how to solve the problems, but he won't try, whereas George can't solve the problems." Lack of working isn't lack of motivation if students cannot do what is asked or if they don't know what they are supposed to do. We assume students can tell what is expected of them and have done similar things in the past when we speak of motivation.

A Variety of Meanings. Traditionally, motivation has been defined as "that which energizes and directs activity." To energize is to increase the strength of behavior—to make students respond more rapidly, with more force, with more persistence, or to get them to respond at all. To direct activity is to bring responding under stimulus control, to make the students less "distractable." If we imagine a classroom, the students whom we call motivated start to work readily and work with enthusiasm and concentration. In contrast, procrastination, short attention span, in fact, any behavior other than working is commonly called lack of motivation.

But working hard in class is only a first step in motivation. The teacher who is interested in the long-range results of education is concerned with behavior outside of class. The teacher may complain. "Yes, John works hard in class, but that's because he wants a good grade. He doesn't seem to *like* the subject. He doesn't pursue it on his own." We not only want to produce behavior now but also for the future. To motivate in this sense is to bring the students under the control of what they themselves produce. We want to make learning *itself* reinforcing for our students. They must learn not for a grade or to "please the teacher" but for the enjoyment they get out of learning, for the natural consequences of solving problems, discovering new things, or creating.

Motivation

is: (1) the contingencies for responding—roughly speaking, the "reasons" for working; (2) the degree to which an individual has been deprived or satiated with a particular reinforcer; (3) the extent to which a student's behavior is controlled by the natural consequences of behaving rather than by artificial reinforcers introduced by others—that is, how much enjoyment the student gets out of working.

The behavioral processes implied by the various uses of the word "motivation" are different. The problems of energizing and directing behavior are problems of using existing reinforcers effectively. Getting students to like a subject, on the other hand, is a problem of making other stimuli reinforcing—of getting students to be reinforced by the products of their own behavior.

Motivation Is Not an Explanation. We have been talking about motivation as something we want to produce, that is, as a *dependent* variable. Unfortunately, it is often used as an independent variable, as in the statement, "Paul doesn't try because he's not motivated." Such statements are explanatory fictions, since the explanation redescribes the problem. It is no help to be told that if we'd just motivate Paul, he would try harder. We need to find the things in the environment that control how hard Paul tries so we can change the contingencies under which he behaves. "Motivation" is a way of describing a *problem,* it is not a cause of behavior.

Needs and Drives Are Not Reasons for Behavior. We are born with physiological "needs" or "drives" in that certain things are necessary for our survival as a species. Food and water, avoidance of pain, elimination of waste, sex, and so on, are needs in this sense. In the evolution of man, individuals who found eating or sex reinforcing and who avoided or escaped pain tended to leave more offspring than others. In succeeding generations the drive for food, sex, and to escape pain became stronger by natural selection. Physiological needs and drives, then, are words used to identify *primary* reinforcers, things necessary for species survival because of our biological heritage. Food, water, sex, and sleep are primary reinforcers.

We also use the words "needs" and "drives" to describe *conditioned* reinforcers, stimuli for which we have no inborn physiological need but which have become reinforcers. The students who "need attention" are ones for whom attention has become reinforcing. The person who is said to "have a drive to dominate" is one for whom dominating is highly reinforcing. When we ask, "How can we develop Thomas's need to achieve?" we are asking, "How can we make achievement reinforcing for Thomas?"

When we *motivate* students we are arranging for them to be reinforced for working. The students will then feel a "need to learn" that subject. In motivating, then, we want to create new "needs." Needs and drives thus refer both to what we already find reinforcing and to reinforcers we want to create. They are not reasons for behavior. Because they add nothing to our analysis, the terms *needs* and *drives* will not be used further.

Needs and Drives

are often used to describe reinforcers, as in the phrases, "He needs a lot of attention" and "She has a high sex drive." Neither needs nor drives explain behavior. Because of their misleading implication of energy originating inside individuals, neither term is used to analyze motivation. Note: "Needs" is also used to describe *behaviors* a student lacks (see page 212), but this is a different use of the word.

Motivation Is Not Teaching Only What Students Are Already Interested In. Some students work when given an opportunity to do so but others do not. We motivate those who do not work by first setting up contingencies under which they will work and then by getting them to be reinforced by their own success. It is *not* motivation simply to change the subject matter.

It is tempting to teach only what students like. If students are not interested in learning to write standard English, why not teach ghetto slang instead? If they do not do their assignments in science, why not teach something they like better, such as "how to repair a motorcycle"? Unfortunately, students are not always eager to learn everything they will need to get along in the world they will encounter as adults. The problem of motivation is not a problem of finding out what students already are interested in but of getting students to become interested in *new* things (see Figure 14.1). You cannot do that simply by changing what you teach.

What Motivation Is. Motivation means several things. At the simplest level, it means to get students to work—to give them a reason for studying. We motivate in this sense when we add "reasons" by setting up contingencies in which working is reinforced by such things as grades, approval, or privileges, or by escape from, or avoidance of, criticism,

Figure 14.1   The problem of motivation is to get students to take an interest in things in their environment which do not, on the surface, look interesting. (Courtesy of Franken, Stock, Boston.)

ridicule, spankings, or other punishments. Motivation also means increasing the reinforcing properties of stimuli. When we talk of students "taking an interest" in something, we mean that it has become a reinforcing stimulus for them. The task of motivating is to *make* it reinforcing for students to learn, to create, to solve problems. They learn to be reinforced by what they produce and by what they find out. But new stimuli cannot become reinforcing unless they are paired with the old. When we motivate, then, we first reinforce students for learning by using existing reinforcers. (The way to do this is covered in Chapter Eight.)

The Bribery Question. The idea of reinforcing students for learning offends some teachers. They feel it is "bribery." They feel students should learn because that is the right thing to do. They feel students should not work for grades, or for approval, or for other "payment." The same teachers do not feel that it is bribery when they take home their monthly paychecks. Both a bribe and a paycheck are money exchanged for work done. A bribe, however, is payment for an activity that is immoral or illegal, that is, that the community punishes. Because of future disadvantages, a bribe is seen as harmful to society and to the individual. Payment for work or for learning, in contrast, does not harm the community and is not, therefore, a bribe.

Let's look for a moment at the alternatives to "paying" students for learning. It is all very well to object to paying people for what they *should* do anyway. But suppose, without some kind of payment, some students don't learn. Are we to ignore them, passing them from one grade to the next and finally out the high school door? Yes, students *should* learn for the love of it but what do we do when they don't? Isn't it our job as teachers to get them to learn anyway—and to get them to enjoy it too?

There is another alternative to "reinforcing working" besides giving up on students, and it is the one most widely used. Rather than reinforcing students for working, teachers punish them when they do not work. The very same teachers who object to having Johnny earn privileges for getting his assignments done on time are not at all opposed to taking away privileges if he doesn't. That is not considered "bribery." But punishing students who fail to work hard does not help them learn to like studying. If anything, it makes the motivation problems worse.

If we don't reinforce students for learning, then, we end up either not producing learning (by not teaching unpopular material or by passing on incompetent students) or we resort to punitive techniques and are back to the discipline of the rod. In contrast, by arranging contingencies carefully, we can shape up working. Once students are working, the control of their behavior can shift so they are no longer dependent on the reinforcement the teacher provides.

Any reinforcer which is provided by the teacher is called artificial, or extrinsic, to distinguish it from the natural, or intrinsic, consequences of behaving a given way. Peer acceptance and teacher approval are artificial reinforcers, as are the usual letter grades, Dean's lists, gold stars, prizes, honors, and graduation itself.

Natural consequences, in contrast, are the inevitable results of behaving. The task of making the stimuli which follow from behavior reinforcing to the person who behaves is a problem of moving from artificial to natural reinforcement. Since students cannot "enjoy" the consequences of studying a field if they do not study, the first task for the teacher of reluctant learners is to get them working. For this we need to change the contingencies under which existing reinforcers are obtained.

INCREASING THE EFFECTIVENESS OF EXISTING REINFORCERS

Deprivation and Satiation. We are concerned with the control by already established reinforcers as well as with creating new reinforcers when we talk of motivation. For the moment we will look at environmental factors affecting the power of existing reinforcers. One of these is degree of deprivation or satiation. Let us take a universal reinforcer—food. Think of a food you like. What determines the control that that food has on you at a particular time? First and foremost, no doubt, is how recently you have eaten it and how much you have eaten: your degree of deprivation or satiation.

Deprivation

is the withholding of access to a reinforcer. A student who has not been able to talk with other students for an hour has had an hour's deprivation of talking with peers.

A certain degree of deprivation is necessary for any *primary* reinforcer to motivate a particular individual at a particular time. To make food reinforcing, for example, we withhold food for a period of time. We do not appeal to hunger or need as causes of the individual's eating. We simply note that by withholding food, we make food more reinforcing. We do not explain the fact that a person eats at dinner by saying that the person is hungry. Instead we look in part at the person's deprivation to account for both the hunger and the eating. Of course, there are many other factors involved too. These include, for example, whether the person is sick or well, dieting or not dieting, active or sedentary. The kinds of foods served make a difference, too, as do other consequences riding upon eating (social approval, saving space for dessert, and so on). But the point is that deprivation *alone* is one way to increase the effect of a reinforcer. We can motivate working for food by depriving an individual of food.

The reinforcing power of stimuli which are not primary reinforcers is increased by deprivation too. Part of what determines how hard we will work for something depends, in other words, on its rarity. Precious stones are more sought after in part because they are more rare. When people have been deprived (however slightly) of gasoline, or toilet paper, or any other goods which had been widely available, those goods become more reinforcing. The energy and cost we will undergo to get them increases.

In the classroom the degree of deprivation also affects the reinforcing power of a stimulus. We cannot use paper as a reinforcer if the students have desks full of it. "Opportunity to talk to friends" will not be an effective reinforcer in a classroom in which everyone chats all the time anyway. Praise from a teacher is more reinforcing when it follows a period of relative deprivation. Lavish approval is often ineffective, particularly if it occurs frequently. A student may say, "It doesn't *mean* anything; the teacher says that to everyone." Even an A grade is valued less if everyone gets one. Students who get A's will also be less excited by it if A's are given to them daily than if they have not had one recently. Note though, that the students used to A's may still feel punished by *not* getting an A grade.

The opposite of deprivation is satiation: "too much." An example of satiation occurred in an elementary school. The teachers of the school wanted to do something nice for the students as a kind of Christmas present, so they arranged to rent movie cartoons. The announcement of the movies was met with cheers. Cartoons were clearly a reinforcer. The last day of school arrived. In the afternoon the lunch tables were put away and chairs were set up in the lunchroom. One hundred and seventy-three students filed in excitedly and sat down to wait for the show. Then it began. Cheers went out as Donald Duck came on the screen. The kids laughed frequently at his antics. Then came Road Runner. More cheers; then there were two Tom and Jerry cartoons. On and on: one short followed another for almost two hours. By the beginning of the second hour there were no more cheers when a new episode began. Several students in the fourth grade were heard to say at the beginning of each cartoon, "Oh, no. Not *another* one!" Satiation had occurred.

Satiation

is the repeated receiving of reinforcement. The longer a person talks with peers, the higher his or her degree of satiation with "talking with peers."

Whenever you are using a particular event or article which you know has reinforced a student in the past, you will find that how well it works at a particular time is partly a function of the recent deprivation or satiation of the student.

Using Generalized Reinforcers. One solution to the problem of satiation is to use generalized reinforcers—conditioned reinforcers which can be exchanged for a variety of other reinforcers. Money is a generalized reinforcer. While we may tire of the movies money buys us or get satiated with the sweets we purchase, money itself remains reinforcing because of the variety of other reinforcers it can buy. In the classroom, teacher attention and approval are generalized reinforcers because of their association with all of the other reinforcers teachers control, from sitting where you want, to good grades, to help in getting a good job or into a good college or university.

If a teacher sets up a point system or token economy in which points or tokens can buy a variety of backup activities or articles, the points or tokens become generalized reinforcers. The greater the variety of backup reinforcers, the less the points or tokens will be susceptible to the fluctuations of deprivation and satiation. If James is tired of film-strips (ten points), he can use his points to rent the basketball at recess.

Using Group Activities as Reinforcers (Field Trips, Parties, and So On). A teacher in a public school set up a point system and planned to use a field trip as one of her reinforcers. She got permission to take only some of her students in case not all earned enough points. The semester progressed and a few students looked as though they were not going to make the required points. Frequently the teacher was heard to make comments like, "You'd better work or you're not going to get enough points to go on the trip," or, "It's really a fun trip. You'll see. You won't want to be left behind all alone. The students last year had a great time."

Something was wrong. The teacher was trying to get her students to want something that was supposed to be a great treat! The problem was, first, that the students had never been on a field trip and didn't know whether or not they wanted to go, and second, having the students go was more of a reinforcer for the *teacher* than for the students themselves. The teacher really didn't want any of her students to miss out.

Needless to say, the point system for the field trip dwindled out in

---

Generalized Reinforcers

are reinforcers which are associated with a variety of other rein-forcers. Money and attention are common examples.

---

effectiveness. If it is more important for you than your students that they should have a certain experience, you should not use it as a reinforcer. There are plenty of other reinforcers to use.

There is, however, a way to increase the desirability of a group activity that you would like to use as a reinforcer. By giving one "free" pass to an activity, you can increase the number of students who will work for that activity.[1] It's like the "free sample" used so often in business. It makes sense that a particular activity or product cannot be very reinforcing to someone who has never experienced it. By having everyone go once, you guarantee that your students have experienced an activity. If you plan to use a field trip as a reinforcer, have everyone go on one at the beginning of the year. *Then* have them work for the next—and make sure that you don't care whether or not every student goes on the second one. If you do care, then don't use field trips as reinforcers—use something else.

To reiterate, you can increase the effectiveness of a given reinforcer by:

---

[1]Teodoro Ayllon and Nathan H. Azrin, *The Token Economy: A Motivational System for Therapy and Rehabilitation*, New York, Appleton-Century-Crofts, 1969.

1. Making sure that students can't get it "free" a lot of the time—that they are under at least some degree of deprivation.
2. Providing for variety to prevent satiation. Use generalized reinforcers (tokens or points) with as many different backup reinforcers as possible. The more things that can be bought with the tokens or points, the more reinforcing they become and the less they are subject to momentary states of deprivation or satiation.
3. Letting all students experience something once "free" before using it as a reinforcer.

MOTIVATION AS GETTING STUDENTS TO PAY ATTENTION

Once upon a time, a boy was having a very hard time getting his donkey to walk (see Figure 14.2). One might call it a motivation problem.
A fellow came up and said, "I can get your donkey to go." The donkey's owner said, "Oh, sir, I would appreciate your help. You see, I've got to help him home before dark." The man looked around, found a two-by-four, and hit the donkey over the head as hard as he could. "Why did you do that?"

Figure 14.2

Figure 14.3 The contingencies in attracting attention are all wrong for motivating studying. After this demonstration, the text the students are supposed to read will seem dull. (Courtesy of Rogers, Monkmeyer.)

asked the boy. "I'll get him to go," said the man, "but first I've got to get his attention!"

One of the most widely held myths of motivation is that before you can teach, you must first attract the attention of the students. Teachers are advised to start lessons with something that will get attention, using demonstrations, enthusiasm, audiovisual displays, current events, or anything which is popular with the students. Any entertaining introduction *will* attract the attention of the students while it is going on (see Figure 14.3). But what then? After generating interest by showing a film of a missile blasting off for the moon to introduce a unit on Newton's laws of motion, will the students be excited by the text you want them to read? If anything, it will be all the duller by comparison.

From an operant point of view, the contingencies in *attracting* attention are all wrong. There is no doubt that attention-getting devices are reinforcing to see. But when is the reinforcement given? A fascinating demonstration which introduces a unit *precedes* any student responding.

If an attention device is thrown in to spark enthusiasm when interest is flagging, you are actually reinforcing students for showing signs of boredom. If anything, you are making your problem worse. If you wish to use some interesting discussion or presentation to motivate studying, you must have it contingent upon some response from your students. Save it for *after* the students complete some assignment you want them to do. Better still, make it explicitly contingent: students get to see the demonstration only after they reach a certain performance level.

Not all of the learning in any field can be entertaining. Even if we could design each class to be exciting, that would not solve the basic problem of motivation. The problem of motivation is to get students to attend to things that are *not* immediately eye-catching. We want them to take an interest in things which initially appear to be dull. They must learn to read books without pictures, to study nature or engineering as it really is, not only as it is dressed up by Madison Avenue techniques.

What makes us pay attention to something? There are hundreds of stimuli in our environment, but we respond to only a few. As Sherlock Holmes pointed out, there is a difference between "looking at" our world and "seeing" what is there. The stimuli to which we respond are those which have been associated with consequences in the past. They may be obvious, like the bell at the end of a school period, or subtle, like a slight smile in someone's eyes that says "yes." If important consequences ride on noticing something, we learn to pay attention to it. If, for example, an important job you want depends on your handwriting—the way you cross your "t's" and dot your "i's"—you would start paying attention to characteristics of your writing that you might not even have been aware of before. You might also start to pay attention to your friends' handwriting.

Teachers who complain that students don't pay attention to what they say might do well to look at what consequences there are for listening. Mr. Jacobs, a teacher who found himself repeating over and over to one particular student, wondered whether the boy was hard of hearing. One day he said very quietly, "Johnny, would you like a piece of candy?" The student responded immediately. The problem wasn't hearing, but attention—there wasn't any reason to hear what Mr. Jacobs usually said.

Putting in Reasons for Paying Attention. If you want your students to pay attention to something they read, to what you say, or to any other stimulus in their environment, you must arrange for responding to that stimulus to be reinforced. The more positive and immediate the consequence, the better attention you will get. Look at the concentration with which quiz show participants listen to the questions they are about to answer. While teachers don't have $64,000 to give for answering correctly, there are other consequences they can provide. Students who read to find the solution to a mystery, or to join a discussion, or to get a check mark in the teacher's records for "remembering" will be more likely to concentrate than other students who will not be asked questions. Those parts of a course which will be on today's test command more attention than things to be on a test which is weeks away. Any immediate consequence will help.

Getting Students to Pay Attention to Lectures. While lectures are probably the least effective method of instruction in use today, they still are common and, since they require far less preparation than a series of exercises for students to do, they will probably continue to be in use for some time. If, someday, you find yourself lecturing, there are some simple things you can do to add consequences for listening. First, you can use a "lecture fill-in sheet," such as the one mentioned in Chapter Thirteen, or the one in Table I which follows. You make an outline of your lecture, leaving out all the important parts of the definitions, rules, examples, and so on. Before starting, you pass out the sheets to the students. As you go through the lecture, you refer to the sheet: "Correlation is a measure of the . . . (see the first item on your fill-in sheet) *degree* of relationship between two or more *variables*. . . ." For some reason, it is reinforcing to have blanks all filled in. Students who normally would be inattentive don't want to miss anything on the fill-in sheets.

A second way to provide a consequence is to give a quiz at the end of each lecture. One instructor, Ms. Ames, had her students make two copies of the answers to a multiple-choice quiz at the end of each lecture. Students handed in one copy and kept the other. Ms. Ames then gave the answers. Those who passed were excused to the back of the room to work on homework or to do whatever they wished (quietly). The rest stayed up front for a review and a second quiz. As the semester progressed, students paid better and better attention until almost all of them passed the quizzes on the first try. Such a strong contingency may not be needed. Even a quiz without students' names is often effective. Just knowing that a quiz is coming the same day (as opposed to a midterm weeks away) is reason enough to attend for many students. Two added advantages of the "no-name" quiz are that students don't get nervous about taking it (since the teacher doesn't know who wrote what) and the teacher needn't take time to correct it. Since no names are attached, students don't expect their papers back. The teacher can just glance through the answers to get an idea of how well students are learning and what should be reviewed. Then the teacher can throw the papers away.

Paying Attention on Written Assignments. If you walked into a school and saw a class of students all working with great concentration and speed, you would probably conclude that they were taking a test. The effort given on tests is in marked contrast to the attention a work sheet

TABLE I Part of a Lecture Fill-In Sheet on Correlation

1. a. Correlation is a measure of the _____ of relationship between
      two or more _____.
   b. It tells the degree to which high measures on one characteristic
      go with _____.
   c. Correlation does _____ tell whether one thing _____
      another.
2. In *positive* correlation high numbers on one measure go with
   _____ numbers on the other.
   In *negative* correlation high numbers on one measure go with
   _____ numbers on the other.
3. Which would you expect to be positively correlated? (Circle the numbers)
   a. Height and weight
   b. Age and miles traveled
   c. Average calories eaten and weight
   d. Darkness of hair and height
4. To get a correlation you must have _____ sets of measures on
   the _____ individuals or days.
5. Which of the following questions could correlation answer?
   a. Do boys or girls learn their numbers first?
   b. Do large boys tend to be more aggressive than small boys?
   c. Do children who do well on matching shapes at age five read better
      at age seven?
   d. Do most children pass through whining and bossing stages?
   e. Do children in general prefer *The Travels of Babar* or *Ferdinand?*
   f. Do more and more children stay home from school as the temperature
      gets colder and colder?
   — and so on —

or exercise commands. One way to increase student productivity is to have everything count like a test. When grading on a point system, each exercise can be given some point value so that it makes a difference how well the students do.

Even more immediate consequences are possible with some of the newer materials which are chemically treated. When students mark with a special pen, they make hidden print appear. (See Chapter Thirteen for examples.) Each time they answer, they get *immediate* feedback. Unlike multiple-choice programmed instruction with visible answers, with this method students cannot see the correct answer without marking a choice (unless, of course, they copy from a paper which has been completed). Such exercises are not limited to multiple-choice responses, and teachers can design their own with special masters which will run off student copies on most ditto machines. The attention these exercises command is quite remarkable—they are fun to do.

USING GRADES TO MOTIVATE

No one wants students to work just for a grade, but students *do* work for grades, and so as long as we give them, we might as well use them to motivate learning. The student who learns "for the love of it" won't be spoiled by also getting an A, and the student who learns because of grades may not learn as much without them.

Grades, however, are usually not used well for motivating students. For one thing, they usually are given in such a way that those who most need to be motivated rarely get reinforced. No one needs to motivate the hardest-working students, but they are usually the ones to get the A's. Whenever a teacher grades on a curve, giving A's to the very best, B's to the better-than-average students, and so on down the line, one student's grade depends on the grades of others. It is a competitive system; one student's gain is another student's loss. When the stakes are high, it can become cutthroat, as in one medical school where students reputedly lock up their notebooks to prevent others from stealing or destroying them. By taking away someone else's notes, you make it unlikely that he or she will do well on exams, thus lowering the curve and making your own exam better by comparison.

Grading on a curve is discouraging to those students who come into a course with fewer skills than the others. Even if they work hard, they are unlikely to do better than the best students. When differences in entering behavior are large (as they usually are), the students with poor backgrounds are faced with a hopeless and unfair task. They must learn much more than those for whom much of the content is review, and they must do so with more limited study skills, reading skills, vocabulary, and so on. Many such students give up at the start.

There are many other systems of grading. A few are listed in Table II. All are "mastery learning" systems in which the grade represents skills mastered rather than how one student stands compared to others.

There are, of course, unlimited variations on the three examples shown. The point is not to advocate one method, but to point out that *how* you grade determines what kind of student behavior you will get. For example, if grades depend in part on meeting deadlines, students will be more prompt than if it doesn't matter when things are done. If students can take a test over and over until they pass, some will take test after test, hardly studying between, hoping that maybe they'll get lucky. If tests can be taken just once, students will study harder before taking them but they will quit studying the material on that test immediately afterward, whether or not they have learned it.

Although no one system is perfect, some suggestions can be made. In general, the more little bits you break a grade into, the more behavior you produce in your students. If, in addition, you offer many opportun-

TABLE II   Some Systems of Grading Besides Grading on a Curve

1. **Grade = Percent of Course Mastered**
   A grade indicates how much of the course students have completed (at 90% mastery level). If they do not score 90% the first time. they may try again until they reach 90%.
   A = all ten units
   B = at least nine units
   C = at least six units
   D = at least five units
   No grade given for fewer than five units
   (Note: All students eventually reach an A if they work long enough.)

2. **Grade = Mastery of Basics Plus "Extra Credit"**
   To get a C, students must complete, at a satisfactory level, all requirements listed as *basic*.
   To get a B, students must do one acceptable paper in addition.
   To get an A, students must do, and write up, an original project which meets course standards.

3. **Grade = Points Accumulated**
   To the Student:
   To get any grade you must earn at least 50 points. Otherwise you will get an incomplete. You can get points for a variety of behaviors—but you have only one try at each. If you are not successful, you can try something else. Point levels for grades are:
   A = 90–100 points
   B = 89–89 points
   C = 70–79 points
   D = 60–69 points
   (Note: Points can be assigned any way the instructor desires; for number of assignments done, tests, getting work in by due dates, speaking up in class, doing projects, and so on—or in any combination.)

ities to better a grade, making it possible for everyone to earn an A, you will more effectively motivate slower students than if you grade on a curve.

Grades, attention, and the things that tokens or points buy are reinforcers that a teacher is constantly giving whether or not he or she is aware of the contingencies involved. How they are given—what contingencies are involved—determines a large part of the enthusiasm with which students work in the classroom. But the use of extrinsic reinforcers is only a first step in motivating. Eventually students must learn for the "love of it," that is, for the natural reinforcers from behaving itself. Only that way will they continue to learn outside of the classroom.

MAKING NATURAL CONSEQUENCES REINFORCING

To get students to enjoy learning, we must make stimuli which students themselves produce become reinforcing for them. The natural consequences of working in a subject area must maintain their behavior.

To become reinforcing, the natural consequences from any learned skill must, in most cases, be paired with stimuli which are already reinforcing. We learn to be reinforced by what we accomplish. Students who have never played basketball are, at first, reinforced by others for getting the ball in the basket. If they are successful and get reinforced for making baskets, they begin to take pleasure from their own skill in shooting. Making a basket has become a conditioned reinforcer. They may then practice alone, maintained by the baskets they make. Maybe later a coach points out that when shooting, they hold their arms out, thus failing to arch the ball. That makes their throws easy to intercept. By reinforcing good form, the coach makes a high arched path a conditioned reinforcer. An already existing reinforcer (coach's approval) thus determines the kind of throw which will reinforce the players. Natural consequences *become* reinforcing by being paired with other reinforcers.

It is the same inside the classroom. In first grade, the reinforcement

---

Intrinsic Motivation

is the control of behavior by the natural consequences of the behavior itself. Natural consequences may be conditioned reinforcers—that is, they may be consequences which were always there but which have become important through their association with other reinforcers. For example, when society reinforces certain kinds of marks, *those* marks become conditioned reinforcers. Thus, after having been socially reinforced for drawing cartoons, the cartoons themselves may become reinforcers for drawing. Our continued drawing is then reinforced by the cartoons we produce, not by social approval. Motivation is then called intrinsic.

---

for reading, drawing, solving problems, and so on, is arranged by other people. The products for which the students are reinforced by peers and teachers start to become conditioned reinforcers. Getting the right answer, for example, becomes important in and of itself, even outside school when answering questions on the backs of cereal boxes or in newspapers.

In most cases the transfer from consequences provided by others to natural consequences occurs without special planning. Peers don't plan to phase out reinforcing good basketball shots, but as newcomers make more and more baskets, they are praised less and less. The same is true for readers. At some point, the words the teacher has reinforced a student for pronouncing begin to make sense. They tell something that the students didn't know before. If students continue to be successful in reading words, what the words say will gain more control over their behavior, and the teacher's approval will become less important. The teacher need not worry about the transition. When students become good readers, they no longer want to be bothered by the teacher telling them they are right.

To help make it reinforcing to learn, some principles can be followed:

1. *Make Sure Students Are Likely to Be Successful by Adapting the Learning Task to Their Current Level of Achievement.* Although you *can* motivate by reinforcing students even when they make a high error rate, you are stacking the cards against the students and against yourself. They will not get the reinforcement of having a perfect or nearly perfect paper. To the extent that mistakes are punishing, you are arranging for the students to be punished for working every time you give them something that is too hard. There is no reason (except convenience for the teacher) to have everyone doing the same exercises at the same time. If the dictum "Treat every student as an individual" has any meaning, it is certainly that you give each student something he or she can do successfully.

2. *Reinforce as immediately and as often as possible and make improvement conspicuous.* Since natural consequences become conditioned reinforcers by being paired with other reinforcers, we need to make sure that each student is reinforced as often as possible for behaving effectively. By making progress conspicuous we draw the student's attention to his or her own progress—which is one natural result of working. Any kind of record or chart will do, although the best ones make it difficult for students to compare with each other. Comparisons of achievement levels, as we have seen, reinforce primarily the better students, not those who need to be motivated.

3. *Have all learners actively participating so they get natural consequences.* It goes without saying that students cannot get natural consequences from their own behavior if they do not behave. It is more reinforcing to *do* a demonstration than to sit and watch one, to try something rather than to listen to how it should be done.

Sometimes a class becomes overly noisy when all students are actively talking, writing, experimenting, and so on. Teachers feel that they are losing control: that they do not have their students' attention. If what the students are doing is worthwhile, that is a good sign, not a bad one. The teachers have lost some of the control of their students' behavior— but the control has been lost to the natural consequences the students are getting from their own actions. They are paying attention not to the teachers but to what they are doing. Passing control from artificial consequences that teachers arrange to natural consequences is what we *must* do if we are to produce students who continue to learn after they leave us.

4. Use the natural reinforcers in a subject area: work them into the learning situation. A teacher of music education used to tell his classes a story:[2]

"When I was a student at college," he'd begin, "a friend of mine said, 'Woody, how would you like to play a game of handball with me?' I said I'd never played handball. 'That's all right,' my friend said, "Come on anyway and you'll learn.' So we got on our sneakers and gym clothes and checked out some funny-looking gloves and a handball, and my friend briefly explained the rules of the game. We started in. Wham! My friend hit the ball and it came zinging at me. Blop! I hit it and it fell right in front of me. My next shot made the wall and bounced obligingly for a perfect slam from my partner, which I, of course, missed. So the game went on. I asked a lot of questions. 'How do you hold your hand when you hit the ball? Where should you aim. Is it better to stand in one part of the court if you can?' Although I didn't win, I enjoyed the game and wanted to play again. Eventually I became a handball enthusiast, often practicing on my own to perfect my serves and devastating shots."

Woody would pause, peering over his glasses. "Now just suppose," he'd continue, leaning back with a slight smile, "that my friend had said to me, 'Oh, you've never played? Well, I tell you what. You go down to the sports store and buy yourself a handball mitt and ball, and you find yourself a teacher to teach you how to hit the ball just so, and you practice at least a half an hour a day hitting the ball. After a year or two of weekly lessons, you should be good enough. Then call me and we'll play a game.'"

Woody would smile. "Now," he'd say, "just how enthusiastic do you think I would have been? Yet that is exactly what we tell our beginning instrument students." It was true. Before I got to play viola with a group, I had taken lessons for two years. The intrinsic reinforcement of playing an instrument is the sounds you make, particularly the music you make *with others.* Woody saw this and designed a course in playing instruments that gave the beginner that reinforcement from the very outset.

Woody would start by holding an assembly. At the front of the room would be chairs set up like a band or orchestra. Each one would have an instrument laying on it. There would be one section leader who knew how to play each instrument sitting among the chairs, and a pianist, and one or two other musicians, depending on how many volunteers Woody could round up. Since I played viola, I was often a section leader for violas for the "string" orchestras. After all the students had filed in for the assembly and were seated, Woody would begin. "Today we're going to give a concert. How many of you have *never* played any of the instruments up here?" Almost all of the hands would go up. "Good," Woody would say. "Now I want you to fix your eyes on an instrument you think

[2]The teacher was Dr. G. Wallace Woodworth, of Columbia University.

you might like to play. When I say 'Go'—not now—I want you to run up and sit on the chair with that instrument." He'd pause. "Please remove the instrument first, though," (laughter) "and try not to bump into any of the other students or instruments. Ready?" (nods) "Ready, set, go." Pandemonium. Eventually all were settled and those who missed out were back in the "audience" seats. Then Woody, in hushed tones only for the "orchestra," would tell in one sentence how to hold the instrument and which string to try to play. Then he'd say, "Now we're going to give a concert. When you think I want you to play, play. And when you think I want you to stop, stop." Then he'd turn to the audience and announce, "Now we are going to give a concert."

He'd walk off and strut back onto the podium like a famous conductor. He'd bow to the audience and then turn to us. Then he'd raise the baton as if he were conducting a hundred-piece orchestra with an opening fortissimo chord. Everybody played, and the sound was fantastic. The newcomers played a one-note drone while the pianist and other players played melody lines. The piece went on, and at the end, Woody made a gigantic cutoff gesture for us all to stop. Inevitably one poor soul wasn't looking, so the concert ended with one big chord followed by a frail note trailing off. (Needless to say, Woody did not have to tell *that* student to "pay attention" the next time.) Then applause, and more applause, and the concert was over. The new players gathered around the veterans, asking, "How do you hold the bow?" "My bow keeps falling off the strings," and so on. Talk about motivation! This introduction was not just a gimmick. The whole course was designed to have students playing decent sounding music from the beginning on. A similar approach—building in the natural reinforcement from group playing—is taken by the Suzuki violin method and by Dr. Robert Pace's method for piano. All motivate much better than the traditional music lessons.

Any subject has stimuli which reinforce those who work in it, but beginners may not encounter them. Courses and curricula for teachers, for example, start with "methods" courses. But why do people go into teaching? To *teach*. The natural consequences of *seeing students learn* is what reinforces teachers' day-to-day behavior. A curriculum for teachers should start by having the students teach a simple lesson. Then they would *ask* for the information that methods courses try to impress upon them as important to learn.

What are the consequences that maintain writing, typing, mathematics, social studies, health, and so on, for professionals in those fields? Although we cannot always provide them in the early stages, we can provide them in a surprising number of cases. If the writer writes to communicate, you can have students read each other's works, perhaps using a class newspaper. The typing class can type real memos or letters. The fifth grade math students can find and solve real problems, such as financing their yearly trip to Washington by selling stationery. Whenever possible have the students' products (typing, mathematical calculating, or whatever) *used*, not just handed in for a grade.

There is a difference between building in natural reinforcers and "attracting attention." The *students* are behaving in the former case, not just passively watching. The teacher isn't changing what he or she wants to teach either. The teacher is still asking students to write, solve problems, and so on, but the instructor is arranging for the students to get realistic, natural consequences for the behaviors they are to learn.

SUMMARY

Teaching is helping people to learn faster or better than they would if left to learn on their own. Part of the help a teacher gives is to reinforce the first attempts of the beginners. Without reinforcement, behavior will extinguish. Beginners in any area are behaving in new ways. Their behavior is weak. At the time they most need reinforcement, they are unlikely to have enough skill to be reinforced by what they produce. The teacher supplies the needed reinforcement to get behavior started. Beginning students are dependent on the teacher not only for encouragement but also for feedback on which of their attempts are better than others. We *learn* to judge our own behavior and its products. At first we cannot tell which of our attempts to accept and which to revise. In some cases, such as beginning reading, there is no way beginners can learn completely on their own. You would not be able to "discover" how to read Chinese just by having a Chinese book around. Someone must already know what the words say so they can tell you when you are right. In other cases, such as shooting baskets in basketball, beginners may "discover" some of the basics, like how to make baskets, but even then, without a teacher, they may learn bad habits which may at first help them to get the ball in the basket but which will hurt their game later. They need a teacher (or coach) to give them feedback. Then there are reluctant students. Students become reluctant by being unsuccessful or by being punished for what they do. Many students try and are punished anyway, perhaps by a thoughtless teacher, perhaps by peers, perhaps only by disappointing others who have unrealistically high expectations for them. Such students, more than most, need frequent reinforcement, since they see what they produce as not good enough. They may also see teacher praise as artificial and may need more tangible reinforcers at the beginning.

Giving frequent reinforcement (encouragement, approval, progress reports, trinkets, or privileges) is the first step in motivation. It is the way parents motivate their children's first words and first steps. It is the way any teacher motivates until the natural consequences of behavior become reinforcing (see Figure 14.4). Artificial reinforcement thus helps students

Figure 14.4 All teaching starts with the teacher giving artificial consequences—but control must shift to more natural consequences if the behavior is to last. (Courtesy of Conklin, Monkmeyer.)

get natural reinforcement. There are many ways to motivate students, but some general principles are clear. To get students responding, we must set up situations which make responding likely, such as assignments in which students *do* something themselves rather than observe others. Then we must reinforce success frequently and immediately—either with attention, or by self-correcting materials, or peer checked progress, or by any other means at our disposal. When the behavior becomes strong— and only then—it is time to slowly withdraw from the picture. If the students haven't already come under the control of what they are learning, we must work at encouraging independence. Only by transferring the control of our students' behavior to natural contingencies in his or her environment can we motivate "for life."

EXERCISES

Concept Check XIVA—Motivation (Objectives A and B)

Which six of the following statements tell what motivation is?

1. How much or how little of a reinforcer an individual has had recently.
2. A cause for behavior, as in the statement, "He works because he is motivated."
3. Attracting the attention of students.
4. How reinforcing it is to study a subject.
5. How much students are reinforced by consequences they themselves produce.
6. The pairing of success in a subject with existing reinforcers.
7. Internal needs and drives which originate in us and move us to action.
8. Environmental history which determines how reinforcing various stlmuli are.
9. Finding what students already like to do.
10. The creation of new "needs" in the sense of making what students find out become important to them.

Answers for Concept Check XIVA

The six statements are numbers 1, 4, 5, 6, 8, and 10. Each of these statements looks at how reinforcing stimuli are to the student, either in terms of the recent deprivation or satiation of the individual (Number 1) or as conditioned reinforcers (numbers 4, 5, 6, 8, and 10.)

Number 2 talks of motivation as a cause rather than as what we wish to produce, and the example used is an explanatory fiction.

Number 3 is not motivation because it does not deal with the problem of making things interesting. Things which attract attention are stimuli which are *already* reinforcing.

Number 7 uses the terms "needs" and "drives" as *causes* for our actions. Since the only evidence for such "causes" is the behaviors they are supposed to explain, "needs" and "drives" used in this way are explanatory fictions. Operant psychologists look for independent variables, such as deprivation, pairing of reinforcers, previous reinforcement or punishment, and so on, to find which ones "move us to action."

Number 9 is not motivation because it does not consider making *new* stimuli reinforcing. The teacher who lets students do what they would do anyway is not motivating them. Motivating is concerned with getting students to do things they *wouldn't* otherwise do.

Concept Check XIVB—Ways to Motivate (Objectives C, D, and E)

Which six of the following techniques would be most likely to motivate *all* students to write poetry and to enjoy writing poetry?

1. Introduce the course with an exciting film of a famous poet receiving a Nobel Prize for poetry.
2. Have students write poems in class that are at a level of difficulty that each can handle—perhaps starting with limericks.
3. Award a meaningful and valuable prize to the student who writes the best poem in the class.
4. Find something in each student's poem that is good or original and mention that, rather than what he or she has done badly.
5. Have your students write poems for a presentation to another class, to illustrate the variety of kinds of poems—short, long, funny, serious, rhyming, nonrhyming, simple, complex, etc.
6. Have students keep records which show weekly improvement in such techniques as rhyming, identifying meter, listing words which a given word brings to mind, and so on.
7. Base the course grade on a final test in which students must write a poem of a particular type, such as a sonnet, and grade the test on a curve.
8. Grade according to points earned and provide a variety of ways for students to earn points, such as writing poems, doing exercises on poetry, bringing in poems they like, and so on.
9. Give assignments which encourage diversity and comment (favorably) on what is unique about each student's poems.
10. Switch to something more interesting when students seem to be discouraged or when they seem reluctant to write poems.

Answers for Concept Check XIVB

The six best techniques for motivating all students are numbers 2, 4, 5, 6, 8, and 9. All of them make it possible for students working at all levels of proficiency to be reinforced frequently. Numbers 5, 6, and 8, for example, provide variety, so that even the poorest student in the class can be reinforced. A student weak in language skills, for example, can, in Number 5, gain social reinforcement for writing a simple, but funny, poem.

Number 1 sets up poor contingencies. The exciting stimulus precedes responding. The movie wouldn't even be a good discriminative stimulus for imitation because it doesn't show the poet writing, just the honors he or she receives later.

Number 3 may motivate your better students, but not the ones who really need to be motivated.

Number 7 may get students to study hard just before the test, but basing a grade on one test does little to motivate studying daily or even weekly. In addition, by grading on a curve you make it impossible for everyone to do well, no matter how much effort is put in. In addition, when a whole grade rides on one hour's behavior (which admittedly is supposed to represent a semester's work), the pressure and anxiety generated are considerable. Such emotions are punishing and create avoidance, not continued study, in the future.

Number 10 reinforces "being discouraged" because you are making "doing something interesting" contingent on it.

PROBLEM-SOLVING EXERCISES (OBJECTIVE E)

Imagine that you teach a high school course called "The World of Working and Living." You see a problem. Your students talk about all the things they are going to buy when they're working, but the jobs they're talking about will not support the style of life they expect. You would like them to be a little more realistic but you don't want to punish them by telling them that they'll never make enough money to live the way they think they will.

Describe a unit which would motivate each student to find out the facts about jobs and the cost of living. Try to include the "natural" reinforcers of deciding what job to take and how to spend money, using the last two principles from Objective E:

1. Have each learner actively participating so he or she gets natural consequences.
2. Use the natural reinforcers in a subject area—work them into the learning situation.

Comments on Problem-Solving Exercises

There is no "answer" for this problem. You might be interested, however, in a unit that fulfills the requirements pretty well.

Ms. Maderich wanted to get students figuring out their wages and expenses and to build in contingencies as close as possible to those for actually making and spending money. First, she had students select a job that they might be able to get, following printed guidelines for types of occupations and the skills, experience, and educational level required to get them. Students then noted down the average salary for that occupation and calculated their likely take home pay.

Next, she got pictures from the local realtor of houses that were currently for sale in the neighborhood and the prices being asked for them. She brought in several Sears Roebuck catalogs and had each student select clothing, appliances, leisure items, and other things that he or she might expect to buy within one year's time.

She had each student figure up his or her mortgage payment and monthly expenditure for the other items.

Lastly, she had each student figure up the amount he or she planned to spend monthly on eating out, going to movies, bowling, and so on.

The students then figured out their total monthly expenses and added a fixed amount for groceries. Throughout the unit students talked among themselves about what to buy and helped each other with their calculations.

(Ms. Maderick did not need to make any comments about the differences between what most students planned to earn and what they planned to spend.)

As you can imagine, this was a "fun" unit. Students were very active figuring out payments, looking up facts in job descriptions, doing a lot of calculating and recording of expenses, and so on. Yet they were learning the same things they might have learned on a series of work sheets on topics like figuring out payments, reading job descriptions, and calculating and recording expenses. The difference between the work sheets and the unit described below is in how reinforcing the consequences of working were. On a work sheet, who cares if a problem comes out with a monthly payment of $12.75 or of $50.75? But if that amount has to come off your mock earnings, then it *does* matter. The information has become an important consequence in that it can reinforce or punish.

Teaching attitudes and values

OVERVIEW

Chapter Fifteen analyzes attitudes and values behaviorally. Some suggestions are given on how to teach favorable attitudes and values.

OBJECTIVES

By the end of the chapter you should be able to:

A. Define *attitude* and *value* behaviorally.
B. Describe the reinforcers which maintain behaviors which show a given attitude or value, such as "a positive attitude toward math" or "honesty."
C. Tell which examples of procedures are most likely to improve students' attitudes and values and which will have little effect or hurt attitudes and values.
D. Suggest changes to improve student attitudes or values in a described situation or course.

Everyone talks about creating positive attitudes as a goal of education. We are not content just to teach Johnny to read and write and do arithmetic; we want him to *like* reading, writing, and arithmetic. Social values are considered an important part of education too. Most teachers would like to help students become more considerate of others, more honest, community spirited, or ecologically minded. To determine how to go about reaching these goals, one must first define what, exactly, they are.

ATTITUDE AS A PREDISPOSITION
TO BEHAVE IN CERTAIN WAYS

An attitude is a predisposition to behave in certain ways. Students with positive attitudes toward school will behave in certain ways when the opportunity arises. They will be likely to talk favorably about school, to stay after school, to continue their schooling after they are not legally required to do so, and so on. Many behaviors can be seen by others. (see Figure 15.1). Equally important, however, are behaviors which can be observed only by the persons themselves. Thoughts, emotions, and feelings of affection or hostility are behaviors which make up part of an attitude even though they are private.

An Attitude

is a predisposition to behave in certain ways.

"Having an attitude" is not a good statement of behavior because it is not specific and it is not active. In contrast, "thoughts about school" or "impulses" are behavioral even though they are private. We can pinpoint the behaviors which make up an attitude even if they are private. Other behavior, after all, may be private, too, even if it is not internal. Talking to oneself, jumping up and down alone, and sending anonymous gifts are just as private as thoughts if no one but the behave sees them occur.

In practice, the teacher can observe only the public behavior of students. The teacher can ask them what they are thinking or feeling, but the answers they give are public behavior, not private. "Thinking" and "reporting what you are thinking" are two different behaviors. Students may report the same phrases that they think, but it is also possible to report something quite different. Students may tell a teacher they like a subject while at the same time hating it in their thoughts.

Behavior and statements about one's own behavior are likely to agree when they are under the same contingencies. The consequences for one must be similar to those for the other. There are usually no particular consequences for thinking one thing as opposed to another. If there are also no particular consequences for saying one thing as opposed to another, students will say what they think. More often, however, expressing one particular view will be reinforced (either subtly, by pleasing someone, or explicitly, as in getting a better grade) while the opposite view will receive punishment or disapproval. When the consequences differ, public statements and private behaviors tend to differ. For example, we may be skeptical when a student tells us, "I never take illegal drugs," or, "I never cheat," when the consequences for engaging in those behaviors are quite different from those of saying that you engage in them. Similarly, the student who is afraid to take drugs or who does not approve

Figure 15.1

of cheating may tell peers that he or she has tried drugs or thinks it clever to "beat the system" when peers reinforce such talk.

When consequences for behavior and for statements about behavior are similar, reports are likely to be true. We tend to believe students who say they love to go to football games because the consequences for liking football and for reporting that you like football are similar in our society. Similarly, we tend to believe the "confessor" because both the misbehavior and the confession generally receive the same kind of consequence, namely, punishment. Of course, we look for other evidence of attitudes besides what students say, but the point here is that we consider the contingencies that students are operating under as well as their behavior when assessing attitudes.

We also look at the source of consequences when we judge an attitude. Students with a positive attitude toward school, for example, must "enjoy school for its own sake"—that is, their behavior of going to school must be reinforced by the school itself. Going to college shows a different attitude when it is reinforced by a generous parental allowance than when it is maintained by reinforcers in the classes a student takes. Similarly, we hesitate to say a student "likes" school, even if he or she *thinks and feels* favorably about it, if the main source of reinforcement is a particular teacher on whom the student has a crush. Students must not only behave in certain ways for us to conclude that they have positive attitudes, they must do so because of the natural or intrinsic consequences of their behavior.

WHY ATTITUDES ARE IMPORTANT

The reason we care about attitudes is because we are interested in producing behavior which will last. If we succeed in predisposing students to read by bringing them under the control of the natural consequences of reading (getting information, finding out what happens next, and so on), they will be likely to continue reading outside school. In contrast, if they read only for teacher approval, reading will extinguish once the teacher is no longer around to reinforce. It is because we are concerned with "education for life" that we are so concerned with attitudes. We want our students to be independent, so that they no longer need a teacher in order to continue learning. When they enjoy learning for its own sake, the consequences they get from learning will maintain that behavior outside the classroom.

HOW ATTITUDES ARE FORMED

People can get the natural consequences of behaving only if they behave. Usually they must do something with a certain degree of skill before any positive consequences are forthcoming. People who love to do puzzles are reinforced by seeing the pieces fit together to form a whole picture. Beginners at puzzles cannot get the natural consequences of seeing the picture gradually emerge if they cannot fit the pieces together. Beginning readers cannot get the natural consequences of finding out what happens next if they cannot pronounce the words. First graders need to be able to pronounce quite a few words before they can get anything useful or entertaining from reading. Similarly, we cannot get the natural consequences from riding a bike, speaking French, performing chemistry experiments, and so on, until we have developed a certain degree of skill.

Before students reach the level of skill required to obtain the natural consequences from performing well, other consequences are needed to get them to behave. Beginners are reinforced by others for getting things right or punished for failure to learn. Which kinds of consequences a teacher uses, and how often he or she uses each kind, determines student attitudes. Our attitudes, in other words, come from the kinds of consequences our behavior receives.

Imagine, for a moment, that you are accustomed to eating with friends in a place that serves fortune cookies. You get into the habit of taking one at the end of every evening meal. You dutifully break it open and read out loud what the note inside says. Your friends do the same. Suppose the first few you get are positive: "You have a great capacity for generosity," "Someone you meet today will be important in your future," "A great opportunity lies ahead," or, "Do not hesitate to do what your heart tells you to do," and so on. Such statements, meaningless as they really are, tend to be reinforcing. They make us like to read the slips inside fortune cookies. Now suppose you start getting fortunes which are not so favorable: "A decision you will make will hurt those you most love," "Your selfishness will cut you off from a great opportunity," "Your chosen path requires more intelligence than you have at your disposal," and so on. Even though these consequences are not important, they tend to be slightly punishing. They do *not* make you enjoy reading fortunes. You may even begin to dislike fortune cookies. You may feel like hitting back at the fortunes by discrediting them: "Who believes in silly old fortune cookies anyway?" You may hit back physically, crumpling up the slips of paper in disgust. Even trivial consequences dealt out at random make a difference in our attitudes.[1]

The consequences we give our students when we teach are not so trivial. Each time you tell students they are not right, they are getting at least as punishing a treatment as an insulting cookie fortune. Their reaction is predictable: "Who wants to learn silly old history anyway?" Moreover, each time you assign them a task they cannot solve, you are setting up a situation in which study and effort will meet with failure. They will, in effect, be punished for trying. Anyone in a situation in which he or she receives frequent punishment and little reinforcement begins to get a negative attitude. Since poorer students experience more failure, they get more punishment. It is no wonder that they tend to become hostile toward school. We don't fail because of a negative attitude toward school; we get a negative attitude because we fail.

CREATING FAVORABLE ATTITUDES

One approach toward making school a more pleasant place for students is to remove the punishment of failure by removing requirements. If students do not want to learn to read, don't make them. If they don't like math, let them study what they like. The teacher in such an approach

---

[1]The fact that the kind of statement one receives determines attitudes is not lost on fortune cookie makers. Most fortunes are highly favorable.

is supposed to make the classroom a stimulating place by providing interesting materials or setting up "interest centers," or "stations." Students are then expected to use their time learning what is of interest to them.

Although the idea of removing punishment is good, there are problems is simply removing requirements. A beautifully laid out reading center may attract attention, but whether or not it teaches reading is another matter. Also, since people tend to like what they do well, students given an opportunity to pursue several subjects will be most likely to pick the ones they already know best—and they will be likely to avoid the very areas in which they are least skilled. They will do, in other words, what they least need and avoid what they need most. Moreover, students who have not already learned to study on their own will most likely switch from activity to activity, rarely spending enough time on one area to learn anything at all.

There is no such thing as free choice anyway. All behavior is affected by previous learning. What students choose in a so-called "free choice" situation depends on their previous experiences in similar situations. If they have not yet learned to use their time for their own long-range benefit, then it is up to the teacher to help them learn to choose better. By simply abolishing requirements and letting students choose what to do, we are programming some students for failure not only because they will not learn needed skills but because they cannot yet manage their own time well. Unproductive students can become frustrated at their own lack of progress in self-management just as easily as they become frustrated at lack of progress in reading. Instead of failing reading, they fail "using time wisely," and their attitude is likely to be negative, as is shown in the cartoon (Figure 15.2).

"Choosing what to do" is learned just like "choosing" the answer to a

Figure 15.2

problem. We can set out to teach using time wisely just as we would teach math or music. Instead of using inefficient methods, such as helping students choose by talking them into one choice or by trial and error (having everyone choose what to do and hoping some succeed in choosing wisely), we can teach self-management (see "self-control", page 283).

One of the aims of the unstructured classroom is to remove punishment and the threat of punishment from the learning environment. An operant approach has the same goals but accomplishes them differently. Instead of removing requirements and then trying to get students to learn by arranging stimulating corners or stations, the operant approach keeps requirements (pinpointed goals or behavioral objectives) but works on getting students to reach them by reinforcing each small step. In a sense, the students still choose what they want to do, but what they choose is determined, at least at first, by the contingencies the teacher arranges.

How to teach effectively (without using punishment) is the subject of this whole book. Insofar as effective teaching makes the student successful, it will also create favorable attitudes.

CONDITIONED REINFORCERS

So far we have been talking about reinforcement and punishment given by the teacher or by success or failure in the classroom. Although these are the main consequences in the classroom, other things associated with reinforcement or punishment acquire the power to reinforce or punish. The schoolroom itself is a neutral place until it is paired with pleasant or unpleasant experiences. Then it arouses emotions—loyalty or hostility—by itself. A particular teacher is just another person until he or she reinforces or punishes. A final exam is no different from a work sheet until it is associated with success or failure in a course. Teachers' marks on papers (circles or checkmarks) acquire power to reinforce or punish by the consequences that accompany them.

Anything which has become a reinforcer, you recall, is called a conditioned reinforcer. Some of what acquires the power to reinforce or punish is the student's own behavior. Suppose we have a student, David, who writes a paper which is easy for him, and we repeatedly praise him for his good work. Perhaps his peers also reinforce him by being impressed with how well he expresses himself. What directly precedes this extrinsic reinforcement is having a completed paper, so completing papers becomes a conditioned reinforcer. Just before completing a paper, the student is writing. His own behavior of writing, then, becomes reinforcing too. (We will assume the completed papers continue to receive approval.) Soon any signs of progress toward completion become reinforcing. The student "enjoys" writing.

Once writing is a strong behavior, it does not need to be reinforced by approval all the time. Only occasional recognition will maintain it. Outsiders, seeing our writer now, would say he has a positive attitude toward writing. They would not see all of the extrinsic reinforcement which built up the attitude. Because no reinforcement is conspicuous, they might say that the writer has "internalized" the value of writing, that he is a "natural-born writer." These are descriptive phrases, but they are not causes. The causes of any attitude are in the student's past history of reinforcement.

In order to become a conditioned reinforcer, any activity which is not biologically reinforcing must be repeatedly paired with another reinforcer. The frequency is critical. If a teacher reinforces often in math and punishes often in grammar, doing math will tend to become a conditioned reinforcer and doing grammar will tend to become punishing. The frequency of being reinforced or punished by a teacher thus affects attitudes, in addition to the effects of success or lack of success in learning the subject itself.

Enthusiastic teachers usually reinforce often. They themselves are in a reinforcing situation if they like their work, so they are not as likely to punish as teachers who dislike teaching. It is not energy level that makes students like an enthusiastic teacher—a sarcastic or critical teacher can have that energy too—but the kinds of consequences the teacher provides. We start to *feel* positive when we are reinforced often.

If you were given the task of making a student like you, you would be sure to reinforce him or her often. Liking a subject is no different; a student must be reinforced often when learning it, both by success and by its association with reinforcement rather than punishment. Only then can the subject itself become a conditioned reinforcer.

VALUES

A value is a set of behaviors, public and private, which a society reinforces. "Holding a value" differs from "having an attitude" in the kinds of consequences the behaver receives. Behavior which "expresses an attitude" reinforces the person behaving, but behavior "showing a value" reinforces someone else. When we are honest, kind, generous, tolerant of others, and so on, the most immediate benefits go to someone else. In the long run we are also likely to benefit, as is society in general, but we get no immediate tangible gain from acting with honesty, generosity, and so on. Table I illustrates the consequences of acting in accordance with some of the more common values in our society.

A Value

is a set of behaviors, public and private, which a society reinforces.

TABLE I   Consequences From Behaving According to Values

Value	Immediate consequence to behaver	Immediate consequence to others	Long-term consequence to behaver and to society
Honesty	—	+	+
Generosity	—	+	+
Tolerance	—	+	+
Kindness	—	+	+
Conservation of Resources (not wasting materials)	—	+	+

The first value, honesty (see Table I), is likely to bring punishment to the behaver. In fact, we don't consider a statement to be honest unless there is possible punishment following it. If a student says, "I had the best paper," we are not impressed with his or her honesty, even if the statement is true. In contrast, we consider George Washington's confession, "I chopped down the cherry tree," an honest statement because of the punishment such a statement usually brings. While the immediate results of being honest may bring punishment to the speaker, the long-term consequences to society are good. In a society where people are honest, one can believe what people say. Trust and openness develop. For the individual, too, the long-range consequences are beneficial. People who are honest may be punished for chopping down cherry trees, but they gain the respect of others and are believed on future occasions. They may even become president.

The same pattern—immediate cost but long-term gain—is also characteristic of the other values in Table I. People who are generous have less themselves as a result of giving. They may later benefit when someone returns a favor, but there is a difference between trading and being generous. The lion in the fable who spared the mouse's life (thus depriving himself of an immediate meal) was generous, since it was unlikely he would ever be paid back. The mouse, however, later returned the favor by gnawing through the hunter's ropes that bound the lion. The lion would not have shown generosity if he had already been bound and had released the mouse in exchange for his own freedom. For an act to be generous, you must end up with less, not with the same amount or more. We do not consider it an act of generosity when a large corporation contributes to a political campaign in exchange for political favors or when a president donates his personal papers to the National Archives —and then takes that gift as a $500,000 deduction on his income tax (thus saving himself over $100,000 in taxes). So it is with the rest of the values. The immediate result of being tolerant, or kind, or of using resources sparingly is more cost than gain. All acts associated with values benefit others in the short run, although the long-range results benefit all.

People who tell the truth, or share, or act in other ways indicative of holding a value must get some payoff, however, or their behavior would extinguish. Although on a given occasion they may be punished for telling the truth or have less of something because of sharing it, they must also sometimes be immediately reinforced in some way. At first, people gain social approval for their honesty, or generosity, or for showing any other value. Later, as they act in honest or generous ways more frequently, their own behavior becomes associated with social approval. "Doing what is right" becomes a conditioned reinforcer. People begin to feel self-satisfaction, or pride, or virtue when they behave well. These feelings do not *cause* the behaviors involved in holding values, they are part of them. Both inner and outer behaviors are maintained by the same contingencies. Feelings, like the public behaviors that accompany them, are learned.

Unlike attitudes which, once learned, are maintained by the natural consequences of pursuing an activity, the behaviors which make up values must be maintained by a group. What the group reinforces (and punishes) defines the value.[2] What is honest, or moral, and so on, therefore, changes from group to group and from one generation to another. The names of the values don't change, only the behaviors which indicate them. An obvious example is sex. Not so very long ago it was immoral for women to show their ankles. Each younger generation has a hard time explaining to the older generation that "times have changed." Different groups *within* the same time period define values differently. What is honest in one group is dishonest from another group's standpoint. The fraternity member, for example, who would not consider ratting when a teacher asked him whether a fellow fraternity member cheated on an exam wouldn't hesitate to report cheating in a contest held by his fraternity. The fraternity member who fails to report cheating doesn't consider himself dishonest, but his teacher may see it a different way. Even such a serious matter as taking another person's life is defined as "murder" from one point of view but as "eliminating the enemy" or "self-defense" from another.

A problem arises when two or more social groups reinforce different behaviors. At home, a student may be reinforced for behaving one way, but at school, the student may be reinforced for behaving differently. Parents or peers, for example, may reinforce racial prejudice while the school is trying to abolish it. Peer groups may reinforce taking drugs while the teacher tries to reinforce *not* taking them. One teacher may

[2]For a similar analysis of "rights," see Ernest A. Vargas, "Rights: A Behavioristic Analysis," *Behaviorism* 3, no. 2 (Fall 1975), pp. 178–190.

reinforce girls for aggressive behavior while another reinforces them when they are passive, yielding, or dependent. Even if a teacher succeeds in teaching students to follow a particular set of values in school, the students may behave differently once they leave school and enter a different social group.

Although it is difficult to teach values that will last, it is not impossible. A value is learned like any other behavior. Frequency of reinforcement, successive approximation, and lack of punishment are just as important for teaching values as for teaching language arts or psychology. Analyzing what behaviors are desirable and looking at their consequences is a start. Some common practices, when analyzed, can be seen to be very destructive. We teach lying, cheating, and injuring others, for example, by what we do. By changing the contingencies, we can instead teach honesty and cooperation. Although different contingencies outside school may support different values, well-established behavior resists change. It can be as difficult for peers to change a behavior established in school as for school to change a behavior established by peers. It is possible for teachers, therefore, to have a lasting impact on their students' values if they manage contingencies wisely.

Honesty. The best way to produce an honest person is to reinforce telling the truth. How often we do the reverse. We get students to tell the truth—to confess to cheating, destroying property, or whatever—and then we punish them. We intend to punish them for their misdeed, but since the punishment follows their confession, we are also punishing honesty. In many cases, students would get out of the punishment if they consistently lied.

Suppose, for example, property is stolen or destroyed—perhaps a microscope is missing, or walls are carved up with obscenities. No one sees the incident, but two boys are suspected because they were seen at the back of the school the night the incident occurred. The two suspects are brought to the biology teacher.

TEACHER: We have had a bit of trouble as you two well know. Last night some school property was destroyed. I'd like you to tell me about the problem. (Silence) We know you two were around the school last night.
DAN: We were jus' playin' baseball.
TEACHER: You were playing baseball at the back entrance to the biology room? Isn't that a funny place to play baseball?

And so on. Half an hour later Dan admits he did it but says Joe had dared him to. If you were to predict what the teacher would do next, what would you predict? Punishment. So long as the boys hold out, they do not get punished. The moment they confess, they are punished.

When punishment is severe, we learn to lie to avoid it. We become literally afraid to tell the truth. For example, if a certain teacher is known to turn over drug users to the police, students will avoid telling the truth if they use drugs. If you were caught with the drug and a needle in your pocket, wouldn't you try to invent a plausible explanation to avoid jail? To avoid punishment, students lie to teachers or to each other; teachers lie to students or to supervisors; husbands and wives lie to each other; politicians lie to their constituencies and to Senate investigating committees.

If you want students to be honest with you, you must reinforce them for telling the truth. You can reinforce honesty by dropping, or at least reducing, the punishment the students normally expect. Usually there is no need for immediate action anyway. You can simply say, "I'm glad you told me the truth," and let it go at that, at least for the time being. Later you can think the whole thing through. The point of punishing is to prevent future occurrences of misbehavior. You cannot change what has already happened but you can help prevent similar infractions in the future. Punishment is not the best way to change student behavior (see Chapter Ten). In addition, it cuts you off from information about what is really going on. The less you punish those who tell about behavior of which you disapprove, the more you will learn the truth from them and from others. It takes a lot of self-control to keep from moralizing to students who suddenly tell you they do something that you strongly disapprove of, but if there was ever a time to hold your tongue and listen, that is it. You can deal with the problem later when you have thought it through.

We need to make a clear distinction between misbehaving and reporting one's own misbehavior. There is a difference between punishing people when you catch them in the act and punishing them when they later tell you they have done something which you did not observe. You want to reinforce telling the truth but not doing wrong. Students will soon distrust you if you pretend to take their side. In contrast, you gain trust by being honest yourself. You may not report a student who tells you about some illegal behavior, but you should not pretend you approve if you do not approve. Some other time you should let the student know what you would do if you caught someone in the act. If you would then report it, you should say so.

Besides reducing or eliminating punishment you can reinforce honesty by any of the techniques described elsewhere in this book. There are hundreds of opportunities in a school. A few examples are listed in Table II. You can probably think of many other ways to handle these or other behaviors, but the principle is the same: reinforce what you want, even when you feel the student should do it without needing reinforcement, and make sure the student does not lose out by being honest.

TABLE II   Some Alternatives to the Punishment Usually Given for Honest Acts

Honest act	Usual consequence	One possible reinforcement
Bringing the teacher money or desirable articles found on the school grounds.	The student doesn't get to keep what he or she found.	Tell the student to hold on to the object found and say that you will ask whether anyone has lost anything. Tell the student that if it is not claimed in three days, he or she may keep it.
Taking responsibility for a late assignment (instead of giving an excuse).	Criticism for not doing it. (An excuse is more likely to get an extension of time).	Give an extension of time for "being honest."
Reporting an unpopular belief (instead of pretending to agree with others or remaining silent).	Disapproval by peers and teachers.	Give public recognition for "having the guts to be honest."
Admitting inability to do something (instead of boasting, faking, or cheating).	Being called stupid, or criticized for not being able to do it, or being forced to try anyway.	"Thank you for telling me." Don't make student "do it anyway." Give alternative on simpler level at which the student can succeed.

BUILDING ATTITUDES AND VALUES

To build any attitudes or values, the teacher must reinforce the actual behaviors desired, not just statements about behaviors. To produce good eating habits, for example, the teacher should reinforce students for selecting milk instead of a soft drink from the beverage machines instead of only reinforcing them for saying, "Milk is better than soda." When too much rides on what they say, students learn to say what teacher wants to hear—but not necessarily to behave any differently otherwise. When reporting and behaving disagree, teachers lose the information they need to help students change. For "good" behavior as well as "bad" behavior, it is better to make consequences follow the behavior itself rather than a report of the behavior.

The problem with providing consequences for behavior rather than for statements about behavior is that you may not be around when the behavior occurs. How can you reinforce your students for eating well or for refusing a cigarette at a party? How can you reinforce generosity at home, or cooperation, or conservation, or all the things which go on outside the classroom? You cannot, but you can influence these behaviors by what you do in class.

SELF-CONTROL

Most of the behaviors classified under the labels "attitudes" and "values" involve working for long-term benefits. The immediate payoff for working at any school is relatively small for most people, compared with reinforcers available outside the classroom. The dropout, for example, can usually get a job at the local gas station and earn more money as a teenager than a friend who stays in school. But having a high school degree has advantages later. Those who give up the short-term advantages gain more advantages later. We have already seen how people who act according to some value stand to lose at first but are likely to benefit in the long run. Students who refuse to cheat may lose the grades their cheating friends obtain, but in the long run they will probably learn more.

Giving up immediate gains for one's future benefit is called *self-control*. We exercise self-control constantly. Every time we give up a sweet, work instead of watching TV, talk politely to someone we dislike, share, and so on, we are denying ourselves immediate reinforcement (sometimes called immediate gratification) for future benefit.

Self-Control

is behavior which has long-term benefits but no conspicuous immediate reinforcement. Such behavior can either (1) decrease the likelihood of future punishment—but result in the loss of immediate reinforcement—or (2) increase the likelihood of future reinforcement—but at an immediate cost. An example of (1) is giving up a reinforcing food to avoid gaining weight. An example of (2) is jogging (which most people find mildly punishing) in order to be healthier in the future.

Self-control is a misleading term because it implies that the control resides inside the individual. What controls students who show good self-control is, of course, no more inside them than what controls anyone else. Such people have learned to work for long periods of time without conspicuous reinforcement but they are maintained by reinforcement nevertheless. What reinforces them are the conditioned reinforcers which bridge the time span from behavior now to payoffs later. They learn this behavior by having reinforcement gradually occur less and less and by having signs of progress toward a goal become conditioned reinforcers through repeated pairing with other reinforcers. None of the behaviors in self-control can appear without this initial reinforcement. As teachers, then, we cannot fade out approval for, say, sharing, until sharing is a well-established behavior. The student cannot feel inner satisfaction at doing a good job without having had approval for similar performance in the past.

Figure 15.3 Too often we talk about creating positive attitudes but dole out punishment as in this cartoon.

SUMMARY

It is not enough to talk about attitudes and values while continuing all of the punitive practices which have been a part of education for centuries. (See Figure 15.3). If you are serious about teaching anything, you need to take the time to specify the behaviors involved, to design sequences of activities to teach them, and to record progress, making sure that it is satisfactory. Attitudes and values are more vaguely defined than content areas like mathematics or history, but they consist of behavior nevertheless. To produce independence, self-control, and all those behaviors which make up attitudes and values, you must design an environment in which your students are reinforced for behaving well. At first you must reinforce frequently, but then, as behavior becomes routine for a student, you reinforce less and less, until natural consequences can take over entirely. The secret to producing positive attitudes and values is to treat the behaviors involved like any others and to shape them step by step.

EXERCISES

Concept Check XVA—Attitudes (Objective A)

Which three of the following statements best tell what an attitude is?

1. The likelihood of a person's behaving in a particular way.
2. What a person says he or she likes and dislikes about something.
3. What an individual thinks, says, and does.
4. The way a person can be expected to act or react to a particular topic.
5. What a standard attitude test measures.

Answers for Concept Check XVA

The best statements are numbers 1, 3, and 4.

Number 2 considers only verbal behavior, which is a small part of what makes up an attitude, as shown in statements such as, "Yes, I know what he [or she] *says*, but I want to know his [or her] *true* attitude."

Number 5 is not a good definition of attitude because responses on a standard attitude test are verbal responses to verbal stimuli. Verbal behavior is only a small part of attitudes (see comments on Number 2). In addition, attitude tests are only a small sample of verbal behavior (they take only about half an hour to about two hours). They are supposed to indicate how and individual would behave in a variety of situations, but their accuracy at doing so depends on the similarity between the contingencies for the actual behavior and for statements about that behavior. (See pages 271–273).

Concept Check XVB—Forming Attitudes (Objective C)

Which three of the following statements describe procedures most likely to create positive attitudes about reading? (Assume that you are the teacher.)

1. Stress the importance of reading and the advantages in life that a good reader has over a poor reader.
2. Give challenging reading exercises and reinforce those who succeed.
3. Have each student read stories (at his or her level) written by other students in the class.
4. Use self-correcting work sheets which slowly become more difficult, making sure that each student progresses successfully.
5. Have students get to do projects of their choice by completing reading assignments tailored to their performance levels.

Answers for Concept Check XVB

The best methods are numbers 3, 4, and 5.

Number 1 is attacking the problem at the wrong end. "Stressing importance" normally precedes responding and is therefore not a consequence for the behavior desired. It is an attempt to convince students that consequences will follow. The way one convinces, however, is by making sure that consequences *do* follow behavior.

Number 2 is a prescription for failure for most students. A "challenging" exercise is one on which there is a high chance of failure. The phrase "reinforce those who succeed" underlines the fact that some may fail. Failure is punishing, and punishment does *not* create positive attitudes. A few students may get extra reinforcement from succeeding at a task that others fail. Reinforcement from beating others, however, is not a natural consequence of doing well, since it depends partly on others doing badly. For a positive attitude the reinforcement ultimately must come from one's *own* efforts and not depend on the behavior of others.

PROBLEM-SOLVING EXERCISES (OBJECTIVE D)

A. Think back over the schooling you have had and see if you can remember an incident or a teacher which you feel had an influence on your attitudes toward a subject, toward school in general, or toward learning. Describe:

1. The incident or what the teacher did (including the setting).
2. The change in your attitude—include as many *specific* behaviors as you can to illustrate the difference in attitude. (For example, instead of saying, "I liked math more afterward," you might say, "Before, I never remember doing any math that was not required, but afterward I remember I asked for a book on math for Christmas and actually read two chapters of it. I also started doing the math puzzles on the backs of cereal boxes. I took math electives in high school and am minoring in math in college. I also make positive statements about math and feel competent in it.")

B. Think back over the course you are now taking for incidents which affected your attitude toward the course and toward operant psychology. Try to think of at least two specific incidents you found which were reinforcing and two which were punishing. Suggest at least two realistic changes in the way the course is run that you feel would improve your attitude toward the course and the subject. What opportunities for reinforcement could be built in? When could you have been reinforced (or did you expect to be reinforced) but did not get reinforced?

Teaching large numbers of students

Few classes at the elementary or secondary school level have more than fifty students in them, but at the college level it is common to find classes with enrollments of hundreds, or even thousands of students. While the principles of teaching are the same regardless of the number of students involved, very large classes pose special problems in management. Part V discusses a technology which is developing to handle large numbers of students while still maintaining the individual treatment of each student so critical for effective teaching.

Individualizing mass education

by Ernest A. Vargas

OVERVIEW

Chapter Sixteen takes a forward look at education, particularly at the problems of mass education. It describes a developing technology which is making it possible to provide the individual contingencies necessary for effective learning, even when teaching large numbers of students at one time.

OBJECTIVES

By the end of the chapter you should be able to:

A. Identify assumptions, procedures, and difficulties of early and traditional educational endeavors.
B. Identify the technological developments that have made possible the individualization of mass education.
C. Identify what system analysis is and its uses and difficulties.
D. Show how operant psychology has made it possible to apply other technologies to mass education.
E. Identify the pertinent characteristics of computer technology and its uses.
F. Identify examples of media and tell how they can contribute to effective education.

THE COMING OF A TECHNOLOGY OF EDUCATION

Organizations transform raw materials into finished products. Some sort of stuff, whether energy or matter, is taken by an organization and converted into something else. The transformation is intended to add value so that the product is useful somewhere else. A large class of organizations is concerned with changing people—for example, hospitals, health spas, mental institutions, nurseries, day-care centers, elementary and high schools, and universities.

Schools are the most common of the people-changing organizations around us. Their basic aims are to socialize people and to shape skills. People are taught to conduct themselves in a civil and moral fashion with respect to others. They are also taught to do things they were not able to do before entering school. What they are able to do and the degree to which they can do it gives them value to others.

What they should be able to do is designated by the curriculum. It specifies the changes wanted in behavior and the stimulus materials to bring them about. The degree to which people can do what is designated is a function of the teaching process. The teaching process is the technology of changing people.

This process, in its institutional expression, has been applied only to a small number of people in most societies. With small numbers of people, teaching has been conducted in the classroom much as it was in everyday life. It has been roughly observed that if events are presented one or more times to individuals, their behavior is changed with respect to the events. As a child, Dick toddles about and throws a small circular object around. His mother consistently hands it to him and says, "Ball." After many handings, the child says "ball" when previously he did not. How this change happens has been unknown for some time.

There has been a great deal of speculation about how people learn, most of it concerned with those mechanisms inside their heads said to be responsible for learning. Methods used to teach people were then justified by the conjectured mechanisms. The few people whose behavior changed under any schooling situation "proved" the efficacy of whatever technology of teaching was being promoted. The burden of failure was thrown on those who did not learn; they were said to lack "inner substance," either neurological or moral. They "didn't have enough brains," "lacked intelligence," "didn't have enough mathematical and language aptitude," or "lacked ambition," "had insufficient motivation," "were not interested," and so forth.

Others had a kinder view of the inner state of the students' character. It was a matter of providing opportunity for the students' "spirit of inquiry to emerge," or for their "imagination to develop," or for "their creativity to be expressed." The younger the students, the more their inner state was defined in this manner. If in later years these qualities were not expressed, it was because the students' "inner qualities" had been stifled or killed by society or by the system. Nothing was lacking in the students—it was the situation that failed to draw out what was best in each individual.

In both cases, the students were presumed to have certain kinds of qualities—aptitude, ambition, creativity—that if missing or suppressed prevented their learning. A distinction was usually made between those qualities dealing with motivation and those dealing with cognition, but in practice the relationship between the two was never clearly settled. If students were concerned and interested, they would try to learn, and if they still did not learn, they were incapable. If they did not try, they were inadequately motivated, and regardless of their abilities would not learn. When the burden was placed on the students, lack of learning was seen as deliberate obstinacy or inadequate intellectual talents. When the burden was on the school, lack of learning was said to be due to the fact that the students were insufficiently motivated by those responsible for their learning.

Neither approach has produced a technology which can handle the problem of individual differences. Differences are not a problem when only a small elite is being educated, especially at the university level. The teacher's style does not change from pupil to pupil, but the good teacher takes into account the rate at which things are learned, the manner of learning, and what is of specific interest. Individual differences are also not a problem when only those who will learn easily are selected to be taught. Groton and other private schools did a great deal for the educational quality and ranking of Harvard, and the homes from which Groton boys came did the same for Groton. The individual who went to Harvard had already had extensive training for the type of education he was to receive. Only those who would be likely to learn were allowed to be taught. Those who did not succeed were given a "gentleman's education" somewhere else.

The difficulties of teaching people in larger groups became exacerbated with the coming of mass education. Education today is largely a matter of "batch processing." A group of students is exposed to the same stimulus or given the same treatment at a particular time. The small classroom of 20 to 30 students and the large lecture hall of 400 to 500 students are the two typical instructional settings in the university. In most cases a lecturer talks; sometimes a film is shown, a record played, or slides presented. In any case, a "common" stimulus is applied. It is assumed that all students will or can react the same way; that is, that all will learn from the common stimulus. This assumption presumes that every individual in the group is much the same with respect to the stimulus or information presented.

Obviously this is not true. Some students do not understand and others are bored. Only a small segment of the group performs as desired when assessed by some sort of test. Large numbers of people have had to be treated alike because there was not a good enough way to consider the special qualities of each one of them.

Education has had to proceed in this crude fashion, processing people in the smallest, most convenient homogeneous unit, because it did not have a sufficiently powerful technology to process large numbers of people on an individual basis. "Technology" is used here in its broadest sense—a way of getting things done. It includes not only the techniques

---

Technology

is a way of getting things done. It includes the use of techniques, tools, and energy.

---

used but also the tools and energy. The larger the number of things to be processed and the greater the detail work to be done on any one of them, the more powerful the technology must be.

Four developments now make it possible to have an effective technology of education when a large number of students must be taught, while taking into account the individual characteristics of each learner. The most important has been an experimental analysis of behavior— *operant psychology*, from which a practical teaching technology could be drawn. Operant principles are being utilized in the fluid and complex situation of the large classroom in more than a hit or miss fashion through the techniques of *system analysis*. Developments in *media* equipment and in *computers* and their accompanying software now make it possible to individualize the delivery of stimuli and the processing of data on each student.

SYSTEM ANALYSIS IN EDUCATION

Anything can be denoted as a system—the body, a car, an engine, an organization, the sun and its planets (the solar system), and so on. The distinctive feature in calling anything or any process a system is that it has components which interact with each other so that changing any one part will affect the others. System analysis is simply a way of talking

---

A System

is any collection of things or processes which interact in an orderly way so that changing one part affects the others in a consistent fashion.

---

about the parts that make up the system. System analysis is a method which delineates all the components in a complex process and describes their relationships over time toward a specified objective. The effect any one part of an operation has on another is denoted explicitly. Using system analysis, the relative contributions of different educational techniques are analyzable at the time of operation or later on. The cost of specific techniques can be weighed against their benefits, allowing an assessment of the relative value of the technique or of the type and number of resources necessary to educate a given number of students and achieve a specific teaching objective.

System analysis methods have been available for some time. Early attempts to apply them to the learning situation within the classroom, however, were not too successful. They were much more successfully applied to nonlearning activities, such as school transportation, inventory needs, and facilities requirements.

Previous Problems in Using System Analysis in Education   The major difficulty in the previous use of system analysis in education has been the lack of a unit of measurement to assess learning. There were crude formulations, such as income over a person's earning lifetime, and they have been used to justify education. A person, on the average, earns more, the more education he or she has obtained. People with eighth grade educations have less earning power, in general, than those with college educations. But this is a questionable way to assess the significance of education. Further, it involves long-term results which, while of concern, do not indicate the immediate results of any teaching process.

It is difficult to get a measure of the effects of teaching when these effects are said to be unmeasurable. For example, how can learning be measured when what the student obtains is an "understanding" of poetry, an "appreciation" of music, a "knowledge" of physics, and so forth? It has been said that test results are merely what a person accomplishes on a test and do not capture the essence of what transpires between the student and the teacher. If the premise of unmeasurability is valid, these objections have merit. It *is* impossible to design a system approach to teaching if learning is unmeasurable, unobservable.

A Behavioral Solution   Any process that specifies outcomes has to have these outcomes denoted in observable terms. Reformulating the learning process in behavioral terms makes a measurable unit available. Changes in the activities of the student—learning—can be directly observed. Treatment effects on learning as it takes place—of media (including teachers), materials, reinforcers—can be immediately studied. The student's progression can be articulated logically and sequentially on the basis of what he or she is capable of doing next. Psychological principles, techniques such as programmed instruction, and statements of behavioral objectives drawn from an operant formulation of learning have made it possible to apply system techniques to the classroom.

The insistence on specifying the learning process in measurable and observable terms does not imply the denial of private events. It is simply a question of their status. It is not possible to build a teaching sequence on events to which there is no access. From an operant point of view, it is not necessary to know all the stimulus events affecting a student in order to organize his or her behavior coherently toward a given goal.

What is observed when a person performs is learning, not merely a performance reflecting some inner essence called "learning." The record of total behavior may be incomplete, but this is a matter of instrumentation and instructional design. The only other dimension that could be directly altered would be physiological. For example, some device such as a biofeedback mechanism could amplify and exhibit brain wave activity and thus indicate different levels of activity as the student studies. But this, for human beings, is not very practical, at least in the immediate future. For a large class of teaching events, physiological intervention may never be practical. Even if it were possible to intervene physiologically, the learning situation would still have to be arranged in terms of a response the person would make, the conditions under which this would occur, and some critical consequence that would follow.

The arrangement of these three factors—some sort of activity on the individual's part, the circumstances under which this activity occurs, and its consequences—is a necessary consideration in teaching any human activity. This is as true for creative or imaginative activity as it is for simple recitation. Creativity simply refers to the fact that the individual's unique history is brought to bear on the product that he or she is producing. There are still standards for any creative product, but not all of the characteristics are specified in detail. In asking for the product we denote the activity and type of thing wanted and provide the setting, so that whatever must be done is highly likely to be done, and then we reinforce accordingly. If one wants a drawing from a child, paint and paper must be provided, as well as attention for anything initially drawn.

The behavioral outcomes for anything desired to be taught can be specified. The objectives for any curricular sequence are therefore behavioral and denote explicitly the effects of teaching. Specifying outcomes behaviorally is therefore an evaluational tool designed not to constrain the learner but to inform the teacher. Examination of the specific contingencies operating on the learner forces attending to what is done to produce change, and therefore highlights the specific effects of different teaching activities and the resources necessary to sustain those activities.

USING THE COMPUTER IN EDUCATION

In addition to system analysis and the experimental analysis of behavior, the third major technological effect on education has been a tool: the computer. The computer may be used three ways in instruction: to keep track of what individuals are doing, to manage their activities, and to directly instruct. All relevant instruction and student learning may be recorded in computer-tracked instruction. Students do so many things over a short period of time that it is difficult to keep a record of what occurs. The computer counts what is occurring and summarizes those data. This information is provided to the appropriate staff, who use it for various purposes. For example, a computer might print out a record like the following to describe in reasonable detail a student's progress:

SMITH AUSTIN   POINTS

Unit number	Date completed	Grade (%)	Unit	Project	Attendance	Total
9	091	95	3	0	0.0	3.0
8	084	100	3	0	0.0	3.0
7	077	95	3	0	0.0	3.0
6	070	95	3	0	0.0	3.0
5	056	90	3	0	0.0	3.0
4	045	95	0	0	0.0	0.0
3	029	90	3	0	0.0	3.0
2	024	95	3	0	0.0	3.0
1	021	95	3	0	0.0	3.0
0	000	0	0	2	0.5	2.5
0	000	0	0	2	0.5	2.5
0	000	0	0	2	0.0	2.0
0	000	0	0	2	0.5	2.5
0	000	0	0	2	0.5	2.5

The teaching staff would use this information to tell whether a conference is necessary with the student and, if so, to locate where difficulties lie.

In computer-managed instruction, the computer manages a portion, or all, of the instructional process. What individuals should do at any step is decided beforehand, and when they reach a choice point, the computer gives them an alternative dictated by the characteristics of their situation. A pretest might be taken at a computer console. After the pretest, the computer might print out something like the following message:

"Your pretest score was 55. Students who make this score should read chapters 3, 4, & 5. The pattern of your errors indicates that close attention should be paid to Chapter 4, especially pages 47 to 54."

Students who score higher might receive a message informing them that they are to proceed to a new lesson.

In computer-assisted instruction, part of the instruction is actually done by the computer. Information is presented to the student, who reacts to it. The next piece of information depends on the kind of response the student makes. The computer may do all of the instructing or it may supplement other methods.

How useful the computer is as its use moves from simply recording to instructing remains to be seen. As a teacher, it is no more or less effective than any other instrument. Its potential lies in being a private tutor. Depending on how it is programmed, it may be a good or a bad tutor. Eventually, it may be possible to have an order of sophistication in the computer's programs which would allow it to respond appropriately to any sort of human behavior.

Whatever the eventual contribution of the computer to tutoring, there is no doubting its advantage for individualizing large courses. Only an army of clerks could keep track of the many steps in the progress of many students in one or more courses. The computer's circuits are that army. It is possible to treat students as individuals only when there is up-to-date information on what they could be doing and what they are doing. When what has been designed is not working properly for a certain student, new steps can be prescribed and a record of their effect made available. The results of each prescription represent a different arrangement of what is known about the student. The computer makes it possible to maintain some order in the quick flow of data on individual students.

THE USE OF MEDIA IN EDUCATION

The fourth major technological change in education is in how stimuli are presented to the student. The use of different media to present information is not new. Various aids have been used as long as there have

---

Media

are the vehicles which present material to the student. Some common media are books, movies, blackboards, and teachers. The singular of media is *medium.*

---

been teaching situations. It is said that an ancient Greek king despaired that his son would never master the 24 letters, from alpha to omega, of the Greek alphabet, "so he gathered 24 young slaves, named them after the letters of the alphabet, and had them live continually with his son as a visual aid."[1] In general, however, old media were not so elaborate and were rather limited to the teacher, the book, and the blackboard. But there is no longer any necessity to be limited to any one prevalent medium. The most appropriate medium with respect to the material and the type of student should be the one used to present the stimulus. Behavior is changed more effectively by using the appropriate form of stimulus delivery. The relationship between media and materials, how-

[1]Martin Ballard, *The Story of Teaching,* New York, Philosophical Library, 1971, p. 12.

ever, is still pursued in an ad hoc fashion, primarily through trial and error, for there are few principles by which to be guided.

The basic aim is to achieve greater stimulus control over the response. Material can be packaged in ways which interest the students. Motivating, or interesting, the students means in part reinforcing them for attending to the material to be learned. Stimuli and sequences of stimuli can be presented in arrangements which are reinforcing, independent of the subject matter. Color, rhythymic sounds, and movement powerfully reinforce attending behavior.

"Colorful" media are useful, but there is a danger that learners may react only to the motivational stimuli and not to the initially weaker instructional stimuli to which they were intended to respond. Flashing lights might simply focus attention on the lights and not on what is supposed to be taught by having attention brought to it. Fancy photography may have the students looking at the camera angles rather than at what the picture is supposed to illustrate. A television monitor that is in an antique casing may have the students admiring the casing rather than watching the program. Eventually, media which reinforce attending must be faded out so that the learners react only to the presence of the instructional material and, finally, only to the changes in their own verbal behavior brought about by the material. A common form of mediated instruction is a book. Other people, places, things, and events are portrayed without the students directly encountering them. Eventually the students must talk or write or think about what the book presents without the book being present.

Mediated Instruction

is instruction in which the student does not directly experience the stimuli to which he or she is to respond, but instead responds to representations of them in picture, word, sound, and so on. A teacher's description of how to do something, for example, is mediated instruction, since the student isn't responding in the situation itself, but to a description of it.

Initially, events surrounding individuals are discriminative stimuli for action, but sooner or later their own behavior must perform this function, as in thinking. Much behavior starts out by being overt but may recede to the covert under the appropriate contingencies and if reinforcement is maintained. When this happens to behavior which is oral, we call it thinking, but it may also happen to perceptual behavior. For example, one may "see" an object in three dimensions without directly observing it. This sort of behavior is very useful because it eventually occurs away from the circumstances which shaped it. However, thinking must be taught, and the use of extravagant forms of media may divert efforts away from teaching it. It is too easy to presume *learning* when only attending is occurring; the form of the two behaviors is too similar. Flashy textbooks for college undergraduates guarantee only that the students will look, not necessarily learn. The results of misusing media are finally obvious when students are tested on what they should have learned. Misuses are, unfortunately, less obvious in those sorts of behaviors, such as thinking or covert perceptual behavior, which are not directly tied to course material.

The child who sees the objects and events described by a storyteller does so only because he has been exposed to complex contingencies involving actual events, pictured or otherwise. (Such contingencies are not as common as they once were. With audiovisual aids and devices the modern child is not often required to "see things which are not really there." He does not visualize very much when being read to from books with pictures in four colors on every page. Moving pictures and television remove practically all occasions for covert seeing. This is education for *Life* or the comics, but it does not prepare the student to read unillustrated materials.)[2]

Media also increase the control of certain characteristics of the stimulus by more closely presenting its actual properties and by adding to the range of characteristics a stimulus has. For example, if something moves, it's useful to show it moving. Something may not have color but it may be useful to add color to highlight it. Media further expedite the learning process through a variety of tools which sharpen the stimuli in the learning environment and enhance the individual's sensory capabilities. Carrels and headphones (see Figure 16.1) cut out extraneous competing stimuli; slide-tape presentations coordinate and sometimes combine the sound and visual aspects of the same information. Television and films magnify an action and maintain it, or by slowing it down or speeding it up, bring out subtle aspects of whatever is pictured.

One last point: using other media besides teachers seems to upset many people. However, other media make possible a human, and sophisticated, use of teachers. They are no longer simply a mobile, low powered amplifying device with a great deal of storage capacity in a small space. They are *that* when they simply recite facts or repeat themselves semester after semester. Man's peculiar feedback capacities can be utilized to correct, amplify, and innovate.

As a medium, human beings are a particular kind of teaching device with certain qualities and characteristics. In instructional design, they are used when certain effects are desired. This is when instructional outcomes call for a certain type of product but cannot specify it in detail; for example, when students are to make unique responses. Teachers respond not only to the behavioral cues supplied by the students, but to

[2]B. F. Skinner, *The Technology of Teaching*, New York, Appleton-Century-Crofts, 1968, pp. 125–126.

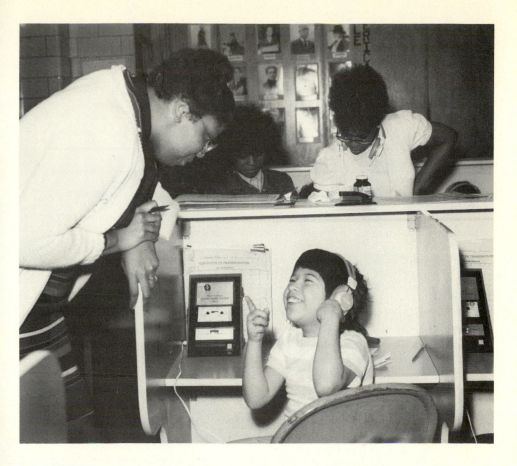

Figure 16.1   Media increase the range of stimuli to which a student can respond. This student can hear a variety of voices, sounds, and pronunciations through the medium of a tape. (Whittier Elementary School, Pontiac, Michigan. Courtesy of New Century Education Corporation.)

the changes in their own behavior initiated by those cues. These changes occur because teachers are members of the same verbal community and therefore attach the same meaning to discriminative stimuli as the persons who emitted them.[3] As yet no machine can do this, and unless it has the same components as a human being, no machine ever will.

SUMMARY

The principles of teaching are the same whether one is teaching one student or hundreds of students. We must look at the behavior of each

[3]For an elaboration of this point, see B. F. Skinner, *Verbal Behavior,* New York, Appleton-Century-Crofts, 1957, especially chapters 1 and 2.

individual in both cases. With the help of the computer, individual records can be kept even on large numbers of students, and instruction can be adjusted according to each individual's records. By looking at behavior and becoming sensitive to small changes in behavior, you as a teacher behave according to each student's progress. It is only then that you can be most effective in helping each student learn.[4]

EXERCISES

Concept Check XVIA—An Operant Approach to Learning (Objective A)

Which three of the following statements illustrate an operant approach to learning (as compared with earlier views of learning)?

1. Learning is observable and measurable.
2. When a student consistently performs differently after doing some exercises, that difference indicates learning, it doesn't just reflect learning.
3. A student's learning is due to the presence or absence of inner qualities that he or she possesses, such as intelligence, drive, or ingenuity.
4. All students could be predicted to respond the same way to a given stimulus, such as a lecture.
5. The progress that a student makes can be changed by changing the conditions under which he or she learns.

Answers for Concept Check XVIA

The operant approach is illustrated by statements 1, 2, and 5.

Number 3 invents "causes" for behaviors observed, resulting in explanatory fictions.

Number 4 ignores the whole science of operant psychology, which is concerned with how an individual's previous history of reinforcement or punishment and deprivation or satiation affects how he or she responds to a stimulus. You would expect different people to act differently to as complicated a set of stimuli as those of a lecture because of the uniqueness of each student's history and genetic endowment.

Concept Check XVIB—Media (Objective F)

Which three of the following are examples of media?

1. A concept
2. An article from a book

[4]For examples of work in higher education from a behavioral perspective, see Laurence L. Fraley and Ernest A. Vargas (eds.), *Behavioral Research and Technology in Higher Education* III, Box 233A, Reedsville, W. Va., The Society for Behavioral Analysis of Culture, 1976.

3. A teacher
4. Chalk and a blackboard
5. How a student responds

Answers for Concept Check XVIB

The three examples of media are numbers 2, 3, and 4.

Number 1 is a set of properties of things which may be presented by media and it is part of the content rather than the vehicle by which that content is presented.

Number 5 is what the student does, not how stimuli are presented to him or to her.

Glossary

Active behavior

Behavior which changes. Running, talking, and writing are active because we can see them progress and change. Even "thinking" is active because the thinker can "observe" his or her thoughts changing. However, "paying attention" and "sitting" are **not** active because they do not specify change.

Active responding

A feature of instruction which requires students to behave rather than to sit and listen. Lessons in which **each** student talks, writes, solves problems, or otherwise responds at a high rate are said to require **active responding.**

Attitude

A predisposition to behave in a certain way. A positive **attitude** toward science is a predisposition to behave in certain ways regarding science, including saying certain kinds of things, spending money or time on science, and so on.

Aversive stimulus

The kind of stimulus we commonly call unpleasant or painful. Technically, any stimulus whose presentation decreases the probability of responding or whose removal is reinforcing. Sometimes called **punisher** or **negative reinforcer.**

Avoidance

Behavior which reduces or eliminates stimuli which in the past have been followed by punishment. The punishment then, does not occur. **Avoidance** is different from **escape** in that in **avoidance** we do not experience the punishment, whereas in **escape** we get out of punishment that has already started. For example, we **avoid** a traffic jam by taking an alternate route before we get in the jam, whereas we **escape** from a traffic jam by taking an alternate route after we have already gotten caught in the jam.

Baseline

The level of a particular behavior before it was changed. **Baseline** is the same thing as **operant level, starting level,** or **pretreatment level.** If these are measured in rate, they are also equivalent to **base rate.**

Base rate

The rate of a particular behavior before it was changed. See **Baseline.**

Behavior

Any action of an individual. **Operant behavior** is behavior which "operates" on the environment, changing it in some way.

Behavior modification

Changing of behavior. While all teaching could be seen as **behavior modification,** the term usually refers to (1) the explicit use of reinforcers to change behavior (as in a token economy), or (2) clinical uses of **respondent** conditioning, such as "desensitization" or "aversion therapy."

Behavioral objectives

Statements of what students should be able to do at the end of a unit of study. They are also called **performance objectives** and **terminal objectives.**

Behaviorism

The philosophy of the science of human behavior. It is the position that we can study behavior scientifically and that we do so by finding the variables of which it is a function. Modern behaviorism is further separated into **methodological behaviorism,** which holds that the behavior we can study is only that which can be measured by two independent observers (thus excluding all inner behavior), and **radical behaviorism,** which includes inner behaviors such as "thoughts" and "dreams" as valid behavior to investigate. B. F. Skinner is the leading spokesman for **radical behaviorism,** which is the position taken in this book.

Chaining

The result when one response alters some of the variables which control another response. For example, the first number a student writes in solving a long-division problem becomes part of the stimuli that control the next number he or she writes. Each number written alters the stimuli to which the student responds. The result is called **chaining.**

Classical conditioning

See Conditioning.

Competency-Based Instruction

Any method of teaching set up to help each student reach objectives that are specified behaviorally. The behaviors required are called **competencies.**

Concept

A property or set of properties of stimuli. For example, the **concept** "red" is a property shared by all of the things we call "red."

Conditioning

The strengthening of a particular behavior. In **respondent conditioning** repeated pairing of a neutral stimulus with a stimulus which already elicits a response results in the neutral stimulus gaining control over that response in a new reflex. In **operant conditioning** a kind of response becomes more likely in a particular situation when similar responses in similar situations have been reinforced.

Contingency

The relationship between a kind of response, the stimuli which precede it, and the stimuli which follow. All three terms must be specified in a complete statement of a contingency. The plural of **contingency** is **contingencies,** or **contingencies of reinforcement.**

Contingency-shaped behavior
Behavior which has been learned by directly experiencing success or failure. **Contingency-shaped behavior** is contrasted with **rule-governed behavior,** which is under control of rules rather than having been shaped by contingencies.

Contingency management
The arranging of contingencies in order to produce specified behavior(s).

Contingent reinforcement
Reinforcement that depends, in some way, on responding. Reinforcement that is contingent on speaking, for example, may not follow *every* spoken response, but it depends on speaking in that it does not occur unless speaking occurs. The particular relationship between responding and reinforcement is specified in the **schedule of reinforcement. Contingent reinforcement** is contrasted with **noncontingent reinforcement,** which occurs regardless of what a person is doing.

Continuous reinforcement (abbreviated crf)
The reinforcement of every response. For example, dispensing machines are set up on a schedule of continuous reinforcement; each response (of inserting the correct change and selecting an item) is supposed to be reinforced by getting the item selected.

Criticism trap
A situation in which criticizing a behavior you dislike seems to work by temporarily stopping it, but which actually reinforces the behavior so that it occurs more often in the future, not less.

Cue
A stimulus which sets the occasion for a particular response. The technical term for **cue** is **discriminative stimulus** (S^D or S^Δ).

Cumulative record
A graph of the running total of responses made. New responses are added on to the old total so that, in a cumulative record, the data line can only go up. How fast it goes up depends on the rate of responding—the more rapid the responding, the steeper the climb. A horizontal line indicates no responding.

Dependent variable
What we are trying to "explain." In psychology, the **dependent variable** is some aspect of behavior that **depends** on other variables in a functional relationship.

Deprivation
The reduced availability of a reinforcer. A student who has not been able to talk with other students for an hour has had an hour's **deprivation** of the social reinforcement of talking with peers.

Discrimination
The process of responding differently in the presence of different stimuli.

Discriminative stimulus (S^D, pronounced **ess-dee**, or S^Δ, pronounced **ess-delta**)
A stimulus in the presence of which a particular response is likely to be, or not to be, reinforced. It sets the occasion for the response. For example the stimulus, "Hi, how are you?" is an S^D for the response "Fine" because it sets the occasion upon which the response "Fine" is usually reinforced. An

S^Δ for the response "Fine" would be the question, "What is your name?" A response of "Fine" to that question is not likely to be reinforced. Both S^D's and S^Δ's are **discriminative stimuli.**

Elicit

Produce as an invariable result. A puff of air on the eye **elicits** an eye blink.

Emit

Produce, but not as an invariable result of any particular stimulus. A student in a class **emits** many responses which are not an automatic response to any preceding stimuli.

Entering behavior

The behavior of a person upon "entering" a program or course. Actually not all of the behavior is considered, just that which is relevant to the program. **Entering behavior** differs from **baseline** (or **operant level**) in that it includes behavior other than that which is to be changed, whereas **baseline** and **operant level** refer only to behavior that is to be changed. For example, in learning to spell second grade words, a student might have a **baseline**, or **operant level,** of zero (the student cannot yet spell any of them), but the person has **entering behavior** which will be helpful, such as the ability to print letters, to follow directions, and so on.

Equal-interval graph

A graph which has lines equally spaced up and down the vertical axis so that when you add or subtract a certain amount, you move up or down the same distance, no matter where on the graph you start.

Equal-ratio graph

Is a graph which has numbers spaced on the vertical axis so that *ratios* will be equal up and down the graph. If you multiply or divide by a certain amount (that is, change by a certain ratio) you move up or down the same distance, no matter where on the graph you start.

Escape behavior

Behavior that is reinforced by getting out of an aversive situation. **Escape** is different from **avoidance** in that in **escape** we start out *in* the aversive situation, whereas in **avoidance** we do not get into the aversive situation in the first place. For example, we **escape** from rain by taking shelter after it starts to rain on us but we **avoid** rain by taking shelter before it starts to rain on us.

Explanatory fiction

Is a statement that has the form of an explanation but whose "cause" is really the same as its "effect." In an **explanatory fiction** the same set of facts is described both by the behavior that is supposedly being explained and by the explanation. An example is, "Sarah doesn't read as well as you would expect from her reading aptitude scores because she is an underachiever in reading." Both "cause" and "effect" describe the difference between Sarah's aptitude scores and reading performance.

Extinction

Is a process in which a response is repeated without reinforcement. When we **extinguish** a behavior, we withhold the reinforcement that has maintained that behavior in the past so that responses go unreinforced. Note that **extinguish** is *not* the same as **eliminate.** There are many ways of eliminating a behavior besides extinction.

Fading
The gradual removal of a prompt or other help or cue for responding.

Feedback
Any indication of the effectiveness of a response. An instructor gives **feedback** when telling a student how well his or her response has met some criteria. **Feedback** is often as simple as a mark indicating whether a response is "right" or "wrong."

Fixed-interval schedule
See Schedules of reinforcement.

Fixed-ratio schedule
See Schedules of reinforcement.

Frequency graph
A graph showing the number (that is, the frequency) of times something occurred during each session a count was taken. For example, a **frequency graph** might have, on its vertical axis, the number of responses, the number of opportunities taken, or the number of correct and incorrect problems solved.

Frequency of reinforcement
How often reinforcement occurs. It can refer to the number of reinforcements per unit of time or to the number of responses that are reinforced out of the number made.

Functional relationship
A relationship in which one variable changes systematically according to the value of another.

Generalization
The spread of effect from a particular stimulus to other stimuli that share common elements.

Generalized reinforcers
Reinforcers that are associated with a variety of other reinforcers. Money is a common example of a **generalized reinforcer.**

Immediate feedback
A consequence that occurs just as a response is being completed or just after it has been completed. To be immediate the consequence must occur before a second response is made. **Immediate feedback** may occur naturally or it may be added. The high jumper gets natural **immediate feedback** for each jump from whether or not the bar falls down. He or she may also get **immediate feedback** that is added by a coach commenting on form as each jump is completed.

Immediate reinforcement
Reinforcement which occurs while the reinforced person is still responding, or at least before he or she has a chance to make another response.

Incompatible behaviors
Behaviors which an individual cannot do at the same time. For example, whistling and drinking are **incompatible.** One cannot do both at the same time.

Independent variable
Any variable that is different from the dependent variable in that it can change **independently** of it. It is something that can change when the de-

pendent variable does not or can remain the same when the dependent variable changes. An **independent variable** can also change in a different direction or at a different rate from the **dependent variable**. (For any **dependent variable**, there are thousands of **independent variables**. In looking for "causes" of behavior, we look for the particular **independent variables** of which behavior is a function.)

Individualized instruction
Instruction in which what each student does, and how fast he or she progresses, depends on his or her performance.

Intermittent reinforcement
Reinforcement that does not follow every response. Only some responses are reinforced.

Interval schedules of reinforcement
See Schedules of reinforcement.

Intrinsic motivation
The control of behavior by the natural consequences the behavior itself produces. Natural consequences may be conditioned reinforcers—that is, they may be stimuli that have become important through their association with other reinforcers. For example, when society reinforces certain kinds of markings, **those** markings become conditioned reinforcers. Thus we become reinforced by seeing ourselves produce the kinds of pictures which have in the past been socially reinforced, even if now no one is around to notice. Our motivation to draw is then called **intrinsic**.

Learning
The change in behavior from living and behaving in any environment.

Mand
Verbal behavior which primarily reinforces the "speaker." Commands, requests, and gestures for someone else to do something are all **mands** because the compliance of the "listener" primarily reinforces the "speaker."

Model
A person whose behavior is imitated by others or a product with characteristics that others try to reproduce.

Module
A unit of instruction, often consisting of a pretest, instructional materials, and a posttest.

Motivation
1) The contingencies for responding—roughly speaking, the "reasons" for behaving. 2) The degree to which an individual has been deprived or satiated with a particular reinforcer. 3) The extent to which a student's behavior is controlled by the natural consequences of behaving rather than by artificial reinforcers introduced by others; in everyday language, "how much enjoyment the student gets out of working."

Natural (or intrinsic) consequences
Stimulus changes which are produced by (and are dependent on) the behavior of the individual who experiences them. **Natural consequences** are contrasted with **artificial** or **extrinsic** consequences, which are provided by (and are dependent on) the behavior of others.

Needs
Behaviors which a person lacks which are necessary in order to function effectively and independently both in the present and in the future.

Negative reinforcement
The reinforcement from the termination of an aversive stimulus. For example, the termination of a baby's crying **negatively reinforces** a mother for picking the child up.

Negative reinforcer
An aversive stimulus. A stimulus which strengthens behavior when removed or weakens behavior when presented.

Operant
A group of responses which produce, and are controlled by, similar consequences. Examples are "eating," "talking," and "thinking about arithmetic." **"An operant"** is roughly equivalent to the term "a behavior," except that it does not include behavior controlled by a preceding stimulus, such as the behavior in a reflex. "Blinking in response to a loud sound," for example, is not an operant.

Operant conditioning
A process in which behavior is "strengthened," in the sense of becoming more likely to occur, through reinforcement.

Operant level
How often, how rapidly, or how forcefully a response was made before a treatment or program was started. Roughly speaking, what the behavior was like at the beginning. **Operant level** is the same as **baseline.** When the **operant level** is measured in rate, it is also the same as **base rate.**

Percent graph
A graph of the percent of correct responses, percent of opportunities taken, percent of times that a response occurred out of the times checked, and so on. **Percent graphs** do *not* show how many responses were made or how rapidly responses were made.

Personalized system of instruction (PSI)
A method of teaching developed by Fred S. Keller. PSI has the following characteristics.

1. Units: Material is broken down into units which consist of:
   a study guide which includes a behavioral statement of what the student is expected to do on a test.
   materials which each student studies on his or her own.
   a test or tests.
2. "Self-pacing" progression thorugh the units: Students may take a test on a unit whenever they feel ready (although there are usually advantages for meeting certain deadlines).
3. "Mastery criteria" students may not go on to the next unit until they have passed the previous unit test at some specified level. Students may take a test more than once.
4. Personal tutoring: Instructors, called "proctors," grade tests (right away) and tutor any student having problems.

Premak principle
The principle that one can use the opportunity to do something that one is **likely** to do to reinforce doing something that one is **not** as likely to do.

For example, one can use the opportunity to play ball to reinforce a person for doing something he or she is less likely to do, such as washing dishes.

Primary reinforcer
Any reinforcer which is necessary for the survival of the species. Food, water, and sex, for example, are **primary reinforcers.**

Probability of response
How likely it is that a response will occur. Since we cannot see a "probability," in practice **probability of response** is measured by frequency or rate of responding.

Programmed instruction (also spelled Programed instruction)
Instruction which is broken down into steps, each of which requires the student to respond. **Branching programs** have a short passage to study and then a multiple-choice item. For each choice, the students are sent to a different section, either telling them they are correct (and giving the next step) or explaining why they are wrong and sending them back to try again. **Linear programs** have very short items, called **frames,** which typically have a sentence to be completed or require the students to draw or construct something. The students are supposed to respond and then uncover the answer. They then proceed to the next item. The amount of active responding required in **linear programs** is greater than that in **branching.** B. F. Skinner wrote the first **linear program** as an attempt to shape the behavior of the student.

Prompt
A supplementary stimulus to help a student respond. For example, if a student cannot remember a technical term we can give a **prompt** by, for example, telling him or her the first letter. Note that later **prompts** are "faded" so that the student eventually responds without them.

Punishment
Any event that decreases the probability of the response it follows; the application of aversive stimuli or the removal of stimuli which are reinforcing. If we punish for something that occurs often, that behavior then has two consequences: whatever is reinforcing the behavior and our **punishment.**

Respondent conditioning
See Conditioning.

Rate
The number of times something occurs within a specified time period. **Rates of behavior** are often reported in "responses per minute," "responses per hour," or "responses per day."

Rate graph
A graph of rate, that is, of the number of responses *per unit of time,* such as problems correct per minute, number of sentences spoken per hour, or the number of cigarettes smoked per day.

Ratio schedules of reinforcement
See Schedules of reinforcement.

Relevance
The usefulness of skills learned—both for a student's immediate life and for the life he or she may lead many years later.

Reinforcement

Any event which maintains or increases the probability of the response it follows. Either the presentation of a positive reinforcer or the removal or reduction of an aversive stimulus.

Resistance to extinction

How long a response will be repeated after it is no longer reinforced or how many responses will be made after they are no longer reinforced.

Respondent behavior

Behavior which is controlled by the stimulus which precedes it. The stimulus-response sequence is called a **reflex.** Blinking at a puff of air, blushing at a compliment, and jumping at a loud sound are examples of **respondent behavior.**

Response

A unit of behavior with a clear beginning and end. **Responses** can be **operant** or **respondent**, depending on whether they are controlled by stimuli which follow them or by stimuli which precede them. How much behavior constitutes "a **response**" is largely arbitrary. We can talk about the **response** of saying one word or of giving a whole lecture.

S^D (pronounced ess-dee)

A discriminative stimulus in the presence of which a response is likely to be reinforced. The end of a concert performance is an S^D for clapping.

S^Δ (pronounced (ess-delta)

A discriminative stimulus in the presence of which a response is not likely to be reinforced. For example, a concert *in progress* is an S^D for clapping.

Satiation

The repeated receiving of reinforcement. The longer a person talks with peers, the higher his or her degree of **satiation** with "talking with peers."

Schedule effects

Effects on behavior which are due to the schedule of reinforcement the individual is on rather than to other factors which affect behavior, such as quantity or quality of reinforcement, deprivation level, difficulty level of the task required, and so on.

Schedules of reinforcement

The ways in which reinforcement is contingent on behavior or, to put it another way, the rules that tell **which** responses are reinforced. The basic **schedules of reinforcement** are diagrammed on page 312. (See Chapter IX for examples and elaboration.)

Self-control

Behavior which has long-term benefits but for which there are no conspicuous immediate reinforcers: (1) behavior which reduces the likelihood of future punishment but results in losing immediate reinforcement, or (2) behavior which increases the likelihood of long-term reinforcement but results in immediate punishment. An example of (1) is giving up a reinforcing food to avoid the delayed punishment of gaining weight. An example of (2) is jogging (which most people find mildly punishing) in order to feel healthier later.

Shaping

The process of building an operant by reinforcing only those responses that are closest to it. When the operant we want is a response to a certain kind of stimulus (such as answers to a question or solutions to problems), shap-

Diagram of Schedules of Reinforcement

ALL REINFORCEMENT

Non-Contingent: Reinforcement does *not* depend on any aspect of behavior.

Contingent: Reinforcement depends on responding in some way.

Continuous Reinforcement (crf: Every response is reinforced.

Intermittent Reinforcement: Only some responses are reinforced.

Ratio Schedules: Reinforcement depends on the *number* of responses made.

Interval Schedules: Reinforcement occurs for responding after a passage of time following the last reinforced response.

Fixed-Ratio Schedules: Reinforcement follows a fixed number of responses.

Variable-Ratio Schedules: Reinforcement follows a variable number of responses.

Fixed-Interval Schedules: Reinforcement follows the first response after a fixed interval of time following the last reinforced response.

Variable-Interval Schedules: Reinforcement follows the first response after a varying interval of time following the last reinforced response.

ing also requires "building" in the stimuli to be presented. The first questions or problems given to students are not as complex as those we expect them to answer or solve later.

Stimulus

Any thing or event. Note that a stimulus exists even if nobody responds to it. What or how much is called "a **stimulus**" is largely arbitrary. One letter of the alphabet can be "a **stimulus**," or one can talk about a whole book as "a **stimulus**." The plural of **stimulus** is **stimuli**.

Stimulus control

The control that stimuli in our environment acquire over the behavior we emit in their presence.

Successive Approximations

The steps the **student** takes as his or her behavior slowly progresses from its initial level to the final level desired.

System

Any collection of things or processes which interact in an orderly way so that changing one part affects the others in a consistent fashion.

Teaching

Changing behavior. Helping others to learn, or to learn faster, or more efficiently than they would on their own. Teaching may be intentional or unintentional.

Value

A set of behaviors, public and private, which a society reinforces.

Index

Index